David
many happy bir[illegible]
Love,
Richard & [illegible]

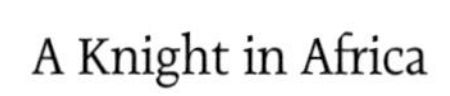

J.K. Chande

A Knight in Africa

Journey from Bukene

J.K. CHANDE

PENUMBRA PRESS
www.penumbrapress.ca

Published by PENUMBRA PRESS.
Printed and bound in Canada.
Copy-edited by Douglas Campbell.
Designed by Mag Carson.

LIBRARY AND ARCHIVES CANADA CATALOGUING IN PUBLICATION
Chande, J. K. (Jayantilal Keshavji), 1928-
A knight in Africa : journey from Bukene / J.K. Chande.

Includes index.
ISBN 1-894131-83-5

1. Chande, J. K. (Jayantilal Keshavji), 1928-. 2. Businessmen--Tanzania--Biography. 3. Philanthropists--Tanzania--Biography. 4. Civil service--Tanzania--Biography. 5. Tanzania--Biography. 6. Tanzania--Politics and government--1964-. I. Title.

DT448.25.C43A3 2005 967.804'092 C2005-904966-9

Dedicated to my parents,
whose love and inspiration helped make my life fulfilling;
to my beloved wife, Jayli; to my sons, Manish, Anuj, and Rupen;
and to my grandchildren, Lonika, Josha, and Polomi
— all of whom continue to give me immense joy

CONTENTS

FOREWORD

This book is an autobiography of J.K. Chande, Round Tabler, Rotarian, Knight of the British Empire. An autobiography seeks to present the life of a person and its author's times. This book meets both demands, admirably.

The early decades of the twentieth century saw the immigration of British Indian subjects into East Africa, some to help construct the East African Railways and others to start a network of commerce in the region. One of these, Keshavji Chande, having joined the adventurous journey in search of fortune, set up what became in the second quarter of the century a leading commercial house, Chande Industries Ltd. His son, Jayantilal Keshavji Chande, popularly known as JK, or Andy, became a pillar of that family enterprise — albeit all too briefly, caught as he was in the wave of nationalisations of the 1960s. Undaunted in spirit, he went on to become a leading figure in the management — although no longer in the ownership — of state-owned commercial and industrial enterprises in Tanzania. This is his story: illuminating, passionate, and challenging.

The description of pre-independence times we find in these pages is rich in panoramas, personalities, and unfolding economic prospects. JK's parents established themselves through careful bookkeeping, a little speculation and risk-taking, and the genuine promotion of empathetic relations with the peasants, who were commodity-producers as well as consumers of finished and imported goods.

Although he chafed at the racially discriminatory educational system, JK made fruitful use of the opportunities presented to him by his devoted family. Building upon his experience, he helped to ensure that the transition to independence was a multiracial and participatory process.

Six years into Tanzania's independence saw the nationalisation of the commanding heights of the economy. It saw the summary acquisition by the state of the Chande family's milling business and other business assets. It is a tribute to Chande's resilience and patriotism and that of his family not only that they acquiesced in the edict, but that he scrupulously agreed to manage the transformation of this critical sector of the economy. Aware of these attributes and of his business competence,

President Nyerere bestowed on him the chairmanship and stewardship of the boards of many public enterprises over many years. With the management of these enterprises in the bureaucratic hands of ex-civil servants, the remit taxed his patience, his skills, and his capacity for hope. His accounts of some exchanges between the principals are immensely amusing — although, in retrospect, they must have been stressful. The tests of his authority and mandate notwithstanding, he discharged his stewardship courageously, imaginatively, and productively.

In independent Tanzania he has held no substantive political post, but his political influence has been immense, and this book amply portrays it. Its outline herein is grossly self-effacing, but its impact is incontrovertible — on the national scale and in the international domain. His connections alone are a true testimony to his eminence.

JK is a man of many parts. No biographical account is complete without an expression of interests, and the scope of his interests and responsibilities is truly overwhelming. I knew him first through his interest in education, when he suborned me onto the Board of the Shaaban Robert Secondary School. Then I learned of his proactive leadership of the School for the Deaf, and the myriad points of benefaction of the Rotary and Freemasonry movements. Here is a person who is a restless philanthropist, not just materially but, more importantly, emotionally and spiritually.

But he has been a dedicated family man as well — his fifty years of lovely marriage to Jayli started as a distance romance, and matured into a fervent bond. An encounter with either touches one with their felicitous devotion to one another and their great love for their three children — all boys. With a father whose pursuit of work and charity has been so energetic as to be near frenetic, this family's unity, a product of love and patience, is exemplary, and truly inspiring.

With this autobiography, JK has given Tanzanians a unique opportunity to remember, to record, to review, and, where necessary, to rewrite the history of Tanganyika/Tanzania. The colonial archives are records of part of our history, but we must also record our own recollections, from our own multiple observation posts. I hope that this venture will inspire his contemporaries of all races to record their reflections.

He has been recognised and honoured by national and international organisations, and he has thoroughly deserved all those honours. I feel gratified to have been associated with the acknowledgement and recognition of the honours that have been bestowed upon him.

J.K. Chande's life spans an epoch — beginning with the early Indian migration to East Africa, continuing with decolonisation and the creation of an independent Tanganyika, and peaking with the establishment of the United Republic of Tanzania, now in the throes of finding a just niche in an integrating East Africa and a globalising world.

I salute a great Tanzanian and a great internationalist.

God bless Tanzania.

God bless Africa.

Benjamin William Mkapa
President
United Republic of Tanzania

PREFACE

My grandfather, I gather, was a remarkable man. He was remarkable for the warmth of his affection toward his family. He was remarkable for his unstinting generosity to anyone who needed help. He was also remarkable for the ineptitude of his speculative stock market trading. Most weekdays my grandfather would send a postcard to his broker in Rajkot giving him instructions in respect of shares in oils, oil seeds, and precious metals. Most weekdays my grandfather would end up buying high and selling low.

The small family farm and trading business in western India could not withstand such persistent losses. Crises would continually break, and be averted only by recourse to desperate remedies. Then, in early 1922, the final denouement came when my grandfather contracted rabies and died. The spectre of bankruptcy that had hung over our family for so long suddenly became an imminent reality, and yet local custom prevented the realisation of the family's only remaining asset of any value, the fifty acres of land they had farmed for several generations. It was then that my father, Keshavji, came to a momentous decision. Aged just twenty-two, he resolved to clear the family's debts once and for all, not at home in India, but by taking a boat bound for Africa, leaving behind his widowed mother, his three brothers and two sisters, and an eighteen-year-old wife and one young daughter of his own.

Forty-five years later, on February 10th, 1967, I was summoned, at two hours' notice, to a meeting with Tanzania's Minister for Commerce. There, in the time it took the Minister to read out two paragraphs of closely typed script, the family fortunes, which had been restored in Africa all those years before, were snatched away again. My assets, all of them, had been summarily nationalised by the government of Tanzania.

Like my father before me, I stared into the abyss, knowing that three generations of my family were financially dependent upon me. Unlike my father, however, I didn't set sail for foreign lands, seeking salvation on another continent. I stayed on in Tanzania, in a country I loved and was a native of, but had now seemingly forsaken me.

This is my story.

ACKNOWLEDGEMENTS

Over the years, my family, friends and colleagues urged me to write about my life. Whereas, it had always been my intention to do so, time and travel always seemed to get in the way of this personal promise to them. In 1995, when I published my collected works on Freemasonry, under the title *Whither Directing Your Course*, I seriously began to apply my mind to fulfil this commitment but again my constant travel made it difficult.

This past year friends' pressure persuaded me to make good my long delayed promise and they helped me get down to the task of recording some memories.

How wonderful it has been to have had such an exciting life in Tanzania. Can anyone have been as fortunate as I have in family, friends and colleagues who have guided and enriched my life and where I have always been the beneficiary?

That said, it is impossible to thank the many people who have been a part of my life and those who helped me to set down my memories. They know me and I know them and they will appreciate that I will be forever grateful for their encouragement, their honesty, their integrity and their generous help. I send all of them my thanks and my abiding affection.

I am grateful to the publisher of Penumbra Press, Dr. John Flood, to Douglas Campbell, my patient and genial copy editor who guided the text, and Penumbra's excellent design artist, Mag Carson.

Dedicating this book to my wife Jayli and my family speaks for itself. Again, I note with joy my good fortune in having Jayli as my companion over much of this journey. I whisper my love for Jayli who, fifty years ago, so generously chose me as her husband.

The President of Tanzania, Benjamin William Mkapa has in most generous terms written a Foreword and for that honour I am in his debt. He has always dignified both the office of the President as well as our country. Most surely President Mkapa is one of the most outstanding leaders in Africa.

ONE

BUKENE: HOMETOWN AND CHILDHOOD

I was born in Mombasa on May 7th, 1928. My father, Keshavji, and mother, Kanku, lived in Bukene, in the Nzega District of the Western Province of Tanganyika, where I was conceived. As soon as my mother was strong enough to travel, it was to Bukene that I returned. In accordance with Hindu custom, it was my father's sister who named me, and she chose the name Jayantilal, from three letters of the alphabet determined by the horoscope, the first of which was the letter 'J'. Less traditionally, however, my arrival in this world was not formally registered in Mombasa until many years after my birth, and only then in accordance with the Hindu calendar (which resulted in a recorded date of August 27th, 1929). Thus, like the Queen of England, I found myself with two birthdays, and, again in common with Her Majesty, each derived from a different year.

Bukene, my home town back in Tanganyika, was no more than a dusty village in what had once been German East Africa. Fifty miles north of Tabora, itself a notorious Arab slave-trading centre and, subsequently, the provincial colonial administrative headquarters, Bukene housed a small, tightly-knit community geared to the growth of rice and maize for mainly local consumption. My father, Keshavji, owned a shop on Bukene's main and only street, selling consumer goods and fuels. But he also traded in local agricultural commodities, acting as a middleman between the local producers and the markets in Tabora and Dar es Salaam. Occasionally he would finance the perennially cash-strapped local farmers, often receiving little but goodwill in return. All too frequently his profit margins were very small, no more than the proceeds of the sale of an empty gunnysack or four-gallon oil tin, the only profit he'd make on the much larger transaction, the sale of the rice. But by the time of my birth, his business, based on firm and prudently laid foundations, was beginning to prosper.

Like all those who have journeyed to Bukene, Keshavji arrived there by a roundabout route. His first stop on leaving his home village of Ged Bagasara in what is now Gujarat state was the port of Bombay. There he caught the SS *Karagola*, of the British India Steamship Company, bound for Mombasa. There, through the business connections of his father-in-law, Nanjibhai Damodar Ruparelia, who was commercially active up and down the Swahili coast from his base in Mombasa, Keshavji found work with an old established Indian merchant company, where, under the watchful eye of the firm's owner, Haji Abdulrahman Issa, he worked for very little.

Mindful of his family's plight back in India, and anxious to hasten the day when his wife and young family could join him, my father worked diligently, putting in long hours and actively seeking extra responsibilities. Within a year he had impressed his new employer so much that he was offered a partnership in the company, an offer he declined. Notwithstanding his unwillingness to tie his future to the firm financially, he had by now placed his family as a whole on a sounder footing. Later, having chosen to live in Dar es Salaam rather than Mombasa in order to limit his dependence on the goodwill of his in-laws, my father started out as a humble trader. Then, in 1924, misfortune struck again. Problems with his eyesight forced him to return to India to seek treatment. He stayed away a whole year, putting his health and his family's trading and farming interests back in order. But all that time Africa was calling out to him, and in 1925 he could no longer postpone his response.

In the late nineteenth century one of his cousins, Juthalal Velji Chande, had travelled with his brothers to Dar es Salaam aboard a dhow, the small, narrow, but swift one-masted sailing boat of ancient design used by countless Arab traders over the millennia. Keshavji, following their lead, travelled to Tanganyika and joined his cousin's firm, which was growing. A railway line linking Mwanza and Tabora had just been opened, and with it had come new trading opportunities in that hinterland of western Tanganyika. For some reason, probably on the whim of some unknown colonial officer at the Provincial Headquarters in Tabora, the tiny settlement of Bukene had been blessed with a station on that route. To Bukene Keshavji came, and within a year he was joined by his wife and daughter.

When my father first arrived in Bukene, the single village street, a sandy-brown dirt road, was just over four hundred yards long. At either end, the dirt road became even more indistinct as it stretched out across flat, almost featureless plains extending for many miles in each direction, a scrubland punctuated by irregular settlements garlanded with fruit trees. Bukene was Tanganyika's answer to the one-horse town, except that by 1925 that single horse had become a car. There were still donkeys aplenty though, and chickens too, grubbing in the dust in front of the houses. The houses themselves, none of them even numbered or named, were uniformly modest and functional, walls and floors made with mud in the traditional fashion, roofed with corrugated iron sheets that expanded and cracked in the unrelenting heat of the six month-long dry season.

It was in one of those dwellings, just fifty yards down from the one-roomed village school, that my father set up his first office cum shop. Later, when my mother and sister arrived, he acquired the house next door for them all to live in. He was not the first or only trader to have been drawn to this part of the Western Province. Other merchants, mainly Indian but some of them Arab, were also attracted to the area by the new railway network and the government-coordinated expansion in local agriculture.

My first childhood memory is of that shop — more precisely, of the machine that stood to one side of the counter, a small device for hulling maize. If I am certain of anything, it is that my lifelong passion, obsession almost, for finding out how things and people can be made to work more efficiently and effectively stems from the many childhood hours I spent on those premises. Every small detail, down to the lid of a tin or the side of a jerrycan, has lodged itself in my memory, preserved forever in sharp focus, distinct, still exerting that primitive fascination even now. In my mind's eye I can still see the four-gallon tins of petrol carrying the logo of the Vacuum Oil Company of South Africa, stacked high in the dirt outside the front of the shop. Inside, laid out in rows on low wooden tables, were the flattened rolls of cotton material that, unbeknownst to our many customers for 'cotton piece goods', became the bed each night for the young and somewhat feckless assistant my father's family had sent him from India. On the cement floor stood hessian bags, each containing two dozen bars of yellow or blue mottled laundry soap, which, once consigned, were re-sold in the villages throughout the Western Province, first as single bars to local entrepreneurs, and thence to farming families in strips, each one a perfect eighth of a bar. As well as the local staple crops of paddy (unhulled rice) and maize, my father dealt in sunflower seeds, cassava, castor seeds, bambara nuts (which the farmers, for want of a more precise term in Kiswahili, called *jugu mave* or 'peanut stones'), 'native' sisal (native, in this instance, as elsewhere in colonial times, being a mildly derogatory term), as well as beeswax and honey, and all were much in evidence around the shop. Beeswax and honey became the barometer for the prevailing climatic conditions around Bukene and Tabora, for it was only when the rains failed that local producers would feel sufficiently desperate to take on the local wild and notoriously aggressive bee colonies. That said, there was a ready market for such local honey and beeswax as could be safely collected, so much so that in later years, during the Second World War, my father used to send regular consignments of honey to the United Kingdom Commercial Corporation, a parastatal of the British government, while beeswax went to the County Perfumery Company in England, where it became one of the principal ingredients of Brylcreem. Even the provincial government latched onto the commercial potential of the local honeycombs, appointing a 'Beeswax Officer' by the name of Smith to a newly created office in Tabora. A regular contact and customer of my father's, Smith was so moved by his experiences among the honey gatherers of Western Province that he later wrote a book about them.

At the age of six, I exchanged the daily routines of the shop and office and home for those of the village schoolroom. At that time there were two schools in Bukene, an Indian Public School with around forty pupils ranging in age from six to fifteen, and a Native Authority School, established by the colonial government for African children. At the Indian school, the medium of education was Gujarati, and all of us fell under the tutelage of a Mr Jagjivan, a man who taught, and lived, in a single-roomed building. At one level, the regulatory at least, Jagjivan got off lightly. For reasons that have never been clearly articulated, the British colonial authorities in Tanganyika were less than enthusiastic about the task of building on the fairly solid foundations of the education system established by the Germans. So instead of taking a painstakingly close interest in the curricula and attainments of educational establishments within their jurisdiction, as colonial administrators did elsewhere in places that were coloured red on the map, the authorities in Tanganyika operated on a *laissez-faire* basis, allowing the Lutheran missionaries who had fanned out across the country under the previous regime to continue to proselytise and educate in unequal measure, whilst the supervision of schools such as the one run by Jagjivan consisted of little more than a cursory half-day annual inspection from Tabora.

But if the schoolmaster's regulatory burden was unusually light, we pupils more than made up for it in the breadth of our abilities and ages. Jagjivan's solution to that conundrum, an open-plan classroom in which pupils of nearly matching ages and/or abilities would cluster in three of the four corners, proved to be both pragmatic and effective. Perhaps none of us came out of that one-room Bukene school as intellectual colossi, but equally, none of us came out without a solid grounding, albeit in Gujarati, in all of the key subjects of the fabled Cambridge Certificate.

My schooldays, six of them a week at that time, were, like those of all children then, and most children now, rigidly timetabled. At around seven o'clock, just after first light, my mother would wake me in the bedroom I shared with two of my siblings. I would clean my teeth, not with a modern toothbrush, but with a traditional Indian vegetable chewing stalk that left my teeth looking surprisingly clean and refreshed. After using the pit 'toilet', complete with a bucket of water for flushing, I would have my daily bath, using water from an old copper tub that was heated with coals from below. When I was young I didn't use soap, but seeds from an Aritha plant, which, when soaked, would produce a thin but efficacious foam. Cleaned and clothed, I would sit down on the floor at a low table in the main communal room to eat my mother's breakfast 'purees', and tea already mixed with milk and sugar. Then came the five-minute walk down the street to school.

I would walk home at noon for lunch and a rest. School resumed at two, as the mid-day heat began to falter a little, and we finished for the day at around five. It was a rare day that my father closed the shop for the day before seven-thirty in the evening. And so, to tide me over until the dinner the family all ate together as one, I would hurriedly wolf down a few of my mother's savoury snacks before heading back to the open yard four doors down from our house, to play volleyball or marbles with my friends. To be honest, I was never much good at either, losing games and thus marbles to my school friends at a rate that would have shamed even my grandfather's old stockbroker. But in a world without newspapers, without radio, with only a wind-up gramophone, which was always more for our parents' pleasure than for ours, the odd losing game of volleyball or marbles, and perhaps, if I was lucky, a look at a much-thumbed and dog-eared Gujarati comic magazine was about as good as it got.

That, of course, and the trains that stopped at Bukene station. Traffic on the Mwanza to Tabora branch line has never been heavy, and those early days most definitely set the pattern for the future. But the sheer rarity value of a long clanking line of goods wagons and, still more, of a passenger train, made certain that their arrival at Bukene was an event that all of the village could savour. In the days of my childhood, freight trains came through Bukene on average about once a day. Passenger trains were a weekly event, on Wednesday night at around eight o'clock, and many of the townspeople, with the Indian station master at their head, would greet each arrival as if it were the first, the station master almost resplendent in his dust-flecked uniform and braided peaked cap. Only one who has been an inhabitant of a tiny settlement like Bukene, in a time like the mid-1930s, can get close to understanding the excitement that was felt by all of us young children as the distant whooping of the engine's whistle proclaimed to the cloudless, star-canopied heavens that eight o'clock on a Wednesday night was almost upon us once again.

The train's arrival was thrilling enough. For it to bring visitors to our home was a thing of much extra pride and joy. In 1938, when I was ten (but in Mombasa's Record Office, still nine) my eldest sister was married in Bukene. The bridegroom, an Hindi, was from Missungwi, near Mwanza, where he had a shop not unlike my father's, though on a smaller scale. The bridegroom's wedding party, which numbered around twenty, travelled from Mwanza to our house by road and by train. The festivities lasted for three days, and on the wedding day itself my abiding memories are of watching the Hindu priest chanting, and of my sister having to sit motionless in front of the fire for almost three hours. To mark the event I wore new clothes, including, for the very first time, long trousers.

The day after the wedding the Ygnopavit ceremony, a special Hindu ceremony, was held, with my young brother and me at its centre. This rite of passage, often timed to coincide with events such as weddings, begins with a ritualistic leave-taking of the male child by a maternal uncle, in which the child is sent on his way into life with a gift of money. Having received my ten-shilling note, I was ushered into the presence of the priest, who presented me with a long white sacred protective thread, about half the thickness of a pencil, which I had to wrap around my body in a loop down to my hip. Ever practical, the priest helpfully demonstrated to me how to wrap the cord around my ear for safekeeping whenever I went to empty my bladder. Cumbersome though it was, I wore the protective white cord under my clothes until I was thirteen years old.

My sister's wedding occurred at a time of rapid expansion in my father's business. In 1935 my cousin Juthalal Velji Chande sold his business to my father. It was my father's first such acquisition, and the springboard for accelerated future growth. Within a year Keshavji had invited his younger brothers, Ratansi and Amratlal, who were still living in India, to join him. Soon he had established a company by the name of Keshavji Jethabhai and Brothers, and was operating out of both Bukene and Tabora. A hard-won agency for sugar (out of Uganda) soon followed, as did the establishment in 1937 of a rice and flour milling business further down on the opposite side of the road to our house in Bukene, and, subsequently, processing facilities for oils and soaps. His acquisition of agencies for the products of Vacuum Oil Company of South Africa Ltd., forerunners of ESSO, and also of Motor Mart and Exchange Limited, Tanganyika franchise-holders of General Motors, opened the door to the nascent truck market in western Tanganyika.

At that time General Motors marketed both Chevrolet and Bedford trucks in East Africa. My father operated this side of the business on a consignment basis, remitting money to Motor Mart only when trucks were sold. His shop window to the world was Livingstone Street in the centre of Tabora, where he had established premises for his newly formed family enterprise. A gleaming example of each truck, which retailed at 3,000 shillings for the three-ton model and 5,000 shillings for the five (then about £150 and £250 respectively), would be parked on either side of the front door of the shop, framing the kerbside display of fully loaded petrol and kerosene cans. The overall effect was less a showroom than a death trap, or at the very least an open invitation to steal. And yet in all the years of my father's truck dealing in Tabora, never once was a vehicle damaged, let alone stolen, and despite all that combustible material lying around in the open, any tragic accident was mercifully avoided.

Back in Bukene I took a close interest in the machinery of my father's business, then being expanded across the road. The installation of a 'Maxoil' expeller, from Rosedowns in England, which churned out twenty four-gallon tins of groundnut oil a day, the 'Dandeker' dehusker and rice polisher from India, the Ruston maize milling machine bought from Lehmann's on Acacia Avenue in Dar es Salaam (a firm that, amazingly enough, still trades from the same address, but under different ownership), the laundry soap machine, which turned out bars in both yellow and mottled white and blue: all of these and more provided fascination aplenty for a young mind eager for novelty and stimulation. Thankfully, my increasing frustration with the finite limits of Bukene society was to be shortlived. At the age of twelve I had outgrown the single-street village, the weekly eight o'clock passenger train, and, most important, the confines of the one-room Indian Public School. Having relocated much of his business to Livingstone Street in Tabora, my father decided that I, as his eldest son, should go there, to continue my education in a town that was fast acquiring what was in colonial Tanganyika a unique but nonetheless well-merited reputation as a centre of educational excellence.

TWO

SCHOOLDAYS

In the summer of 1940 I moved to Tabora, where I stayed with my uncle Ratansi. By that time Hitler's war machine had rolled across much of Western Europe. The Battle of Britain had just begun. The war in the Atlantic shipping lanes was intensifying.

To me, in western Tanganyika, all this seemed a long long way away. Unlike the Great War, in which German East Africa had been the setting for a series of sharp engagements on land and sea—the Ice Cream War, as it was later dubbed—the Second World War made no great impact. But true to form in an empire run on the principles of bureaucratic homogeneity, some of the formalities of the distant war were being observed nonetheless.

For the general public, rationing was the most obvious measure. Unlike in Britain, however, this was a paper exercise that had little or no impact on daily life. For my family, as merchants, the introduction of price controls and the establishment of regional strategic storage depots were much more far-reaching steps. Both policies were designed to guarantee supplies and inhibit profiteering. But to an awakening economy in desperate need of guaranteed local markets, they were an unintended blessing. Suddenly we were no longer as dependent upon the prevailing conditions in distant export markets. There was now a consistent demand for whatever crops and refined goods we could supply.

But the wartime measures were not merely economic. Tabora was designated, alongside Arusha, as one of two Tanganyikan holding centres for Axis POWs. To Arusha went the Italians, who settled quickly, and subsequently masterminded the rapid expansion of the country's road-building programmes. Tabora, meanwhile, got the Germans, a handful at most, who were kept out of sight under house arrest somewhere to the west of the town. In contrast to the Italians in the north, whose sole interest was in making money, not planning escapes, the Germans kept themselves to themselves, seeing out their incarceration in absolute inactivity. Not once did I see any evidence of the German POWs in Tabora. Indeed, the townspeople more generally paid little or no heed to them, not even in the committee that my uncle had been co-opted onto to promote

Indian recruitment into the King's African Rifles, under the overall direction of Dr S.B. Malik, Director of Manpower — Asian. My father, meanwhile, with his business rapidly expanding, was more conscious than I of the potential ripple effect of the conflict in Europe. He thus bought himself a Zenith radio, a truly wondrous device, which he listened to avidly each evening, tuning in to the BBC World Service news bulletins, tracking the progress of the far-off war. As the war progressed, he would also listen to the tragicomic broadcasts of the infamous Lord Haw-Haw.

But all this was largely inconsequential in our daily lives. Mussolini's grubby one-sided campaign in Abyssinia back in 1936 had made much more impact on my part of the world than the Second World War ever would. The invasion of Abyssinia, obscene in both concept and execution, had genuinely unsettled the people of East Africa, the flows of refugees southward having been yet another stark reminder, if one was ever needed, of the absolute vulnerability of our little world to the caprices of imperialistic dictators and their successors.

But if world history was passing me by, my own personal history was suddenly made much richer when I moved fifty miles south. Tabora became a place of many wonders to a sheltered village boy approaching his teens. The town bustled, with streets fanning out in every direction, not just two. It was cosmopolitan in religion and race, with the Muslim population matching that of the Lutherans, Catholics, and Anglicans. And if agriculture and the Nyamwezi tribe still dominated, as they did back home in Bukene, the breadth of both peoples and activities was much greater than anything Nzega District could ever offer.

If my surroundings had changed, so too had my treatment at the hands of my father. To him I was now a young adult, a protégé in the making, and he now actively encouraged me to take an interest in the family business, giving me little jobs to do when I came home from school, such as counting cash at the desk in the back office. School, too, was markedly different, and immeasurably better. The Haridas Ranchod Memorial School, an academy for Indian children that exists to this day, may not have matched the educational attainments of the elite Christian schools of Tabora in the 1930s, but against any other standard in colonial Tanganyika it was an excellent school. At the Memorial School my hitherto limited education broadened immeasurably. My awareness of Tanganyika, and more precisely of how it was administered, broadened also.

Tabora gave me my first real taste of Tanganyika's colonial administration. In Bukene, the only white people I saw were occasional visiting civil servants, who set up camp at the end of the main street for the duration of whatever study they had been instructed to carry out. In Tabora, however, the Provincial Headquarters, the ruling white community was neither transient nor invisible. My uncle Ratansi, who dealt with government on a regular basis, had established good relations with successive district and provincial commissioners. He also had good contacts at lower levels, in particular with Mr Ambalal K. Patel (later made an MBE) in the Provincial Commissioner's office and Mr Ambalal B. Patel in the District Commissioner's office. Within a few weeks of my starting school in Tabora, the existence of three separate streams of colonial humanity, white, brown, and black, became all too apparent to me. The white stream, narrow but strong and fast-flowing, sustained its dominance by channelling the other two. Across the country, the black stream was largely directed toward agricultural or other menial labour, though Tabora, almost uniquely, was at that time subconsciously bucking that trend by providing excellent schooling for what later proved to be the first generation of independent Tanganyika's leaders. The brown stream — Indians, as we were called then — had already consolidated a tight hold on the marketplace, but the sons of those merchants were being directed, where possible, away from commerce and toward the local civil service. The waters of all three streams mixed but little, and then only on terms of benefit to the white, and the separateness of the three began in early childhood, with education. The whites sent their children to English schools, to be taught in English, the browns to Indian schools, to be taught in Gujarati, and the black Africans to 'Native' schools, there to be taught in Kiswahili. But occasionally, as happened elsewhere across the British Empire, the overriding requirements of evangelism and of cricket cut across these three separate streams and opened up rare channels of genuine dialogue between the races.

It was of no consequence whatsoever that I was not a natural cricket player. We Indians, as a race, had mastered the game in the previous century, and in Tanganyika our Indian teams regularly inflicted heavy defeats on the local British. During these games, and in the subsequent discussions in which we picked apart each aspect of the game, the prevailing hierarchies were set aside. And it was in those brief interludes that I discovered a vocation, a gift if you like, for establishing lines of communication that went beyond the mere exchange of mutual pleasantries. The three racial streams might be flowing separately in colonial Tanganyika, but in my discussions of cricket then, and of business and governance in later life, I found I had a genuine and apparently rare aptitude for navigating between the separate streams, and often mixing the waters together, to wider benefit.

Gradually my life in Tabora took on a settled pattern. My school was about a half-hour walk from our house. I would often play volleyball with friends, as in Bukene, or cards in the evenings and on weekends. There was a cinema, too, the Tabora Talkies on Mbama Road, where we would pay fifty East African cents to watch old Hindi movies, eating peanuts we had bought from the roadside vendors. But most days I would return to my uncle's house on Livingstone Street after school was over, often stopping, on my way through the shop to the living quarters, to pick up a task I had left unfinished the night before, or just to sit and listen to my uncle talking about business.

Then, one afternoon some eighteen months after my arrival in Tabora, my uncle was waiting for me after school at the door of the shop. He had had a telephone call from Bukene just a few minutes earlier asking him to tell me that my mother was dead.

Even now I find it hard to write those words and then just move on. That morning in Tabora in 1942 my mother had been alive and beautiful and still mine. By late afternoon, she was gone, gone forever, and not a day has passed since then without my thoughts turning to her in some slight or profound way. Perhaps if I'd known then that she had fallen ill, seriously so, things might have turned out differently. Perhaps if I'd been given the chance to prepare myself for the blow that was about to fall, the pain might somehow have been lessened. But I doubt it. I loved my mother with that fierce devotion that only a first-born son can feel, and to lose her at that age, in the prime of her life but before mine had really started, seemed utterly unbearable then. Even now, some sixty-three years later, the pain is fresh, the wound not fully closed, and the numbing effects of time have not managed to dull my senses.

In the hours that followed I came to learn the full tragic circumstances of her death. From a single mosquito bite she had contracted cerebral malaria, that deadly scourge of Tanganyika, past and present. The first symptoms had manifested themselves but days before her death and, as ever in such cases, the deterioration in her condition had been mercilessly swift. With no doctor, let alone hospital, in Bukene, the medical assistant from the District Headquarters in Nzega, some twenty-two miles away, had been summoned to her side. The assistant's diagnosis had been swift and without equivocation, and the arrangements for my mother's transfer to Nzega had been put in place. But even before she could leave Bukene, what life she had left had quietly ebbed away. Just thirty-five years old, she left behind nine grieving children, three boys and six girls.

The last photograph ever taken of my mother now sits in a frame on my wall. It captures both her beauty and her compassion as I remember them. But that picture also acts as a constant reminder of just one of the many instances of motherly love that bound me to her so closely. Among other things, my mother was justifiably proud of her hair, which was thick and lustrous, and she sought to ensure that we too had luxuriant heads of hair. Once a week my mother would massage our scalps with a concoction that was imported from India, a sweet-smelling treacly liquid that went by the name of 'Brhami Hair Oil'. Once anointed, our heads would be wrapped in a short roll of cotton cloth, much like gauze or muslin, to make sure the oil soaked in overnight as we slept. Then, just before breakfast the following morning, she would wash the heads of all of us in turn, telling each of us in her soft small voice just how much good the twelve-hour soaking in the oil was doing for our locks. My own strong head of hair, which has lasted well into my seventies, may thus be a potent testament to the invigorating qualities of 'Brhami Hair Oil'. But for me, the significance of the memory lies not in the apparent efficacy of the product, but in the tenderness of a ritual that was part of the love that my mother showered on all of us, in a life that ended too quickly, too cruelly.

The weeks after my mother's cremation in Tabora now seem to me to be part of another, more distant life. My three uncles, including my uncle Liladhar, who was then living in India, and two aunts drew even closer to my father, to sustain him in his loss. I, too, moved closer to the heart of the family, assuming responsibilities I had never anticipated, growing up quickly even as I mourned. We coped as best we could, but however hard we all tried, the parallel, sometimes conflicting responsibilities of running a successful business and bringing up nine children could not be successfully discharged indefinitely. After six months of struggling to make things work, the family reluctantly decided that two of the children, the eldest boy and one of the younger sisters, would have to move the five hundred miles southeast to Dar es Salaam, to live with relatives. When that decision was finally acted upon, I was just fourteen years old.

My arrival in Dar es Salaam in the autumn of 1942 was very different from my arrival in Tabora just two years earlier. The youthful exuberance I'd felt on leaving behind the petty constraints of village life had long gone. In its stead had come a sense of responsibility, and of purpose. I was not yet a man, but I was no longer the carefree boy I'd once been.

My younger sister went to live with my mother's brother Karsandas Nanji Ruparelia. I took up residence in the house of Ramji Velji Chande, a cousin, albeit once removed, of my father. He lived in a two-storey building on what was then the Bagamoyo Road (now the Morogoro Road). Shortly after my arrival in Dar es Salaam I was enrolled at the Indian Central School (now known as Tambaza Secondary School), the most prestigious Indian school in the country, whose headmaster was the celebrated disciplinarian, H.D. Naik. There I did tolerably well, passing mathematics, English, chemistry, geography, history, and civics at Cambridge Junior Certificate Level.

My life in Dar es Salaam quickly took on many of the routines of my existence in Tabora. After school I would help my father's cousin, whom I called Uncle, with the business in the office downstairs. I began with the most menial of tasks, the reuse of envelopes in accordance with the recommendation on the back flap of all colonial (and indeed all post-colonial) official correspondence. I was assigned a desk and a pot of glue and a brush, and my job was to paste plain white labels over the addresses on incoming letters. From that I graduated to errands, and in time to routine drafting of correspondence. I shared a bedroom with one of my cousins. And on Sundays and the hours after school I found myself working alongside an older Indian named Dayalal Bhatt. Now for reasons best known to himself, Bhatt liked to be known as 'Niranjan', which roughly translates as 'happy frame of mind'. Niranjan was fluent in French and English as well as Gujarati, and he worked as the middleman between my uncle's business in Dar es Salaam and its office in Ujumbura (now Bujumbura, in Burundi). Niranjan may not have quite lived up to his own self-billing, but he was still a good source of amusement, even if sometimes he provided it unwittingly. As a creature more of habit than of happiness, Niranjan would stop working at precisely ten past one each day and head upstairs to one of the bedrooms, where he would carefully remove his trousers and lie down to sleep for exactly fifty minutes. One day we followed him upstairs, waited for ten minutes or so until we were absolutely sure that he was fast asleep, and then moved the hands of his alarm clock forward to two o'clock. When the bell jangled, Niranjan got up, put his trousers back on, and rushed downstairs, dishevelled and confused in equal measure. It was not until much later that afternoon that he came to realise he'd somehow gone and mislaid a full forty minutes of his daily siesta. But even then, my cousin and I never owned up to what we'd done.

Several months after my arrival in Dar es Salaam, it was as plain to my uncle as it was to me that I would never be a star pupil at any school I attended. On one occasion the District Commissioner from Tabora, a Mr Robinson, sent word to him that he would come calling at his office to enquire after my scholastic progress in Dar es Salaam. When Mr Robinson arrived, my uncle was, as usual, sitting at his desk in the corner of the office. Mr Robinson was ushered in, and my uncle looked him up and down. It was a clash of cultures, the Indian in his white Gandhi cap and loose-fitting dhoti, the English colonial officer in his long khaki shorts and socks. Mr Robinson recognised the awkwardness of the situation and quickly moved to the point. On being asked about my success in the recent school exams, my uncle looked down and fiddled with his cufflinks. Eventually, having given the impression that he'd been thinking long and hard about his answer, he announced portentously that I was 'in the first rank of the class but counting from the left side.' In saying this he was, of course, using the Gujarati convention of reading, and ranking, from right to left. But my uncle did not realize that Mr Robinson had completely misinterpreted his reply. On his return to Tabora, he confounded my father's low expectations of me by telling him that I was doing very well at school, so much so, in fact, that it would be 'an awful waste' to let me follow him into the shopkeeping business. This eulogy aroused my father's suspicions, and he asked whether the unexpectedly good news about my academic attainments had come from the horse's mouth. Hearing that instead it was his cousin, my uncle, who had been the source hardly allayed my father's suspicions. It didn't take long to discover the truth of the matter, that I was in fact 'the best of the worst'.

Despite my lack of brilliance, I enjoyed my schooling in Dar es Salaam. I enjoyed the lessons, especially in mathematics and history, and quickly made friends. At recess time we would eat skinned oranges and peanuts and drink Coca-Cola. Sometimes the local goats would steal our food, while at other times vervet monkeys would come down from the trees to scavenge. It was in Dar es Salaam that I got my first taste of beer, a bottle of India Pale Ale, or IPA as it was known the world over. And it was in Dar es Salaam that I first became aware of girls.

In Indian families in those days there was a strict taboo preventing boys from coming into close contact with girls. This extended as far as such innocent pursuits as conversation, which made the eternally mysterious process of falling in love even more complicated than it usually is. Nevertheless, thanks to the good fortune of living in the same city as my younger sister, Vijya, but without my parents, I found myself able to meet a number of girls without falling foul of traditional mores, and I became fond of one of them, a friend of Vijya's, an enchanting girl named Chandraprabha. Luckily for me, I think the feeling was mutual. Unluckily for both of us, the fact that she was my sister's friend gave us only limited licence. In the brief time that I knew and thought I loved that wonderful girl, we never exchanged anything more than the most commonplace of clumsily expressed words. And yet, as is the case with all first loves, even such flat and uninspiring prose was subtly transformed into poetry, and as such the memories linger.

In early 1944, my father went to India to re-marry, and brought his new wife back to Tanganyika. Her name was Rumkunver and, unusually for that time, she had been divorced from her first husband. Our first meeting was awkward, if not uncomfortable, for both of us. I was old enough to recognise the difficulties my father faced in trying to meet the demands on his time and attention both at home and at work on his own. After all, my move to Dar es Salaam at a tender age had come about because of those pressures. I was also keenly aware of the needs of my youngest siblings, who were crying out for the love and affection only a mother could give.

It is to my stepmother's great credit that she earned the respect of all of us children from the outset. She behaved with such tact and tolerance and kindness that we came to like her, and then love her. She made my father's life whole again, and brought up the youngest children as her own. Most challenging of all, she made for herself a special place in the hearts of the eldest children without ever attempting to displace the memories of our lost and adored mother. By her warmth and gentleness, my father's essentially pragmatic decision to re-marry was transformed into something deeper and more transcendent.

But my days in Dar es Salaam, and in Tanganyika, were, unbeknownst to me, coming to an end. By 1944, my father's ambitions for my future education were increasingly focussed on India. As he saw it, and as he explained it to me at the time, the facilities for undergraduate study in the motherland were far broader in scope and richer in quality than anything colonial Tanganyika could offer. Besides, the move to India would help to broaden my hitherto limited horizons, while at the same time giving me direct exposure to the culture and heritage of my forefathers.

But how far he wanted me to go in that voyage of personal discovery has always been open to question. My father had watched with a mixture of pride and concern as my interest in Indian philosophy and religion had deepened over the years. He recognised more clearly than I ever did that I took after my mother in wanting to nurture the romantic and idealistic side of my nature. But at the same time, he knew that I had to temper this with the practicalities of professional qualifications of use to the family business interests, and with a commitment to the long hours of hard work that would be necessary for me to consolidate and build upon his many commercial achievements. Hence my going to India to study represented something of a calculated risk for him, a gamble of the sort more naturally associated with his late father than it could ever be with him. I guess he hoped that if my interest in the esoteric world were given much freer rein, one day I would come to recognise that my true destiny, like that of so many Lohanas (a subcaste of Hindus that originated in Lohar Pradesh, which covered a large part of what is today Afghanistan, Pakistan, Kashmir, and the Hindu Kush, and that migrated in the eleventh century to Saurashtra and Kutch, now a part of Gujarat state in India) before me, lay in the field of commerce, and not in scriptures and legends.

Dilemmas such as these were still far in the future when I booked my passage to India in 1945. The excitement of that first trip to my motherland remains fresh in my mind. I can still picture the ship I boarded at the port in Dar es Salaam, the SS *Takliwa*, of the British India Steamship Navigation Company. I can still recall the seven-day journey to Bombay via Mombasa. And most of all, I remember the day of my arrival in Bombay, when, after the tumult of greetings from my father's family, I went out in the evening with the cousin who was later to become my official guardian, and we sat in a restaurant owned by an old Iranian friend of my cousin's father and chewed betelnuts and drank spicy tea and talked long into the night about our plans for the future, starting with the day after, and my need to resume my schooling as soon as I possibly could.

My cousin was of a practical frame of mind, so much so that his immediate advice to me was to abandon secondary education and immediately enrol in an accountancy training course. Having been sent back to India to complete my formal education, I was hardly going to change my plans within twenty-four hours of my arrival in Bombay. Instead I struck a compromise, which saw me applying for accountancy training in order to make productive use of any time it might take to find a suitable secondary school. Of the two local institutions that offered me places in their accountancy courses, Davar's College of Commerce and Batliboi's Accountancy Training Institute, I chose Batliboi's, with my family covering the costs.

But I wasn't destined to stay very long at Batliboi's. Within weeks of my arrival in India I found a place at the quaintly named Scottish Orphanage Society's High School, which was situated in Mahim, an outlying suburb of the city. To get there, I had to take a train each morning from the Churchgate Station, a one-hour journey on an electric service run by the Bombay Electric Supply and Tramways Limited. From the first day, I regretted my decision to abandon Batliboi's. Not only did the travelling time extend an already long school day, but the school itself was experiencing an accelerating decline. The staff were an ill-matched assortment of Anglo-Indians, Indians, and English. The students were an equally mixed bunch, whose commitment to study had clearly been affected by the sustained collapse in the school's fortunes. Instead of consulting an educational adviser on the choices before me, I had made my own mind up, on the basis of an exaggerated prospectus.

There was nothing for me to do but to leave. Luckily, by that time I had been in Bombay for almost six months, and I now knew how to avoid making the same mistake twice. This time basing myself on good advice, I enrolled at the St. Peter's Boys' School (previously the European Boys' High School) at Panchgani, a hill station in Satara District, about 160 miles southeast of Bombay.

Panchgani derives its name from the five hills that surround it. It is a quaint and often breathtakingly beautiful town situated at an altitude of just over 4,000 feet, with a mix of old colonial and Parsee buildings that criss-cross the sloping roads in a jumble of unplanned construction. Eleven miles away, at the end of a switchback road that looks out across both the Coastal Plains and the sacred Krishna River, stands the even more imposing and prestigious hill station of Mahabhaleshwar, Bombay's summer capital, and the long-time refuge of the city's rulers, both native and imperial. And ninety minutes away by the State Transport Service bus lies Poona (now Pune), where the Aga Khan had his palace and where Mahatma Gandhi was for a time interned, and which was a three hours' train ride from Bombay aboard the 'Deccan Queen'.

From the moment I arrived in Panchgani, I knew I had made the right decision. The town itself was charming, a veritable haven after the heat and bustle of Bombay. The school was well run and hospitable. My schoolmates all seemed friendly and bright and hard-working. And the relationships between the pupils at the several boarding schools in Panchgani were warm and open, including, for the first time in my experience, between boys and girls. There was, however, one major problem.

At the time of my enrolment, the school had insisted, as they did with all boarders, that a parent or guardian be close at hand and contactable should any problem arise. I initially assumed that this was yet another instance of Indian bureaucracy that I could somehow wriggle past. But it was not. It became clear to me soon after my arrival at Panchgani that this was a firm requirement that could not be eluded.

My first reaction was one of despair. The thought of returning to Bombay, and an establishment such as the one I had just abandoned in haste, filled me with genuine dread. At the same time, with my father two thousand miles and a continent away in Tanganyika, my chances of satisfying the requirements of the local school authorities seemed slim. In a state of high anxiety, I turned for advice to my eighteen year-old cousin in Bombay. In my hour of need, he didn't let me down. In fact, he wrote back by return of post, introducing himself to the Principal at St. Peter's as my legally appointed guardian.

As subterfuges go, it was a difficult one to pull off. After all, my perplexed state on first being told of the school's requirements had almost given the game away. But if anyone could pass himself off as the legal guardian of someone roughly his own age, my cousin could.

The first clue to this complex and creative character came with his name. He was called Satyavan Juthalal, which breaks down, in translation, to 'epitome of truth' and 'perpetual liar'. Quite why he was given this contradictory combination of names remains a mystery to me, but whether it was by accident or by design, he grew up seemingly determined to live up to the qualities of both.

His self-appointment as my guardian was by no means the most audacious of his gambits. With a father who shared the family predilection for gambling, it was inevitable that my cousin would take risks whenever he could. Satyavan got into the habit of changing his schools like shirts, moving on whenever he judged that his latest bit of academic fakery was about to be uncovered. The most spectacular coup concerned the hallowed School Certificate. For his final examination in the Ardhamagadhi language, he exercised his right to choose a distant examination centre, and employed a native Ardhamagadhi speaker to sit the exam for him. Unsurprisingly, he did extremely well, so much so that the suspicions of his school were roused. They took to writing postcards to his father, expressing their fears that my cousin had pulled off his worst stunt yet. Needless to say, these were all intercepted before they reached the father, and progressively more emollient replies were supplied, until at last a card got through the net. His father replied in all truthfulness that he had seen little of his son for the previous few months, and that any explanation for his wonderful achievement was possible.

My cousin remained my guardian in India until I finally came of age. In all that time, I hardly saw anything of him, even when I went back to Bombay to stay with him. His waking hours began when mine finished, and vice versa. Later, he went off to East Africa and thence to the Congo. I have always felt indebted to him, both for pulling me out of a hole when all seemed lost, and for teaching me the valuable life lesson that on some rare occasions the natural dictates of conscience and integrity must be tempered with a little pragmatism and creativity.

Once I had surmounted the hurdle of guardianship, I was allowed to integrate myself fully into the life of St. Peter's Boys' School. I was assigned to Red House, which meant that I was installed as a resident of Lawrence Villa, together with about thirty other boarding students. We roomed in threes and fours (I and two other students were housed in the veranda), with Edgar Glancey, a middle-aged Englishman, as our housemaster. Glancey, who eventually retired to Australia, was a kindly man, with an even kindlier wife, and together they made sure that I soon settled in comfortably at the school. The principal of the school, O.D. Bason, another Englishman, was equally welcoming, and my affection and respect for him, which began with his failure to question my cousin too closely as to his age and circumstances, increased over the years as I came to know his work and methods. For Bason was in charge of the school at a tumultuous time in Indian history, when the 'Quit India' campaign to get the British out was at its height, and when the local arrangements for self-governance short of Independence were beginning to make their presence felt. The school, which as I have said had been known earlier as European Boys' School, operated according to an entrance quota system, whereby a large percentage of students were Anglo-Indians and the rest were others — many were sons of the Rulers and Princes, and a few, like me, were from overseas. The school continued to reflect the predominant ethos even after it changed its name, and attendance at the Sunday service at the School Chapel was mandatory for all. This latter, religious aspect of school life created difficulties for me. A couple of fellow pupils, who were Muslims, successfully petitioned the principal to be excused from Sunday Christian service, and a Muslim tutor was found to instruct them in the Koran instead. I followed their lead, and was slightly surprised to be excused as well. I was even more surprised and, I have to say, disconcerted to discover that a Hindu priest had been found to give me one-to-one instruction for the duration of the Sunday service.

The Sunday service at the School Chapel was clearly the high point of the week for the majority Christian community in our school. With the girls from the neighbouring Kimmin's Girls' School joining, naturally a great deal of effort went into keeping the boys and girls as separate as possible. But in the event, segregation proved almost impossible to enforce. Thus it was that, just when my agitation for separation from services on Sunday on religious grounds was reaching its height, I met a Parsee girl named Aloo Davar at the Chapel. We first set eyes on each other across the heads of a number of our fellow pupils. But it wasn't long before we were formally introduced, thanks to the kind heart of an Anglo-Indian girl named Gloria Bright, who had perspicaciously recognised the subtle signs of a mutual attraction, and had acted upon them.

Aloo changed my view of the Chapel overnight. Perhaps taking a leaf out of my cousin/guardian's book, I quickly went from staunch opponent of Chapel to one of its fervent devotees. Such was my interest in Aloo that I volunteered, unsuccessfully it turned out, to become a member of the choir, given that the vantage point this offered would have given me an unrestricted view of my beloved for the entire service. Shrugging off this temporary check on my ambitions, Aloo and I agreed to pass ourselves off to the teacher on duty as distant cousins, thus ensuring that our brief and innocent meetings after each Sunday's service would be officially sanctioned by the powers that be at our respective schools. In helping ourselves, we helped others too, in the way we had previously been assisted by Gloria Bright. It soon became established that each of our cousinly conversations in St. Peter's School Chapel would be accompanied by a surreptitious exchange of letters from enamoured fellow pupils who had not been blessed with either the wit or the good fortune to have declared themselves cousins in the early days of joint services at the School Chapel.

Meanwhile, my studies progressed. I made many friends at school, among fellow pupils who were drawn, in the main, from the families of doctors, lawyers, colonial officers, and the rulers of vestigial empires that had once flourished in post-Moghal India. Here too I met the scions of well-connected families from across Asia and Africa, including one Ugandan boy from a wealthy family whose favourite foods were dispatched regularly from Bombay in hampers.

I thus ate well, and I think learned well too. As ever, I wasn't a student of the first rank, even counting from the left side. But by applying myself, I made the most of the high-quality instruction that was on offer. Again, beauty had its own inimitable way of imparting wisdom. Perhaps the youngest teacher, Eunice Salisbury, was also the most attractive to us boys. Her youthful poise, her blonde hair, and her piercing blue eyes were a guarantee of rapt attention, and thus, for most of us, high marks.

Sixty years later I returned to St. Peter's Boys' School, not with Aloo but with my wife Jayli on my arm. It was December 4th, 2004, and Jayli and I were there along with about 1,500 others, including a number of Old Boys, many of them from outside India.

At the banquet on the last day of the celebrations — a crowning conclusion to the school's first one hundred years — I was the guest of honour, and was asked to recount some of the tales of my schooldays. I was very happy to take that journey down memory lane, to meet students both old and new, spanning more than two generations, and especially to meet one of my former teachers, a Mr Davis.

I was pleased to note that the building was well maintained, and that the garden and the surrounding landscape were all in prime condition. In one of the dormitories in Lawrence Villa I saw the bedroom I used to sleep in some sixty years ago, although our beds had long ago been replaced by bunk beds in order to meet the increasing demand for space at the school. And in the centenary photo exhibition I saw a picture of my old girlfriend Aloo.

After the three days of celebration, Jayli and I came back to Bombay (now Mumbai) and invited the Secretary of the Board of Management and his wife for dinner. As we reminisced, I felt as if my time in the school had happened only yesterday.

The emotional awakening I experienced at St. Peter's went hand in hand with a growing spiritual and political enlightenment. In Bukene, Tabora, and even Dar es Salaam, my studies had been Eurocentric. Even at Indian schools, the set books had focussed almost exclusively on British and occasionally continental European history. But here in Panchgani the curriculum suddenly changed. I had access to books about Indian history, Indian culture, Indian religions. My eyes opened as never before, and books by such historians as Sir Vincent Smith and Father James Gense S.J. changed my perspective of the world, and of my place in it. A fateful confluence was established between my new thirst for Indian learning and what was happening all around me in India. I got caught up in the excitement of those last eighteen months before Independence, in the youthful exuberance of the 'Quit India' campaign, in the fever for impending nationhood, and in the concurrent outpouring of resentment at the excesses of the British Raj. Fate was to ensure that I was to be a witness to the independence of both my family's motherland and of my homeland, Tanganyika, and my formative experiences in India undoubtedly shaped my perceptions of independence in Dar es Salaam some fifteen years later. Thus the teenage boy who wrote letters to *The Times of India* seeking an early end to British rule in India became the man caught in the undertow of Britain's sudden withdrawal from East Africa in the early 1960s. On both occasions, vast countries that had hitherto been run by small numbers of dedicated, super-skilled Britons were, in haste, made masters of their own destiny. On both occasions, that haste bequeathed a poisonous legacy. In India and throughout the region, haste spawned division, discord, and conflict that has persisted to this day. In Tanganyika, haste left a system that was ill prepared for the onerous responsibilities of nationhood, a country founded in a crippling dependency, reinforced by a chronic undercapacity that continues to blight the country's future.

But any feelings I might have had about the gaining of Indian independence were swept away in the tide of nationalist fervour that swamped the region. Besides, I had more important things on my mind than any youthful assessment of British de-colonisation. My secondary school career had successfully come to a close in 1948 with passes in the Cambridge Higher Certificate in History, Civics, and English. It was time for me to move on to university education.

For this, I went to Poona (now Pune). At the Nawrosjee Wadia College (a part of the University of Poona) I enrolled for a B.A. in Indian History. From the first day, it was clear to me that my studies would be a challenge like no others I had ever faced. The College principal, a Mr Joag, was an exacting scholar. To survive, let alone prosper, in that more rarefied intellectual atmosphere I had to work much harder than ever before. And this time there were no piercing blue eyes to spur me on.

An additional complication was my lack of accommodation. There was no room at the hostel attached to the college. In consequence I moved from hotel to hotel, squeezing myself in among the tourists and business travellers. Eventually I struck up a friendship with Homi Irani, who was a part owner of the Napier Hotel in Poona. Homi allowed me to negotiate a discounted rate for a long stay, and at last I began to settle. I bought myself a bicycle, and began to go out to the local theatre and cinema. With friends from college and with Homi, I started going to restaurants, and explored the town. My other spare-time interests were walking and stamp-collecting, pastimes that would be inexplicable to my grandchildren, but were commonplace then among my peers.

Despite the advantages of my discounted rate at the Napier, I was still on the lookout for living arrangements that felt more like a home. Eventually I struck it lucky at a most unlikely place. An Armenian businessman, John Alyanak, perhaps the only one of his kind in the whole of Poona, had recently established himself as a trader in motor vehicles. His business was just about breaking even when we happened to meet at the Napier Hotel, and on hearing of my perennial problems with housing, he and his wife Eva offered to take me on as their paying guest. Though the cost of board and lodging at their house at 6, Staveley Road took more than forty percent of my weekly allowance, I didn't hesitate to accept their offer. My bicycle and my single suitcase, which by then had lodged in rooms all over Poona, had at last found a permanent resting place.

The Alyanaks turned out to be perfect hosts. Though their house was very basic, with a toilet that could only be cleaned from outside, they and their Goan servant, a man called Augustine, treated me as one of the family. John was an early riser, often leaving the house before dawn, and I would invariably breakfast alone. But in the evenings we would almost always eat dinner together, as a family. Living with the Alyanaks gave me the stability I needed to make a success of my university studies. As 1949 became 1950, I felt I had truly established myself in Poona.

Then, suddenly, in January 1950, I received a letter from my father telling me that his younger brother, Ratansi, living in Dar es Salaam, had been taken ill. For some time now he had been suffering from appalling pains in his head. Eventually he'd been advised to have all of his teeth removed. But even after he submitted himself to such a drastic remedy, my uncle's pain had persisted, and it had been agreed that he needed an extended leave of absence to try and sort the problem out. But this decision created a crisis for the family firm. With the Dar es Salaam end of the operation embarking on a sustained period of rapid expansion, a new milling plant having been set up at a cost of six million shillings, someone was needed to help the uncle run the business until he was fit to return. That someone, according to my father's letter, was to be me.

I was very reluctant to break off my studies less than halfway through a four-year course. Equally, I knew I had no choice but to comply with my father's request. I therefore went to see Mr Joag and his deputy, Mr Suri. I explained the situation and asked if my place could be reserved for me until I could return. Mr Suri eyed me with suspicion. He had had a bad experience at the hands of an Indian student from East Africa, and he wanted to know more. 'Are you from Zanzibar?' he asked. 'Tanganyika,' I replied, and his attitude softened. Nevertheless, he wouldn't give an assurance that my place would held open for me, and both were adamant that in the event of my being allowed to return, I would have to repeat the whole of this second year of my studies.

It was thus with a very heavy heart that I bade leave of the Alanyaks. I went directly to Bombay, in the hope of getting an early sailing to Dar es Salaam. But bad luck continued to dog me. It took a month of applications in Bombay, and the intervention of the Dar es Salaam branch of the shipping agents, Smith Mackenzie, to finally secure me a berth. In February 1950, I finally set sail on MV *Vasna* for Tanzania, travelling toward an uncertain future, and leaving behind an unfinished past.

THREE

THE FAMILY BUSINESS: APPRENTICESHIP

I came home fully expecting to be pitched immediately into the running of the family business in Dar es Salaam, which by then had expanded and diversified. Besides exporting sunflower and castor seeds the company traded in palm kernels, pulses, and cereals, as well as beeswax and honey. The company also dealt with cotton piece goods and hides and skins. The family firm was the largest exporter of coffee beans and honey, mainly to Europe. But as it turned out, my father had other plans. Perhaps concerned that the spiritual side of my character had been overfed for the past six years, he decided that I needed to return to the original base of operations in Bukene, to learn about the business from the bottom up from my other uncle, Amratlal. This change of plan only served to magnify my sense of disappointment at returning home. Leaving my studies and friends in Poona for Dar es Salaam had seemed bad enough. To leave all that for Bukene, to go back to square one if you like, was a bitter blow. My memories of Bukene were inextricably linked to my early childhood and to Mother. But now both of them were gone, irretrievably so.

But the resilience, and perhaps also the nascent ambition that had carried me through the many upheavals I had already experienced in my young life, now saw me through this latest chapter. On arrival in Bukene, I found that little had changed in the ten years since I had left. The passenger trains still stopped at the station at eight o'clock on a Wednesday evening. Donkeys and chickens still dodged the occasional car or truck on the dusty single main street. And Mr Jagjivan still ran his rotating classes at the old schoolhouse just down from our family shop. Perhaps the only momentous change had been in the scale of my family's food processing and milling operations.

My father's business had prospered since I left for India. From having been one of the main produce buyers in Nzega District, his foodstuffs and trading empire was now growing to be of national importance. In Bukene, to the original rice mill my father had established in the early 1940s a soap factory had been added, which produced laundry soap in yellow and blue mottled bars, a maize mill, which produced a rich flour known locally as 'Dona', and a plant for extracting oil from seeds and nuts. All these, when put together with the expanding trading operations across Tabora Western Province, had been the backbone for the expansion of the family's operations in Tabora and Dar es Salaam.

Backbone was a word my uncle would have used often. Both he and my aunt loved me dearly, I had no doubt about that. But he was a stern taskmaster, expecting me to join him at an early breakfast, often at dawn, the precursor to a working day that always extended beyond seven-thirty in the evening. This was a crash course in commerce and I learned quickly. My grasp of Swahili, already firmly established, improved immeasurably. So, too, did my drafting skills in English and Gujarati. Most important of all, I began to understand what made our business tick, and how wealth could be generated from a solid platform of hard work, good market knowledge, close working relationships up and down the supply chains, and, above all, more hard work.

In the three and a half months I was to spend in Bukene in 1950, time off from work was at a premium. What few leisure hours I had were usually spent at the old family home, which had been renovated and extended since I had grown up there. But occasionally I found myself with time on my hands, and it was then that I would wander out to the temporary encampments that would be set up at the outer fringes of the village. Here a steady stream of colonial officials from the Public Works Department and the Agricultural Department in Tabora would pass through, officers in ones or twos spending the weeks studying the local transport and foodstuffs networks with a view to improving crop quality and availability. Some evenings I would spend talking into the night with the British Agricultural Extension Officers, all of us grateful for the chance to talk at the end of a long and arduous working day. Often on a Sunday I would take these officers little bundles of Indian food from the house, to supplement the more basic fare they got at camp. Again, as in earlier days both here in Tanganyika and in India, I found myself able to build relationships with people from different backgrounds and different interests, in a spirit of partnership and equality.

When, after fourteen weeks, my uncle declared me fit to return to work in Dar es Salaam, I wondered whether the chance was presenting itself for me to return to my studies. But it wasn't. Instead I found myself drafted into the family team in Dar es Salaam. I won't deny the disappointment I felt at that. At the same time, I had for the first time acquired a genuine taste for business. The short apprenticeship back in

Bukene had convinced me that my long-term future lay not in Indian History in the motherland, but in commerce, here in Tanganyika.

My first responsibilities in Dar es Salaam were largely clerical. Businesses such as ours in the immediate post-war era were heavily dependent upon cablegrams and codebooks such as Bentleys and Acmes L. My role was to draft messages to be sent through Cable and Wireless, and to make out invoices for goods supplied. I also had to prepare Bills of Exchange and Promissory Notes, using an old Imperial manual typewriter. I don't need to point out that none of these tasks was very exciting. But they were necessary groundwork for my taking over responsibility for shipping arrangements for our expanding export trade. The firm used to import copra from Mafia by dhow, and it was my responsibility to ensure that the main supplier, Fazal Bhanji Jessa, loaded the copra on time and that the goods were discharged at Kurasini dhow jetty without delay—and to take care of the insurance. The only risk one could insure against was 'the total loss of goods through total of loss of a vessel'. No insurance company would give any other cover. One afternoon a person in tattered clothes walked into the office and told me that he was *nahodha* [coxswain] of dhow M65, that he had been bringing in copra for us, and that the dhow had sunk. It then dawned on me that I had failed to take out an insurance policy. I telephoned one Mr Pillai in the office of J.M. Jaffer and Company Limited, the firm's insurance brokers and the sole agents for a New Zealand firm called the South British Insurance Company Limited. I told Mr Pillai that I needed to talk to him urgently and that I was on my way to see him. When I got there I explained how I had overlooked taking out a cover for this shipment. In my presence he booked a telephone call to the general manager of the South British Insurance Company at their headquarters in Mombasa. It took quite some time to get the call through. When he managed to make contact, he explained the situation. Mr Pillai was instructed to issue a *nunc pro tunc* cover note and debit the premium to Chande Brothers Limited. This was done by the insurers as a gesture of goodwill, taking into account the substantial business it received from the family firm. I was advised to keep the *nahodha* in Dar es Salaam and arrange for him to swear an affidavit before the District Commissioner explaining the circumstances surrounding the sinking of the dhow. This required a tracer investigation at all East African ports to establish that the vessel was definitely lost. Eventually the claim was settled. Following this incident the South British Insurance Company arranged for my firm to take out a declaration policy covering shipments for the year, and to give a monthly advice of the shipments made under the policy. My uncle Ratansi never learnt that I had goofed.

By 1950 the family had become the largest exporter of coffee from Tanganyika. Entire trainloads of produce from Bukene would make their way to the Princess Margaret Quay in Dar es Salaam port and coffee from Moshi to Tanga port for transshipment to Britain and mainland Europe. But in addition to coffee, as I mentioned earlier, we were also major exporters of palm kernels, cotton, oil cake, oilseeds (mainly sunflower and castor), beeswax, and honey. It fell to me to ensure that these products reached their destinations.

The shipping lines to our part of the world were all incorporated into a cartel known as the East African Conference Lines. Headquartered in London, with the regional office in Mombasa, this cartel encompassed the Union Castle Line (whose local agents were Smith McKenzie), Lloyd Triestino (whose local agents were Mitchell Coutts), and Clan Hall and Harrison Lines (whose local agents were the African Mercantile Company Limited). Each of these lines would offer a loyalty discount (which they described as a 'deferred rebate') of around nine percent, and each would compete for the right to carry our freight. But the Conference Lines cartel, a licence to print money if ever there was one, also did what it could to keep on the right side of key customers such as ourselves. I remember an early visit to London in my new role that included a spectacular lunch at the Ritz with the Chairman of the Lines, preceded by pink gins at his club. But the lavish entertaining masked a serious intent. The shipping operations to East Africa in those days were run with great honesty and thoroughness. The precision with which each stage of the operation was run meant that we, as major exporters, could always rely upon the efficacy and efficiency of all of the cartel's shipping lines. Thus the major challenge for us, in a country with as weak an internal transportation infrastructure as Tanganyika's, was getting the goods to the port in good order and on time.

It was around this time that my father and my uncle began to think of restructuring their growing business empire. The real hub of activity had become Dar es Salaam, not least because of the acquisition of new business premises and a sizeable plot of land on the old Pugu Road. In 1952, he decided to move permanently to the capital, and in doing so sold the old shop and office on Livingstone Street in Tabora. These were acquired by my brother-in-law, Vijya's husband, who renamed the operation Tanna Brothers, after his shop in Mwanza.

My father's move to Dar es Salaam enabled me to get to know him properly, almost for the first time. I came to recognise his brilliance as a businessman, his eye for detail as well as for the strategic picture. Most of all, though, I came to know him as a man who was humble, devout, and almost ascetic, a person of absolute and unwavering integrity. Keshavji neither smoked nor drank and was a strict vegetarian. He worshipped at the temple regularly and supported many local charities, both in western Tanganyika and in Dar es Salaam. He paid his workforce fairly, and treated his employees with respect. His outside interests were simple. He liked to walk, and he liked to be with his family. And, importantly for the business, he too had a knack for getting on with people.

Through the extensive contacts that my father and my uncle had in the business and official worlds, and then through my own, I began to play an increasingly active role in local society. I joined the Dar es Salaam Cultural Society, the only forum in the city at which all three races were able to mix freely without fear or favour. Culture was rarely, if ever, on the agenda, the Society having been euphemistically named. We met one Saturday each month under the presidency of J.P. Moffett, the Colonial Commissioner for Social Services, and gathered in the premises of the British Council, because no hotel was willing to play host to such a mongrel grouping. There we took tea together and discussed the issues of the day. Later, as I became more active in the Society, and was voted onto the Committee and then appointed Acting Secretary, we invited distinguished guest speakers to address us. By the late 1950s we had listened to such luminaries as the Aga Khan, who talked to us about war in a city whose name meant 'Haven of Peace' (an irony that was not lost on the speaker), the Vice-President of India, Dr Radhakrishnan, who spoke to us on the future of civilisation for forty minutes without notes in a spellbinding performance at the old Avalon Cinema, Mrs Indira Gandhi, the Rt Hon. Iain Macleod, The Hon. Mrs Golda Meir, and His Grace the Archbishop of Canterbury, the Most Rev. Arthur Michael Ramsey.

By then I knew the inside of the Avalon all too well. In the early 1950s I had become a regular cinemagoer. Not as a paying customer, however, as in the old days with my school friends at the Tabora Talkies, but as a member of the grandly titled Territorial Film Censorship Board. This was my first-ever public appointment, and it had come about because I had become more active on the local scene, and my profile had become more visible. I found myself acting as one of three local censors reporting to Percy Everett, the Territorial Film Censor, who in turn reported to Barclay Leechman, the member of the local Executive Council (EXCO) responsible for Social Services. Percy Everett, a portly man who drove an Austin car in his day job, was a director of the local branch of the East African wholesaling group, Gailey and Roberts (now owned by Unilever), and he was nothing if not a character. Among other things, he had a soft spot for parrots, which raucously filled the house he shared with his wife Queenie. Percy ran the Territorial Film Board for almost a decade before going on to even better things, becoming the first appointed mayor of Dar es Salaam and taking an active interest in the Chamber of Commerce and the Chamber of Industries.

At that time, the mid-1950s, Dar es Salaam boasted a total of five cinemas. In addition to the aforementioned Avalon, there were the Empire, the Empress, the Odeon, and the Amana, of which only the latter was located in the so-called 'native' area. At the beginning of each month the viewing members of the Film Board would be sent a note by the Secretary to the Censor informing them of their assignments for the next four weeks. Mostly this involved at least three of us (the quorum that had been established for the Board) attending a special private matinee performance at one of the city's five cinemas, which we visited in rotation, of a film destined for local general release. We were advised not to sit together, but to take seats in different areas of the deserted auditorium (presumably in case certain salacious images were only visible from particular vantage points!). Our instructions in respect of content were equally straightforward. We were to look out for, and report back on, any scenes of a sexual nature, or of criminal activity. But there were no guidelines whatsoever as to race or religion. When we reported back with an agreed recommendation, the film would be granted a 'U', 'A', or 'X' certificate. And for our pains we received no payment other than a token twenty shillings per assignment toward travel expenses.

At first I undertook my new duties with due seriousness and diligence. I would report to the appointed venue and sit through Hindi films with no discernible plot that were often more than three hours in duration. I would sit through an entire Abbott and Costello epic. And I became something of an expert in the less bankable output of Alan Ladd and Tyrone Power and Stewart Granger.

In the circumstances, it didn't take long for the absurdity of what I was being asked to do to become apparent. After all, in the 1950s the US film industry had been so cowed by the activities of Senator McCarthy and his cohorts that almost every Hollywood film was about square-jawed heroes and white picket fences and motherhood and apple pie. The British film industry, meanwhile, was in no better shape, turning out largely insipid versions of old Ealing standards. And the nascent Bombay film industry was operating under such tight moral codes that the distributors' constant effort to dupe the masses into thinking they were about to see something truly salacious was always very wide of the mark. Even kissing was taboo in those days.

But even if none of these constraints had been in place, the fact is that all the films that wended their way so slowly to the distant shores of Tanganyika had already been subject to the most rigorous government censorship processes in the US, the UK, and India. The notion that we on the Territorial Film Censorship Board would, one quiet afternoon in a cinema, spot some incitement to criminal or sexual activity that all of these other boards had somehow missed was frankly risible. To be honest, our little Film Board was yet another example of the British colonial system replicating domestic bureaucratic structures on a global scale without ever asking the obvious question: why? Maybe if we in Tanganyika, just a couple of years after the Mau Mau rebellion in neighbouring Kenya, had been instructed to look out for scenes that might upset the uneasy local harmony between the races, our work might have been of some genuine relevance. But we weren't, so it wasn't.

Unsurprisingly, my commitment to the censorship process eventually became less than total. With the connivance of the cinema managers, whose only interest was the rubber-stamping of their features for the coming weeks, I would sneak out of the darkened stalls about ten minutes into most of the screenings, returning only in time for the final scene and the closing credits. Thanks to the management, and the way we were widely dispersed across a darkened cinema, I got away with my alternative approach to film censorship for a number of months. Then one afternoon a colleague, the wife of a barrister unfortunately, caught me in the act.

I was immediately reported to Percy Everett, and a telephone call from him quickly followed. Everett began the conversation in a very formal manner, saying that he regretted to say that a complaint about me had been lodged. According to his source, he went on, I was no longer fulfilling my responsibilities in an appropriate manner. 'In what way?' I asked, feigning innocence and buying time. After a pause, as if to weigh his next words, Everett told me that I had been spotted leaving the cinema just after a film had started, and it had been put to him that this was a regular occurrence. Now it was my turn to pause. It was true, I admitted, that once or twice during the course of one of those long Hindi films in a stuffy auditorium with nothing by way of air conditioning, I had been forced to step outside for a quick breather. And on one occasion I had even gone so far as to seek medical attention. But these had been isolated incidents against a backdrop of sustained fulfillment of my duties to the Board. Given the gravity of the accusations, I continued, it might be better if we were to arrange a formal meeting, together with my accuser. That way, she would be able to provide chapter and verse and I would be given a chance to present my side of the story.

At that, Everett paused again. The fact that I had readily identified my accuser as female was of real significance to him. Both of us were aware of rumours circulating in the city that one of the women on the Committee was anxious to secure an additional place on the Board for a friend. Creating a vacancy by means of my dismissal would of course have served that purpose, but at the cost of some embarrassment to the Board. Everett cleared his throat and then told me, in a voice less serious than the one he had used before, to carry on with my assignment. 'But be more careful in future,' he added, conspiratorially. I agreed, and I was.

My responsibilities within the family firm meanwhile continued to grow. In my uncle Ratansi I found an able tutor, and he found in me, I think, a willing student. From him, I learned how to manage staff and to run a production line. I got to understand the intricacies of the milling and extraction processes. I became adept at negotiation with both suppliers and customers. And by these means I began to build a reputation in the local business community. I owe a great deal to both my uncles, who always evinced interest not only in my welfare but also in my learning the tricks of the trade in a proper way. In both Bukene and Dar es Salaam they gradually entrusted me with more and more responsibilities.

As a result, I was approached by some of my more senior commercial contacts with a view to my helping them set up a Round Table in Dar es Salaam. The Round Table movement, a philanthropic enterprise that had started life in England and had grown to become the Round Table in Ireland and the British Isles, was by then just beginning to make its presence felt in Asia and Africa. In East Africa, Round Tables had been established in both Mombasa and Nairobi, and by 1954 there was talk of following suit in Kampala and Dar es Salaam. Thanks to the enthusiasm and persuasiveness of Alastair Niven, the local Union Castle staff, and Ron Hornsby, a local income tax assessor, a set-up meeting was held in Dar es Salaam, and I went along. The Dar es Salaam Table was officially established soon afterwards and allotted Number 4, even though we beat Kampala, allotted Number 3, to the punch. And I was formally inducted as the first non-white Round Tabler in the whole world.

I won't deny that I felt honoured to be recognised in this way. But I didn't dwell too much on self-congratulation. The world had moved on since the foundation of the Round Table movement, and their recognition of those changed circumstances was overdue. I am glad to say that my appointment was but the first of many for non-whites. In Dar es Salaam alone, I was quickly joined by Noorali Sayani, an Ismaili attorney, by Tony Almeda, an architect, by Al Noor Kassum, also an Ismaili barrister, who joined Nyerere's cabinet, and by the now legendary broadcaster Hamsa Kasongo of the Tanganyika Broadcasting Corporation. Today, thanks to the efforts of pioneers in cities such as Dar es Salaam, the Round Table movement worldwide has become truly representative of the global business community and of those it seeks to serve. Sadly, global membership, like that of similar organizations, including Freemasonry, is going down.

My involvement in Round Table activities increased as the 1950s wore on. In 1956 I was appointed Secretary, with Ron Hornsby as Chairman. Our work together brought home to both of us the different skills we needed in our respective careers. Given the rigid structure of the club meetings, I took to producing the draft minutes of the forthcoming meeting alongside those for the meeting just gone. The first time I presented both documents to Ron, he looked at me as if I had just arrived from another planet. But once he got used to my methods we made a good team, and the following year I was appointed Vice-Chairman, moving up to Chair in 1958.

In my year in charge, the Round Table raised a record sum of money for local charities. The highlight of the year, and by far the biggest money-spinner, was the so-called 'Mannequin Parade' in the property in Oyster Bay owned by Prince Aly Khan. Thanks to the kind sponsorship of BOAC, three of London's top models were flown out to Dar es Salaam in the company of the celebrity hairstylist, Mr 'Teasy-Weasy' Raymond. Needless to say, late-1950s Dar es Salaam was a world away from the catwalks of London, and the culture shock began at the airport. No sooner had the visitors disembarked after their long journey than they were detained by the Tanganyika Customs Service, together with the costume jewellery they had brought with them. It was only after some careful negotiation, in which I was ably assisted by the local BOAC manager, that Teasy-Weasy, the three girls, and all their luggage were allowed to continue their journey into Dar es Salaam.

The London fashion team were lodged as guests of the New Africa Hotel. Needless to say, it had emerged at the series of preparatory meetings in advance of their arrival that there would be no shortage of local volunteers willing to assist the models in whatever way possible. Predictably, however, Mr Teasy-Weasy took charge of all chaperoning and dressing room arrangements, and the men on the local committee didn't get so much as a look in. I can't say I envied Mr Teasy-Weasy in his task. The circumstances of their arrival threw the girls off balance, making them skittish for the remainder of their stay, and the New Africa was witness to a never-ending round of tantrums.

On the day itself, I had roped in a compère from the local amateur theatre group, the Dar es Salaam Players, a man who, if I recall correctly, later struck up quite a friendship with our celebrity crimper. The technical team in charge of the event had set up a temporary runway on the veranda of the house for the girls to parade on, and laid out the chairs and bar for what promised to be a memorable night of unprecedented glamour. The catering arrangements were first-class, as were the acceptances from the original guest list, which included the Governor, Sir Richard Turnbull, as well as the Mayor of Dar es Salaam, David Howarth. Unfortunately, the one thing that none of us had taken into account was the Dar es Salaam weather.

Anyone who has ever been to Dar es Salaam — and, more pertinently, out to Oyster Bay — will be aware of the gentle and cooling breezes that often blow in from the sea. That morning, the day of the Mannequin Parade, the gentle sea breeze was more like a gale. It was a wind that shook the struts of the temporary catwalk, a wind that no hair lacquer known to man could have withstood. We committee-members panicked, and thought of bringing the event inside, but by then it was much too late to put together a Plan B. All we could do was keep the news of this latest development from the visiting party at the New Africa Hotel, where the nerves of even the normally jovial Mr Teasy-Weasy had already begun to stretch (the previous night I had had to intervene when he'd berated a waiter for his slowness in bringing his gin, threatening to take him to London for 'proper training'). Up at the house in Oyster Bay we kept a worried vigil, hoping the wind would drop.

Come nightfall, at around six o'clock, the wind suddenly died away. And so the show went on, with a full complement of local dignitaries, and it was successful beyond our wildest expectations. Only once did the Governor and his party, his wife resplendent in a feathery hat and long white gloves, get an inkling of what we'd all been through to get the event off the ground, when a momentary lull in the proceedings was interrupted by the sound of the girls quarrelling shrilly among themselves in their makeshift dressing room. The next day we were on the front page of the *Tanganyika Standard*. And the money we raised made it possible to establish the Dar es Salaam District Nursing Service, to minister to patients in the outlying areas of the city.

My business activities naturally drew me into the Dar es Salaam Produce Exchange, where I was quickly elected to the Management

Committee, and of which at one time my uncle served as Chairman. I also became a member of the Dar es Salaam Chamber of Commerce and Agriculture, which had been established in 1921, in the early months of the British Mandate. By 1960 I had become its first non-white president. But four years before that, I was approached by the Governor, Sir Edward (later Lord) Twining, with a view to my taking over a six-month vacancy in the local Legislative Council (LEGCO), following the departure of one of the Indian members for an extended leave of absence. LEGCO had been established in Tanganyika in 1926 to advise the governor on a range of issues. In 1948, in common with LEGCOs across the newly rebranded British Commonwealth, a handful of unofficial members from the main local ethnic groups were also invited to participate. In Tanganyika, LEGCO expanded to accommodate four new unofficial African members, and these, together with unofficial Asian counterparts, perfectly equalled the number of existing British representatives, thereby creating what the old Colonial Office was wont to call a 'balanced representation'. As was the case throughout the British Empire, and later the Commonwealth, Tanganyika's LEGCO worked in tandem with an Executive Council (EXCO), which acted as a form of cabinet to the governor of the day.

The offer for me to join LEGCO was thus a signal honour. But before committing myself in any way, I went to seek advice from my father. Somewhat to my surprise, I found him to be implacably opposed to my taking up such an appointment. He told me that I should devote my energies to business and avoid any entanglement with politics. He also made it clear, without actually spelling it out, that he was concerned about the knock-on effect an appointment in the gift and service of the colonial administration might have on the family firm's burgeoning relationships with leading African businessmen and politicians, such as John Rupia and Dossa Aziz, from whom our firm was purchasing paddy and to whom advance payments were often made.

Another reason for my father's concern was that by 1956 the political landscape in Tanganyika was changing. Back in 1920, the British government had been charged by the League of Nations with the responsibility of administering Tanganyika with a view to preparing it for nationhood. A new generation of black Tanganyikans, led by the visionary nationalist, Dr Julius Nyerere, had taken it upon themselves to prepare for their homeland's future independence. Educated at Edinburgh University, and close friends with and influenced by a whole generation of Fabians in the British Labour Party, Dr Nyerere had by 1956 established a proto-political party, the African National Union (later TANU), and was already well on the way to international as well as national political significance. Nyerere was a humanist, without a racist bone in his body, but there were other senior members of his party who had begun to agitate not only for the departure of the colonial power but also for an end to 'Asian exploitation' of black Tanganyikan workers. The economic roots of these feelings were perhaps understandable. At that time, the average annual income of a European in Tanganyika was just under £1,800, against just over £500 for an Asian and a mere £75 for an African. But the way these figures were being translated into a political agenda was unsettling, to say the least, because at the same time Governor Sir Edward Twining had given his blessing to the formation of the United Tanganyika Party (UTP), which was funded by local Asian and expatriate British interests in support of old colonial ideas about what might constitute racial parity in an independent Tanganyika. Supporters of the UTP included two leading Asian families, and influential individuals such as Tom Tyrell and Col. Sterling, later of the Capricorn Society. The UTP was soon to be joined by some British officials, including, in 1957, the Governor himself, in denouncing TANU as racist (on the grounds that, among other things, it excluded Europeans and Asians from membership), even though the moderate wing of TANU, led by Dr Nyerere, was at that time quietly courting the Asian community. Local Asian businessmen such as ourselves were thus being pushed from all sides — and were sometimes pulling on all sides — of this highly charged political (and racial) debate.

My father was more conscious than most of his peers of this continuing build-up of pressure. He was also, I have to say, deeply cautious when it came to anything to do with politics. Since his move from Tabora to Dar es Salaam, he had deepened his already keen interest in social and charitable works. He used to tell me that when you give something away, your left hand should not know what your right hand is doing. This disinterested approach to philanthropy won him recognition and respect in the local Asian community, and he was elected President of the Lohana Mahajan. In black African circles, too, his contribution was recognised, not least by his willingness to work in genuine partnership with newly established black businesses, such as the Aziz and the Rupia paddy growers. But his focus was exclusively commercial and philanthropic, not political, and he wanted me, as the likely future champion of the family's business interests, to follow in his avowedly apolitical, if not anti-political, footsteps.

After our one-to-one meeting, I took my father's advice and turned down the Governor's LEGCO offer. But in doing so, I was acutely conscious that my father and I maintained irreconcilably different perceptions of the wider implications of our undertaking acts of public service, and that these differences could only widen over time. For even as I shared my father's reluctance to become actively involved in politics, and would stick to this separation of business and active political involvement throughout my life, I knew that my deep commitment to public service could not find an expression in my homeland without exposing me to risk or incurring some cost. Whether it be in an advisory capacity during the last days of the colonial administration, or in a similar role under successive governments of independent Tanzania, there would always be the chance that a small minority of people who didn't know me well might somehow seek to misinterpret or misrepresent my own entirely selfless motives.

The year 1956 may not have seen me installed as a temporary member of LEGCO, but by then I had more than enough responsibility in the family firm. By 1952, my control of the export side of the business had seen me appointed, by my father and uncles, as Manager of Chande Brothers Limited. Most of the production side of the business was still concentrated within the separate entity of Chande Industries Limited, whose fifteen-acre plot on the Pugu Road was now being quickly developed. We had acquired the land, the headquarters of what was to be the National Milling Corp., on a ninety-nine year lease from Sheikh Ali Bin Said, who in turn had bought the site in the 1920s for next to nothing from the Custodian of Enemy (i.e., German) Property, and we had already built a number of mills and oil extraction plants. My side of the business, Chande Brothers Limited, had meanwhile not only become the largest exporter of coffee from Tanganyika, but had risen to second in the ranks of beeswax exporters, and into the top ten in the lucrative oil seed/oil cake market, against some serious multinational UK-based competition in the shape of Unilever, Gibson and Co., and the Steel Brothers.

In 1957, a misunderstanding between my uncles in Bukene and Dar es Salaam came to a head. Generally, friction in families is caused by jealousies amongst wives of brothers or of sons, often over property. Family feuds often result. In our case, however, property wasn't a factor; the problem was the brothers. The root of the dispute lay in the growing sense of isolation felt by my youngest uncle, Amratlal, out in Bukene. Although none of us realised it until too late, he felt out on a limb in that tiny village in western Tanganyika. Small problems that were a regular feature of life out there, such as the difficulties involved in obtaining permits or securing space on freight wagons, were allowed to grow to such large proportions in the absence of sympathetic attention from his brother Ratansi in Dar es Salaam that my uncle Amratlal eventually said that he wanted to break away from the family firm.

Efforts by my father and my uncle Ratansi to dissuade him from this course of action were to no avail. And so a division of the assets was finally agreed upon. This proved simpler than any of us had expected. The Bukene operation was about equal in size to each of the businesses held under two family companies in Dar es Salaam, so it was given to my uncle Amratlal; my uncle Ratansi retained Chande Brothers Limited, which dealt with the export of coffee and other produce, and my father took over Chande Industries Limited, which owned flour and rice mills in Dar es Salaam. The three brothers continued to serve on the Boards of the three companies.

My uncle Ratansi wound up his business in the early 1960s and established a coffee exporting business in Bangalore, India, with the assistance of his three sons. At about that same time my uncle Amratlal also left, and started a new business in Secunderabad, India.

The year after the division of the companies, my father appointed me Chief Executive of Chande Industries Limited. The now exclusively Dar es Salaam-based company was primed for a new phase of accelerated expansion. A new and, in my eyes, more enlightened governor, Sir Richard Turnbull, was appointed to administer Tanganyika. And it wasn't long before a renewed official approach, this time an invitation to join both LEGCO and EXCO, came my way.

On this occasion, I was determined to say yes. But before I did so, I wanted to bring my father on side. I therefore approached my uncle Ratansi, and he in turn talked to my other uncle in Bukene. I also talked to some of my father's friends. And then the process of getting my father's agreement began. This time, the collective pressure was much more successful than my previous solo efforts had been. My father gave me his blessing, but on one condition, which I immediately accepted: that I should not receive any allowances, emoluments, or other benefits arising from these appointments.

My appointment to EXCO took me into the inner circle of the British rule in Tanganyika. Like the cabinet back in Britain, we met every Thursday morning, with the papers circulated in advance by locked dispatch box. My original intention had been to add the EXCO papers to the workload of my secretary at Chande Industries Limited. But when that secretary failed to obtain the requisite clearances from State Security, the wife of a junior Treasury official was seconded to my staff on a part-time basis to handle my paperwork. I soon realised my good fortune in gaining that extra pair of hands. The volume of EXCO work was such that it would have quickly swamped my business secretary.

When he appointed me to EXCO, the Governor had hoped that I would agree to cover commerce and trade. But instead I opted for agriculture. There was little that a Tanganyikan EXCO could do to improve upon the terms and logistics of trade within the Commonwealth. But there was plenty to be done about Tanganyikan agriculture.

Learning from the mistakes of the groundnut scheme was top of that list. This was the only instance of significant British government agricultural investment in the entire history of colonial Tanganyika. Yet within months of its launch in the early 1950s, groundnuts (more popularly known as peanuts) became a byword for gross incompetence, and that connotation has lingered to this day. The post-war British Food Minister, John Strachey MP, was ostensibly the prime mover in the scheme. But the true architects were the local Unilever representatives, whose failure to anticipate many of the obvious problems that dogged the scheme from the outset condemned all concerned to ignominy, if not disgrace. To begin with, the suitability of the topography and soil in the new areas in southeastern Tanganyika designated for cultivation had not been definitively established. On top of that, there were major communication problems involved in getting the produce from farmer to market. A new railway from the interior to Mtwara Port, quickly nicknamed the Groundnut Line, had to be built at enormous cost. Then Mtwara itself had to be redeveloped, with the local wags renaming it Stracheyville after the British Food Minister mentioned above. Yet even with all of that new investment, the meagre returns from the new groundnut fields were always going to be vulnerable to the sharp practices of local groundnut traders anxious to protect their existing market shares. Unilever may have built the coffin for the groundnut scheme, but it was these local Indian middlemen who hammered home the final nails.

But before I could begin to address the many problems in agriculture, I found myself heaped with other responsibilities. The first and perhaps most difficult of these was my appointment to the Capital Sentence Remission Committee. John Fletcher Cooke, the Chief Secretary to the government, undoubtedly the most important civil servant in colonial Tanganyika, made the initial approach, seeking my agreement to serve on this four-man committee. I played for time, being extremely reluctant to get involved in this kind of work. But as a relatively new member of EXCO, I was in no real position to resist when a second and more insistent request was made. In four short years I had gone from watching Disney on behalf of the government to reviewing death sentences.

I approached this work with a sense of foreboding. It was not misplaced. The committee's role was to advise the governor on each of the capital sentences handed down by the courts. Our recommendations were based on a set of four reports: from the Commissioner of Prisons; from the Social Welfare Officer; from the law courts (consisting of records of the proceedings all the way up to the Appeal Court); and from the religious leader deputed by the court to visit the prisoner in the condemned cell. In the main, the cases concerned ritual murders related to witchcraft, and it was often difficult to gain a clear understanding of what had actually happened and why. We therefore reviewed our four separate dossiers in great detail, taking pains to form a collective judgement that all of us could stand by, which judgement would then form the basis of our recommendation to the governor. The options themselves, given our place at the end of a process, were simple and to the point: uphold the sentence or commute to life. Complications would arise only in the event of the governor's disagreeing with our advice. He would then have to lay our report and his dissenting opinion, backed with evidence, before the authorities back in London.

The one common strand between my earlier film censorship duties and my new role in the judicial system was the absence of much freedom of manoeuvre. Just as the censorship systems inside both the film industries and the governments overseas had already made up their minds for us, so had the pre-independence Tanganyikan legal system. I was conscious from the outset of a presumption within the system that our committee would uphold most, if not all, of the capital sentences handed down by the courts. The presence of Attorney-General John Cole as a full member of the committee certainly reinforced that impression, and I soon became aware how difficult it would be for us to challenge a judiciary system that was confident of the robustness of its own internal checks and balances. In consequence, my time spent serving on this committee pained my conscience more than any other public duty I ever undertook. The only small comforts I could ever draw from my two-year tenure was the knowledge that I did my utmost to ensure that no decision to uphold was ever taken lightly, and the fact that we managed to successfully recommend commutation more often than the system had ever expected us to.

Two other tasks were allotted to me during my time on LEGCO and EXCO. I was appointed a 'Visiting Justice', with a remit to review prison conditions throughout Tanganyika. I was also made a member of the Eastern Province Advisory Council, which met in Morogoro once a month under the chairmanship of the provincial commissioner. In the former role, I managed to bring about some minor improvements to the prison system in respect of new systems of skills training for prisoners (previously they had done only unskilled manual labour) and an expansion in the number of prison farms. In the latter capacity, I made my presence felt by helping to accelerate new road-building plans (especially in rural areas).

By 1959, my workload had increased exponentially. In addition to my official duties on LEGCO and EXCO, I had assumed much more responsibility for the day-to-day running of Chande Industries. My father, meanwhile, had taken up much more of a strategic role, guiding my hand on the bigger issues while consolidating our networks across the region. His health was not what it had been. But, working in tandem, together with my uncle, we were thriving as a business, and thriving as a family. I had no inkling at all that my father was seriously ill. And then suddenly he was.

The initial diagnosis, subsequently confirmed by a specialist, was pancreatic cancer, and the disease was already well established. Knowing that time was not on our side, we hurriedly scoured the world for a specialist who might yet save my father's life. We found one in Boston, USA, a man of global repute who had already successfully treated Anthony Eden. The family made arrangements for my father to be transferred there immediately.

The first leg of his journey was to Nairobi. There, the intention was that my father would recuperate at Parklands Nursing Home before flying on to Boston via Rome. But on reaching the Kenyan capital, with an opportunity at last to think things through after an emotive week of frenetic activity, and on the advice of a friend, a Mr Anderson, my father changed his mind. He decided that he didn't want to go to Boston for treatment after all. He was all too aware how far the disease had taken hold, and he just didn't want to risk dying alone in the States. So he came back to Dar es Salaam, to his family.

After that the end came mercifully quickly. He was able to spend his last weeks surrounded by his loved ones, and with the support and comfort of his many close friends. Representatives of commercial and official Dar es Salaam, including the Chief Secretary to the government, came to pay final calls on him. And when he died, he did so peacefully and happily, having spent many of his last precious hours in the company of his beloved first grandson, Manish.

August 1959, the month of my father's passing, had been tumultuous in a wider sense. There had been a recrudescence of virulent anti-Asian sentiments among some senior members of TANU. The poison of racism was again seeping into the body politic. And yet, in spite of all this, my father's funeral became another spontaneous manifestation of the tribal, racial, and religious tolerance that has always been the bedrock of Tanganyikan society. People from all walks of life, from all faiths, from all communities, flocked to my father's funeral. Hundreds of messages of condolence poured in from all over the country, from ordinary people he had met in the paddy fields of Western Province right up to the Governor of Tanganyika himself. John Fletcher Cooke, the Chief Secretary of the government, perhaps summed up the feelings of many in the note he sent me afterwards: 'Your father was well-known in Dar es Salaam for his kindly and cheerful personality and for his many contributions to the public life of the capital. I know that he will be greatly missed, not only by his immediate family and his community, but by his many friends whom he numbered among all sections of the population throughout Tanganyika.'

Keshavji had come to Tanganyika all those years before to redeem his family's name and fortunes. He had done that. But then he had gone on to achieve much more. His piety, his wisdom, his integrity, and his many kindnesses would live on down the years in the hearts of many; they would also act as my guide.

FOUR

MARRIAGE: MY WONDERFUL JAYLI

The death of my father was a bitter blow. Our relationship was of a kind that young people today, even those brought up in the Lohana tradition, would simply not understand. My love for my mother had been unconditional and free. With my father, the emotion we felt for each other was undoubtedly less intense. But the bond between us was made up of much more than just feeling, enriched as it was by the traditions, the piety, and above all the sense of mutual duty that tied together the father and his first-born son in my native culture. And so when that bond was finally broken, my sense of loss went to the heart of my identity. Had it not been that I had a wife I loved dearly, and a young first-born son of my own, my father's death would have left a gap in my life that would have been hard to fill.

Then, as so often in my life, my wife Jayli's love helped me see all things in their proper perspective. By August 1959 we had already been married just over four years, and our three year-old son Manish, the first of the grandsons on the male side of the Chande family, had already enriched the last few weeks of my father's life, his presence around the house having done much to soften the final blow. I was no longer living with my father in his house on the Upanga Road, for we had our own home by then, a cosy apartment on the United Nations Road.

As I said, Jayli and I had been happily married for just over four years. The thought of my marriage, however, had been around for a lot longer than that. Eight years before my father died, and not long after I hurriedly returned to Tanganyika from India, the notion of my getting married had first entered the head of my uncle Ratansi. I say entered Ratansi's head, because my uncle was very much that kind of man. Oh, I certainly liked girls well enough, but my interest at that time was not really in the practicalities of sustaining the family dynasty. My uncle Ratansi, however, though a warm and kind man, was also intensely pragmatic and orderly, and he was the first in the family to recognise, as he recovered from the illness that had brought me home, that his nephew Andy had reached a time in his life when he might soon need a family of his own.

He first broached the subject of my getting married with my father back in 1951. In those days such conversations were not out of the ordinary, for arranged marriages were very much the rule, not the exception, in the Indian diaspora. For a time, the two brothers pondered the way ahead, thinking through the possible options, before eventually agreeing that the time was indeed ripe to start looking for a suitable wife for me. First, though, they took it upon themselves to watch me closely, in order to find out if there was any special liaison already in my life. At that time I was leading a very busy social life in Dar es Salaam, often dining out and going out drinking with friends, much to my father's dislike, and taking frequent weekend trips to Zanzibar. But throughout that time I had no special girlfriend. Then my uncle heard of a young Indian girl living in Kisumu. Her father was known to my family, and was a member of the Lohana community. It wasn't long before contact was made, and the girl and I were both told of our respective fathers' intention that we should meet. But as preparations were still being made for that momentous first meeting, tragedy struck. When crossing a swollen river in a motor car, the girl from Kisumu was swept away by the current and drowned.

That setback put the family plans on hold for a while. But after a decent interval, some months after the awful accident, my father and uncle felt ready to return to the matter at hand. This time their attention turned further north. For more than thirty years, my father had known the Madhvani family, who lived near Jinja, in Uganda. The Madhvanis were business people, and on a grand scale, too, being one of the most prosperous families in Uganda, if not the whole of Eastern Africa. Like my father, Muljibhai Madhvani was prominent in the Lohana community, even more so in fact, and on his many visits to Tanganyika Muljibhai would often stay with my father at the house in Tabora. Over time, the shared interest in business grew into a genuine friendship, a relationship of warmth and trust that was to last all their lives, and my father was appointed agent for the Madhvani sugar interests in Tanganyika. In time I, too, got to know the Madhvani businessmen, and struck up a friendship with Muljibhai's eldest son, Jayant. Like me, he served as a member of LEGCO, in Uganda. Not surprisingly given the family's undoubted flair, some would say genius, for commerce, the Madhvani family crest is a gilded cogwheel. But between the Madhvanis and the Chandes the talk was increasingly as much about kinship as about business.

It is hardly surprising, therefore, that the issue of my marriage was eventually raised with both families. As was the custom, the subject was not introduced directly by the two fathers, but came about through the intervention of middlemen. But once it was broached, the two fathers quickly agreed that I should travel to Uganda to stay with the family and meet Muljibhai's third daughter Jayalaxmi. At the time, I was twenty-five years old and one of nine children, whereas Jayalaxmi was a mere sixteen years old, and one of twelve children. Before I left for Jinja, my father told me of the underlying motive for my visit to Uganda. Significantly, though, Jayalaxmi, or Jayli as I called her, was not told.

This discrepancy in our knowledge of what was afoot made for an interesting first encounter, to put it mildly. Knowing what I did, I was nervous at the prospect of meeting Jayli, so much so that I declined the family's offer to stay at their estate near Jinja, preferring to base myself in Kampala, where I already had many friends. But at least I had the advantage of knowing what exactly was going on. Jayli had no such inside knowledge, and the way I behaved on the day did nothing to make things any clearer, for her or, indeed, for her family. Perhaps I was over-anxious. Perhaps I was too easily flummoxed by her obvious self-possession, which manifested itself immediately to me in so many small ways, most disconcertingly for me, oddly enough, in her driving her own car at such a tender age. Perhaps I was overawed by the grandeur of the Kakira Sugar Estate, which covers twenty thousand acres at the heart of the Madhvani commercial empire. Whatever the reasons, the day came and went with precious little progress to show for it. Jayli's parents were at a loss to understand what I had really thought about their daughter. Nor, I have to say, could I tell myself with any great clarity what I was thinking about the proposed match, even though I had quickly concluded that Jayli was a very nice girl indeed. As for Jayli herself, I doubt whether I made much of an impression on her that day either. In fact, I know I didn't.

And yet, despite all this, on my return to Dar es Salaam I quickly began to warm to the idea of marriage to Jayli. My first impressions, obscured somewhat by the confused events of that day in Jinja, soon settled into a warm and positive feeling about the match. My uncle, undaunted by the mixed reports coming back to him from the Madhvani family, resumed his advocacy of a union between these two prominent business dynasties, and I listened closely to his advice, as always. But it was only the intervention of the Ridleys, English friends of both families, that helped me finally make up my mind. Robert Ridley was the head of Standard Bank of South Africa Limited in East Africa, and as such was both banker and trusted confidant to the Chande and Madhvani families. His wife Mary was a good friend of all as well, and the couple's combined support for the proposed marriage, based on a deep personal knowledge of both Jayli and myself, removed any lingering concerns I might have had.

Jayli and I accordingly became engaged on March 28th, 1953. The two families then set to work planning the date and arrangements for our marriage. Before they could get very far, however, worrying news came down from Uganda that Jayli's mother had been diagnosed with cancer. With local doctors unable to contain its spread, she was flown to a hospital in New York, where, sadly, the specialists confirmed that the disease had taken such a hold that she had but weeks to live. And so she died there, her family by her side.

This awful loss put off all thoughts of marriage for the next twelve months of official family mourning. It was not until the second half of 1954 that the two sides were able to begin planning again. But again a family bereavement put a stop to the planning process, this time on my side of the house, with the death of a cousin in the Congo that saw my family going into official mourning for another six months.

By early 1955 Jayli and I were at last free to plan ahead again. Our long engagement had unfortunately been a time of great sadness, especially for Jayli, but the two of us had stayed in touch throughout those many long months, resolute in our commitment to a marriage that had already been postponed twice. Our friends, however, were perhaps less sanguine about our prospects, joking to me that the forthcoming union with Jayli was less a marriage than a mirage, moving further away each time we got close to it. Others wondered aloud, again in jest, I hope, whether the Madhvani family had at last discovered some skeletons lurking in my closet, and were now having second thoughts. Thankfully, all such ribaldry was finally put aside when May 5th, 1955 was set as the date of our marriage in Uganda.

The wedding guests travelled to the Madhvani estate near Jinja from far and wide, arriving by plane, by car, and even on foot. My father chartered a twenty-eight-seat DC-3 from East African Airways, and our family was flown from Dar es Salaam to the tiny airport at Jinja. From there we travelled the nine miles to the Madhvani estate in vehicles provided by the bride's family. I remember precious little about either journey, caught up as I was in the excitement bubbling up from my family around me. All I can recall of that day is the exactitude of the arrival arrangements laid on for us at Jinja airport, the almost military precision with which we were ushered to the line of waiting cars, which then set off, as if in convoy, to the Madhvani estate, a foretaste, it turned out, of the days to come, the precursor of a wedding ceremony in which nothing had been left to chance, in which every last detail had been meticulously planned and provided for.

The exactness with which everything about our arrival had been prepared perhaps gave me the courage to do some forward planning of my own. For people of other faiths, it is perhaps difficult to comprehend the exhaustive — often exhausting — nature of Hindu weddings. My own personal experience, especially of my sisters' weddings, had alerted me to the privations as well as the pleasures of a ceremony that was drawn out over three whole days and evenings. Of most concern to me at the wedding was the part of the ceremony when the bride and groom have to sit almost motionless for several hours on very small stools in front of a large open fire. Having seen how my eldest sister and her husband had struggled to get through this part of the ceremony, I took the earliest opportunity I could find to have a quiet word with the Hindu priest Mr Keshavlal Monji Joshi, who would be officiating at the wedding. If he could find a way to hurry that part of the ceremony forward, I said to him, I was sure that many people in both families would subsequently find ways of showing their appreciation to him.

I must admit I was quite heartened by what I took to be the priest's sympathetic response. I was less heartened by what he did next. He went straight back to Jayli's eldest brother, Jayant, and told him every last detail of our conversation. As Jayant told me afterwards, the line the priest took with him was that 'your future brother-in-law wants to take shortcuts.' Needless to say, we didn't take any shortcuts on the day. And, thankfully, my trusted friend Jayant took a charitable view of my proposed alternative ceremony, and said no more about it.

The wedding itself was a very grand affair, as perhaps befitted a union between members of two of the foremost Indian families in East Africa. The cream of Ugandan society had been invited, and was on hand. Although the Governor himself was unable to attend, he sent a message of congratulations, as did Uganda's Chief Secretary, but the Provincial Commissioner of Uganda's Eastern Province was in attendance. The ceremony was held in the main bungalow on the Madhvani estate, which had been opulently decorated with silks and flowers and garlands of every colour. The outdoor open-sided structure in which the wedding itself was held, a converted carport I suspect, was similarly garlanded, with burnished brass and silver jars in each corner. Jayli herself was resplendent throughout in a series of richly brocaded saris, while the guests in attendance, both family and friends, were a picture of elegance. In something of a break with tradition, Jayli was given away by her two eldest brothers, who had pressed their father into giving them that honour jointly. Another surprise came in the form of the speech of thanks from my family, which was delivered with great élan by my young sister Vijya Tanna. I say it was a surprise, because I don't think any of us knew that she could speak so well in public, and all of it without notes or prompts. Meanwhile the friends of mine who had travelled across to Jinja from Dar es Salaam, Nairobi, and Kampala all enjoyed themselves immensely, even though I got the strong impression that they were more beguiled by their surroundings and the attendant opportunities for sightseeing than by anything that happened during the wedding ceremony itself.

Gifts we received in profusion. Most of them, like wedding presents the world over, have since sunk without trace into some dark abyss of my memory. One alone, a Favre Leuba gold watch with a gold strap that was given to me by my bride's family, has stayed with me ever since, in my heart and on my wrist. Since the day I was given it, that watch, Swiss-made and of undeniable quality, has never been opened, let alone serviced, even though I have often enquired, without success, about the chances of at least getting the dial cleaned. Even now I wear it daily, although the watch face has been stained by damp and the lettering faded by age, and its original gold strap has long since been melted down and turned into cufflinks. Only on trips abroad is that beloved wristwatch put away in a drawer, to be replaced by a much more practical one with two separate dials that my daughters-in-law clubbed together to buy me, a watch that is a not-so-subtle reminder, from the days before standard trunk dialling, that telephone calls booked at daytime in my hotel in one part of the world might be answered at nighttime, almost invariably in the middle of it, in London. Besides the wristwatch, we still use a part of the tea set given to us by the Ridleys, and a clock given by the staff still adorns the sideboard in our dining room.

But back to the wedding in Jinja. At last, after two lengthy postponements, Jayli and I had finally been married to each other, with due ceremony and amid great happiness. The time thus came for us to make our return journey to Dar es Salaam. My uncle had planned that stage of the trip with almost as much care as a Madhvani, electing to make our return more of a procession than a journey. Instead of returning directly to Dar es Salaam, our chartered DC-3 would fly instead by way of Kisumu, Nairobi, and Mombasa, with extended stops at each point to allow those family members and friends who had been unable to make the long journey to Jinja to meet us all, still arrayed in our wedding finery. But by the time our plane reached Nairobi that scheme of my uncle's had fallen apart, when the local manager of East African Airways summarily reneged on the charter agreement. As soon as we touched down at Nairobi airport, with family and friends already gathering beside the aircraft, we were informed that we had to offload some of the wedding party so as to free up space for some passengers the airline had overbooked on their scheduled flights. Needless to say we were having none of that, and a stand-up row developed. Eventually, after a delay of some hours, the airline relented and we were allowed to continue our journey. But with our schedule now hopelessly derailed and darkness closing in, the last leg, to Mombasa, had to be abandoned. We flew directly back to Dar es Salaam, thereby disappointing all those who had been waiting for hours in vain to see us.

Had the manager of East African Airways in Nairobi known that someone of the character and calibre of my uncle Ratansi was on board our plane, he might have thought twice, even thrice, about chancing his arm with us that day. As soon as we got back to Dar es Salaam, my uncle filed a judicial claim against the airline for damages in respect of breach of contract. The court in Dar es Salaam duly found in my uncle's favour and awarded him both costs and damages. At that point, East African Airways decided that the court ruling in favour of my uncle set an undesirable precedent that could cost the company dearly in the future. He took the case on appeal all the way up to the Judicial Committee of the Privy Council in London, only to lose it there as well. Thus it was, thanks to the overbooking of cabin space in Kenya and the perseverance of my uncle Ratansi, that my marriage to Jayli in Uganda in May 1955 became a part of the official records of the Privy Council.

Our return to Dar es Salaam was marked by more than judicial proceedings. My father had arranged another round of lavish receptions, at which local officialdom, led by Sir Rex Surridge, the Chief Secretary, turned out in force. Then, with my uncle already turning his attention to the lawyers in Dar es Salaam, Jayli and I set out on our honeymoon. Our first stop was the Queen Elizabeth II Park in Uganda. After a few days of game-watching there, we moved on to Ruanda (now Rwanda), Burundi (today known as Urundi), and Belgian Congo, and spent the best part of two weeks sightseeing in that strange and turbulent country. Communications in that part of the world then were hardly on a par with those in Dar es Salaam, and the lack of any word from us to the Madhvani estate back in Jinja caused growing concern for our safety. Eventually Jayli's father got in touch with mine, to find out if my father had heard from us. When our holiday in the jungle highlands was finally over, we emerged unscathed from that heart of darkness, oblivious to all the fuss we had caused, and returned to Dar es Salaam and my father's house on the Upanga Road.

That house had been a fine place for me to live in, well situated next to the Upanga Sports Club and very close to the well-manicured and verdant Commonwealth Cemetery. But it wasn't as well suited for a pair of newlyweds, and despite my father's warm welcome, we didn't stay in Upanga Road for very long. Some months before the day of our marriage I had acquired an apartment much closer to the centre of town, on the United Nations Road, and it wasn't many weeks before we made it a home of our own. It was on the United Nations Road that, in the first few months of our marriage, it became readily apparent to me just why it was that the Ridleys had spoken so highly of Jayli as a potential bride. Her family was many miles away in a different land; she was just eighteen years old, with little experience of the wider world; she had been brought up in a life of privilege, if not luxury, with staff in attendance on her at all times. And yet she took to her new life in Dar es Salaam with an enthusiasm that was genuinely uplifting, with nary a murmur of complaint. She soon took complete charge of the running of our lives, turning out to be an excellent cook, a vivacious hostess, and an intelligent partner from the very first days. She also had the priceless knack of knowing just what to say to me to keep me on an even keel, in good times as well as bad. Before long she had become very close to my stepmother, and then to my sister in Dar es Salaam and my youngest brother as well, and it wasn't long before she was making up for my deficiencies in keeping in touch with my own extended family. In short, I soon became convinced just how lucky I was to have married her.

Our happiness was complete when Jayli became pregnant, and she gave birth in Kampala to a healthy baby boy, whom we named Manish. The night before his birth, on February 23rd, 1956, she had sat up late into the evening with her friends, playing cards as usual, causing several of them to predict that she was about to bring an inveterate gambler into the world. As it happens, they were wrong, though Jayli herself never lost her own love of playing cards. Once mother and child were declared fit to travel, their return to Dar es Salaam was a time of great rejoicing, both for me and my father, for at last he had been granted the first grandson on the male side, so greatly prized in our community.

These events seemed to mark the onset of a truly golden era, for me, for Jayli, indeed for my whole family. And though my father's death on August 19th, 1959 brought that epoch to a sudden end, in time another such followed, and that in turn became golden, too.

FIVE

TANZANIAN SOVEREIGNTY

In India, I had been fortunate enough to be present at the birth of a nation. Now, in the late 1950s, it was becoming all too apparent to me that I was about to witness the emergence of another.

No matter that Tanganyika had been woefully under-prepared by its colonial masters for the responsibilities of nationhood. No matter that Mwalimu [the Teacher] Nyerere, the visionary leader par excellence of the Tanganyikan nationalist movement, had been confidently predicting, as late as 1957, that independence was still a generation away. No matter that the local economy was chronically underdeveloped, with an almost frightening dependence upon the skills, markets, and capital of the soon-to-be-departing colonial master. The simple, all-important fact was that Harold Macmillan had committed himself to letting the winds of change blow down the slowly crumbling walls of British imperialism in Africa, and he was going to make sure it happened, irrespective of the lessons history might have taught him not only about the benefits to the subjects of such rapid divestment, but about the costs as well. Perhaps Macmillan's able Colonial Secretary, Iain McLeod, summed up the new mood in Whitehall most succinctly when he said to me, during his visit to Tanganyika in 1958, 'If a mistake is being made, it is better that it happens when it is going forward.' And go forward is what the British government fully intended to do.

The first step in this process had been the first-ever democratic elections in Tanganyika. When Governor Sir Richard Turnbull had announced that the first round of these would be held in 1958, the vast bulk of the local African nationalist movement had reacted with unveiled hostility. Not because they didn't want self-government; after all, the notion of *Uhuru* [freedom] had been coursing in their veins for a long time. The simple fact was that they could not bring themselves to trust the avowed intentions of the colonial power.

Two anecdotes demonstrate the gap that existed between the natives and the colonial masters. Although within the colonial administration there were many progressive, committed, and hard-working government servants, one occasionally came across officers who were just marking time, and these tended to be patronising. I once heard a young man recite the following verses at a function in Arusha, where the settler community had considerable influence:

> This is the land of changeless heat,
> Where time slops easily under your feet,
> And only the carrion crow is fleet —
> The land of *Bado Kidogo* [There is always a tomorrow].
>
> The shauri begins, but where are the men?
> The desk is prepared but where is the pen?
> The safari is coming — but when?
> You must wait for — *Bado Kidogo.*
>
> But you would teach me a harder creed
> Of what shall be gained by infinite speed;
> But who am I, that I should heed
> In the land of *Bado Kidogo*?
>
> For why should a man be always in haste,
> And worry if many things must be faced?
> There is plenty of time — and enough to waste
> In the land of *Bado Kidogo.*
>
> And he is foolish who is oppressed
> When life was meant to be a jest;
> Be what you may — and leave the rest;
> 'Tis the way of *Bado Kidogo.*
>
> For yesterday's sun was the same as today's
> And tomorrow's is still behind the haze,
> Why, then, worry? The best of ways
> Is the land of *Bado Kidogo.*
>
> This is the land of changeless heat,
> Where time slops easily under your feet;
> And I, who live but to sleep and eat,
> Am the soul of *Bado Kidogo.*

I recalled that young man when in the early sixties I heard the story of a conversation, through an interpreter, between a French agricultural economist and a peasant who was resting under a tree:

> The economist: Why don't you get some fertiliser, put in some extra effort, and work in cooperation with your fellow peasants? In a short time you would double your production.
> The peasant: What would it bring me?
> The economist: A better quality of life, extra leisure time, and happiness.
> The peasant: That is precisely what I am enjoying now!

Cultural diversity and individual difference certainly played their part in poisoning attitudes on both sides. But more substantial factors were at work in creating mistrust between the races in Tanganyika. The recently departed governor, Sir Edward Twining, had done much to further sour relations between the colonial power and the Tanganyika African National Union (TANU) when, in May 1957, he had characterised the African nationalist movement, in his usual bombastic way, as 'racist'. He'd argued that the future of the country's traditional (i.e., tribal) leaders was being threatened by 'those who base their appeal on the emotional attractions of extreme nationalism, which in effect is nothing but racialism.' Then there was the not insignificant matter of Twining's own political party, the UTP, which had been created to be, and was now operating as, a check on the long-term political ambitions of TANU. The slow progress of African advancement in the civil service and in academia had been a further factor in TANU's opposition to the proposed elections, blighting, as it did, its assessment of the good intentions of the colonial administration (at the time of independence, there were only a handful of black university graduates in the entire country). Finally, there was the make-up of the ruling bodies, which had been adjusted in the 1950s to take account of reforms in LEGCOs and EXCOs worldwide, but which still did not give African nationalists any real say in the way the country was run.

It was therefore no surprise that the bulk of African nationalists were deeply sceptical of the usefulness of elections. They had had enough of empty promises and accommodations with the colonial system, and in general were reluctant to find common cause with most of the European and Asian residents of Tanganyika, who were to be specifically excluded from membership of TANU until a year or so before independence had been finally gained.

It was in the midst of this difficult and seemingly dangerous situation that Mwalimu Nyerere's qualities as a statesman-in-waiting were first truly tested. Unlike many of his peers in the African nationalist movement, Mwalimu had always recognised the need to build the widest possible base of support for Tanganyikan nationhood, whatever membership policies the party itself might have. This was perhaps best exemplified by his acceptance of financial support from the Asian community for his trip to New York to address the UN in 1957, or the technical advice he sought from Asian lawyers when he was on trial in 1958. For, unlike many of his peers, Mwalimu had quickly recognised that a policy of boycotting the colonial power's new self-government initiatives could prove to be self-defeating, opening the political door to opportunistic parties such as the UTP, whose commitment to the best interests of the majority of Tanganyikans was in doubt. Unlike so many in Tanganyika at that time, black, brown, or white, Mwalimu was at once a man of unbending principle and a moderate, a man who would tirelessly seek to bring an end to colonialism across Africa, and indeed the globe, but wherever possible without recourse to violence.

I had seen something of such a man before, back in India in the 1940s. Mahatma Gandhi had also been a man of great principle, and one similarly opposed to the use of violence as a means to a political end. Like Mwalimu, he too had insisted on the creation of a society based on the rule of law, in which all men and women had equality of rights and opportunities. And he too had had to help guide an independence movement whose impatience with the slow progress and apparent duplicity of the colonial master sometimes got the better of its own long-term interests and good judgement. In India, I had had brought home to me the risks that such men of principle and moderation often ran in the pursuit of their principled and moderate policies. I could still remember hearing the news in Poona that Mahatma Gandhi had been assassinated, not at the hands of a colonial British assassin but, after independence had been won, by one of his own countrymen, a Hindu affronted by the manner in which the Indian Congress Party was showing its tolerance of Muslims.

But if Mwalimu himself was aware of these risks, he did not let his concern colour his judgement. For it was in these crucial years in the run-up to independence, in that highly charged situation of standoff between nationalists and colonists, that Mwalimu's genius really flowered. For this was a man with a rare gift, unique in my experience, of making men and women of all ethnic groups not only feel comfortable in his presence, but also intimately involved in his decision-making processes. Everyone who attended a meeting with Mwalimu went away from the encounter believing that he or she, and not Mwalimu, had been the one to come up with the truly bright ideas. By drawing the best out of people, he was able to convince those around him that they were all included in his plans for the future, that they were all making their own distinctive contributions to the collective thinking of the party and the government, indeed to the entire national debate across the breadth of Tanganyika.

And it was by this means that Mwalimu began the process of trying to convince a deeply hostile TANU of the wisdom of participating in the first round of the elections called by Governor Sir Richard Turnbull. The date for the first round was set for September 1958, and for the second some five months later, in February 1959. Under the Governor's plan, each of the country's three main ethnic groups was to receive ten of the thirty seats in the National Assembly that had been designated for free election. Given that this proposed division of spoils was in no way based on the ethnic make-up of Tanganyika (at that time, Asians and Europeans combined made up just over one and one-half percent of the total population of around ten million people), it was perhaps inevitable that the question of race would become the first battleground for the internal TANU debate.

The lines for this battle had been drawn in the previous two years. Ever since the legalisation of political parties in Tanganyika some years before, concerns about the inequalities, both political and economic, between the ethnic groups in Tanganyika had been the driving issue in local politics. Some TANU activists had rebutted the Twining allegations of racism by pointing to the disproportionate wealth of local Europeans and Asians, contending that their concern was not about the colour of peoples' skins but about economic egalitarianism. Some local party organisers went beyond these arguments, talking about the need to repatriate minority communities to Britain or India or Pakistan after independence was achieved. Others went still further, using public denunciations of Asian businessmen as exploiters of African farmers as a weapon in an attempt to gain control of the merchandising sector by force, as happened in some areas of Sukumuland (near Lake Victoria), where Asian middlemen were excluded from cotton marketing. Much of this anger and frustration was perfectly understandable in the circumstances. But as Mwalimu clearly recognised, any failure to channel this anger into sustainable policy-making ran the risk of unnecessary bloodshed and prolonged suffering. As a *Kenyan Weekly News* editorial of the day put it, somewhat sanctimoniously, 'No-one supposes that Mr Nyerere supports or approves the hot heads or rowdies among his followers but some pretty severe disciplining is going to be necessary if the whole is not to become dubbed as irresponsible and dangerous.'

Nyerere's problems were further complicated by the format of the proposed elections. Not only were most Africans disenfranchised by the narrow definition of the suffrage chosen by the Governor, but all of the candidates, irrespective of race, were required to compete for votes among all of the races, with the electorate being similarly required to cast their ballots for candidates of each race. None of this was consistent with the creation of a level electoral playing field, even though the arrangements being put into place were a true reflection of the economic realities of the day (with Europeans in Tanganyika earning an average annual income of £1,560, against £654 for Asians and £75 for Africans). Not surprisingly, given all of this, even Mwalimu at first baulked at the idea of contesting elections on the basis of racial parity. But as the internal debate wore on, he suddenly changed his mind, as he so often did when faced with compelling arguments, and argued that TANU had to fight these elections, however flawed they might seem. As he explained sometime afterwards, 'My party was opposed to participation in the elections. They said, "Even if we win the African seats, we are going to be dominated by the ten Asians and ten Europeans." But I said, "Don't be silly. Don't sit here and assume that all members of the Asian community, or all members of the European community, are opposed to what we are doing. Many of them are more committed [to independence] than some of us here."'

The party's annual delegates' conference debated participation in the elections for four days. The debate was heated throughout, but never spilled over into violence. By the end of it all, Mwalimu had managed to persuade a slim but nonetheless significant majority of the delegates (thirty-seven out of sixty) to support him. But the bitterness of those who had consistently advocated a boycott lingered on. In the aftermath of the conference, amid an acrid public debate fomented by those hard-liners who contended that Mwalimu's participatory approach was based on weakness, not principle, a new and explicitly anti-European (and anti-Asian) party emerged. This was the African National Congress (ANC), and this new party chose the vigorous and vociferous Zuberi Mtemvu as its leader. ANC, in its founding pronouncements, asserted that in any African country such as Tanganyika, 'the interests of Africans are paramount, and should prevail over those of the members of other races.' Mwalimu might have won a signal victory in TANU, but now risked being outflanked by the ANC.

The outcome of the party debate on participation in the first elections in Tanganyika was but one of several defining moments for Mwalimu. Among other things, his victory contributed to a signal change in the attitudes toward his leadership of the nationalist movement on the part of the European and Asian elites in Tanganyika. Previously, there had been much suspicion of TANU, largely based on fear and prejudice and ignorance. Mwalimu, too, had had his fair share of doubters. But once the detail of the TANU decision-making process had been made public, and people began to see how hard-won but how democratic Mwalimu's victory had been, attitudes began to change, and change quickly. Sitting inside the inner counsels of LEGCO and EXCO and moving around the East African, Asian, and European business circles of that day, I was able to see at first hand the impact that Mwalimu's victory was having on perceptions. And it was not just perceptions that were changing. Mwalimu's victory laid the foundations for a significant shift in voting patterns, both in the dual elections in Tanganyika of 1958-59 and in the later general elections of 1960. In the 1958-59 elections, TANU put up candidates for, and then won, all the available contested seats, obtaining over 67 percent of the total votes cast, with many Europeans and Asians opting to swing their support behind TANU. Asian candidates supported by TANU — the likes of Sophia Mustafa, Mohamud Rattansey, and Mwalimu's close friend Amir Jamal — all won seats with large majorities. In contrast, the Twining-sponsored UTP was effectively wiped off the political map, while the ANC, refusing on principle to participate, denied themselves the chance to test their strength.

From then on, the pace of constitutional reform suddenly picked up. A committee was established under Sir Richard Ramage to reshape the legislature and executive so as to increase the proportion of black Tanganyikan representation. The Governor began to consult much more closely with Mwalimu over the roadmap for future political and administrative change. Mwalimu nominated five elected TANU members to serve on EXCO (which ran concurrently with the Council of Ministers), Derek Bryceson, Amir Jamal, George Kahama, Chief Fundikira, and Solomon Eliufoo. And general elections were called for August 1960, with a view to the granting of independence at the end of the following year.

It was in the run-up to these elections that I became aware of the interest TANU were now showing in me. One afternoon I received a message from a TANU official, Kasella Bantu. He told me that he had a message for me from Oscar Kambona, the Secretary-General of TANU. The gist of that message was that both Kambona and Mwalimu were looking to me to make a public commitment to the African nationalist struggle, and that I should deliver this support to TANU by standing as a candidate in the forthcoming general elections. At once I could see that behind this appeal lay the desire by TANU's leadership to allay the concerns of a still nervous Asian business community, to reassure them that under Mwalimu's leadership an independent Tanganyika would be a country in which commercial opportunities would be available to all, irrespective of their racial or religious backgrounds.

I thought long and hard about the Kambona appeal. But still mindful of my father's advice not to mix business with politics, I eventually refused to make such a commitment. It wasn't that I lacked faith in Mwalimu personally, or in what he and the TANU leadership were trying to achieve. But I drew a careful distinction between my serving on LEGCO and EXCO as a representative of the community at large, and my pursuing a career based on an explicit identification with a political party. It was my firmly held belief that the best way I could support the emerging nation of Tanganyika was by working to build up much firmer economic foundations rather than engaging in full-time political activity.

I don't think the subtleties of that argument were readily understood by either Kambona or Mwalimu. After all, they were still contending with unceasing pressure from a significant minority of hard-line nationalists within TANU who, against Mwalimu's opposition, were still sustaining the ban on European and Asian membership in the party. Indeed it became clear to me, only two months after that offer to stand for TANU was made, that Mwalimu was not happy with my refusal to take it up. We both found ourselves attending a lunch at the Aquarium Restaurant in Dar es Salaam in honour of the Kenyan Minister for Works, Ibrahim Nathoo. During that meal, Mwalimu openly complained to Nathoo that I was more than happy to join the colonial government by agreeing to become part of both LEGCO and EXCO, but that I had no intention of throwing my support behind TANU or playing the sort of role he wanted me to play in an independent Tanganyika. There was little I could say or do at the time to placate him. I had based my decision on what I thought were sound principles and I was going to stick to it. By then any opportunity I might have had to enter the TANU lists had already passed. An alternative Asian candidate, Mahmoud Rattansey, had been selected for the Tabora constituency that would have been offered to me. A public show of support would have done me no good either, and would have compromised my principles. I therefore had to bide my time and wait for future opportunities, in my dealings with Mwalimu and the TANU leadership, to try to bring home to them my own personal commitment to an independent Tanganyika, and my readiness to serve the new nation should the call ever come.

The election campaign of 1960 proved to be a tumultuous affair. Even though Mwalimu criss-crossed the country during the campaign, always appealing for calm, constantly reminding the electorate that once independence was achieved, foreign investors would be looking for peace and harmony, there were outbreaks of racially motivated violence in the Northern Province, as well as racist editorials in the TANU newspaper, *Uhuru*, attacking Asian and European 'exploiters' of the African people. But the campaign wasn't as hot or as violent as many in the European or Asian communities secretly feared. And as Mwalimu continually insisted, in a campaign message clearly aimed at an outside audience as well as at the minority elites, an independent Tanganyika under his leadership would never turn out to be 'another Congo'. That message and others aimed at reassuring the minorities must have got through to the local Europeans and Asians, because on August 30th, 1960, 1.1 million voters gave the TANU candidates, under their campaign slogan 'Friendship for All', an overwhelming victory. TANU won seventy out of the seventy-one contested seats. Given that under the electoral procedures, eleven of those seats had been reserved for Asians (with Rattansey sweeping home in Tabora) and ten for European candidates, this outcome represented a major vote of confidence in the egalitarian approach espoused by Mwalimu. And yet, in another sharp reminder to him of the internal challenges he still faced, hardliners continued to block attempts to allow the twenty-one Asian and European candidates from officially joining TANU.

Three days after the election, on September 2nd, 1960, Dr Julius Nyerere was officially sworn in as Tanganyika's first elected chief minister. In his subsequent radio broadcast he said that nationalism had been combined with a smile and good humour. 'The people of Tanganyika became fervent nationalists without becoming racialists.' Despite his victory, he refused to join the interim government, preferring instead to make his nominations to the new Council of Ministers (formerly EXCO). Meanwhile, under an agreement he negotiated with Sir Richard Turnbull, all official and nominated members of the National Assembly/LEGCO and EXCO, like myself, were to continue in office until Tanganyika became independent, on December 9th, 1961.

That last year of waiting for independence passed quickly indeed. The feeling of anticipation, as 1961 wore on, became increasingly palpable. Like many others, both inside and outside LEGCO and EXCO, I continued to worry in private about the pitiful infrastructure that was being bequeathed to the new nation by the British. But I also knew, from my time in India as well as in Dar es Salaam, that freedom, once scented, cannot be delayed or denied. Tanganyikan independence might not have been won at the cost of recent bloodshed, as it had been in India just fourteen years previously, but it was no less prized for all that.

I still remember clearly the independence celebrations on December 9th, 1961. At midnight a spectacular fireworks display lit up the port of Dar es Salaam, where an expectant crowd in their hundreds of thousands had gathered to watch. Moments before, the Union Jack had been slowly run down the flagpole at Government House, to be replaced by the new green and yellow and black Tanganyikan flag. People were in a festive mood all around the country, dancing in the streets and hugging each other. In the villages people were huddled around radio sets to hear their new leader proclaim, 'We, the people of Tanganyika, would like to light a candle and put it on top of Mount Kilimanjaro which would shine beyond our borders, giving hope where there was despair, love where there was hate, and dignity where there was only humiliation.'

Tanganyika, my homeland, was a nation at last.

SIX

MWALIMU NYERERE AND THE UNITED REPUBLIC OF TANZANIA

Forty-four years have passed since Tanganyika gained its independence. Looking back to those early days of nationhood from the peace and calm and growing prosperity of present-day Tanzania, I sometimes wonder at the unwavering resilience and good nature of the people of this land of mine. Mwalimu kept his promise to the outside world that the newly independent Tanganyika would never be 'another Congo'. And yet, in common with most if not all countries in Africa that have emerged from the shadow of colonialism, we Tanzanians, all of us, had to endure much hardship and indignity, especially in those early and volatile decades. There was no template for a successful decolonisation, no master plan that we all could follow. Instead, with respect to every determinant of stability and growth, be it economic, social, or simply human, the newborn Tanganyika began the race for development so far behind the industrialised nations that I am often surprised that we have managed to stagger as far as we have without once descending into utter chaos. We entered this new world as dependents, and every policy option we have pursued since independence has only served to deepen our sense of reliance on others for our very survival. Whenever our leaders looked to the outside world for assistance in solving our own peculiar problems, as they had to almost constantly for the first forty years of our nationhood, we fell prey to the machinations of power politics, to the whims and fancies of academics or retired politicians hell-bent on social re-engineering, or, perhaps most painfully of all, to the failure of our well-meaning friends to trust us with consistent, unconditional funding — instead, they forced us to spend their money according to their national interests and fads, rather than our own. Even now, in my most sombre moments, I find myself fearing for Tanzania, and for all developing countries like Tanzania, bobbing, as we all are, on the tides of globalisation, perhaps no longer caught up by proxy in any superpower confrontations, but still at the mercy of forces that no one in the world can pretend to control, but that almost inexorably make the rich countries richer, and the poor countries poorer.

But now I move back to the early days of our nationhood. As I said earlier, my concerns at the sudden rush toward independence were founded in the fragility of the economy, the failure of the colonial power to train and educate the African people for self-rule, and the potential combustibility of the race question. Lo and behold, within days of Mwalimu's taking up the reins of power, the latter two combined to throw his newly installed administration off course. The first-ever debate in the new parliament turned out to be about race and citizenship; it concerned a new bill that set out a graduated approach to the acquisition of citizenship for all people other than second-generation true-born Tanganyikans. The government's seemingly fair proposals, which allowed, over time, for all long-term residents to become citizens, ran into immediate and fierce opposition from some TANU MPs, who wanted 'Tanganyika for the Tanganyikans'. Mwalimu's riposte was short and sharp. He accused the opponents of the bill of behaving like Nazis. As he later summed it up, 'If we in Tanganyika are going to divorce citizenship from loyalty and marry it to colour, it won't stop there. We shall go on breaking that principle ... going downhill until we break up the country. We glorify human beings, not colour.'

This parliamentary debate soon escaped the bounds of Karimjee Hall (the then House of Parliament), spreading across the country like an uncontrollable bushfire, with the trade unions, who had stood shoulder to shoulder with TANU throughout the struggle for independence, joining with the parliamentary militants in outright opposition to the draft Citizenship Bill. Within weeks of his assumption of power, Mwalimu found it necessary to submit his resignation as prime minister and hand over the reins of power to his deputy, Rashidi Kawawa. Instead of running the country as prime minister, Mwalimu found himself forced to go back to his roots, and those of his party, travelling the length and breadth of the country to engage in a new political debate with his people. The fact that he had to do this was a direct consequence of Britain's failure to prepare the African people for the responsibilities as well as the rights of power. The pitifully small elite of educated cadres in TANU had all been promoted into key positions of responsibility within the central government on the first day of independence. This had denuded the party of trained and educated activists, leaving the rest of it, in the regions and at the grassroots level, in the hands of party members who, pretty much of necessity, had a much more visceral approach to politics. Mwalimu thus found his rule under direct and immediate challenge from these people, and had to resign his post temporarily in order to reconnect his government to the people it now served.

While Mwalimu was away touring the country, the policy of Africanisation was pressed forward by the government now run by Kawawa. Several prominent European civil servants were made compulsorily redundant, albeit with compensation. A further 260 non-African (mainly Asian) civil servants lost their jobs, and a further 600 Africans were taken on. At the same time a crash training programme for junior civil servants was put in place.

Similar policies were implemented in the police service. By June 1962, some forty percent of the expatriate workforce had left government service. These actions did much to calm the rising tide of discontent in the majority population, who were demanding swift action by the government to remedy the imbalances and injustices of the colonial era. But the need for greater control than was possible through dialogue or limited institutional change saw, in June 1962, the passage by the National Assembly of new legislation limiting the powers of the trade union movement and handing the government the right to preventive detention.

By that time, Mwalimu had already completed his many tours of the countryside, reassured the party's supporters of his bona fides, and rebuilt the national organisation of TANU. In August 1962, he was unanimously selected as TANU's presidential candidate, and was duly elected, in a vote notable for low registration and turnout. The first crisis had passed. Thanks to a combination of traditional African methods of dialogue with the people and tough laws, the critics of what had been mistakenly perceived as pro-European and pro-Asian policies had been held in check.

But this proved to be only a lull in a longer campaign. In August 1962, the former trade union leader Christopher Kassanga Tumbo resigned his job as High Commissioner in London to form the People's Democratic Party (PDP). That same month, strike action flared in the sisal estates, which before independence had employed over thirty percent of all Africans who were in formal employment. Mwalimu's response to both of these developments was to open up membership of TANU to all races, and then to institute a one-party system. The All-Muslim National Union of Tanganyika (AMNUT) called for a referendum on the single-party system, but without success. The Preventive Detention Act was used to bring all other political parties into line, and Tumbo fled to Kenya. Union leaders, especially those responsible for the strikes on the sisal estates, were also detained without trial.

Despite the crackdown, union leaders continued to foment resistance to the government, using what they saw as the slow pace of

'Africanisation' as the stick with which to beat it. Mwalimu and his government tried to deal with this pressure by a mixture of further preventive detentions and policies designed to equalise opportunities for employment. By early 1964, he had had enough of trying to square this circle. On January 7th, he circulated a letter to all ministries, declaring, 'The nation must use the entire reservoir of skills and experience. The skin in which this skill is encased is completely irrelevant. This means that discrimination in civil service employment as regards recruitment, training and promotion must be brought to an end immediately. We cannot allow the growth of first- and second-class citizenship. Africanisation is dead.'

Four days later, revolution broke out on Zanzibar, as a result of the intervention of a little-known Ugandan, John Okello. In less than forty-eight hours, amid total chaos in the streets of Stone Town, something between fifteen and twenty thousand Arabs and Indians had been slaughtered. The Sultan's government had sought assistance from the British government, but it did not materialize, although London made arrangements for evacuation of the Sultan, his family, and others closely associated with him. Thirteen days later, on the mainland this time, an army mutiny broke out and key buildings were seized, including State House in Dar es Salaam. The rebellion soon spread to the barracks at Tabora, with the ringleaders openly challenging Mwalimu's approach to reform and race under the guise of demands for higher pay and the removal of British officers. It took intensive negotiations by Mwalimu's ministers, and then a crucial intervention by the British army, to quell that six-day uprising. Both events, the revolution and then the mutiny, underlined in the most graphic way the fragility of the local situation in post-colonial times. The mutiny in particular, which saw the former colonial power having to intervene to save Mwalimu's administration, was the most potent reminder of the limits of even Mwalimu's authority, some three years after independence. Mwalimu felt a sense of humiliation that he was forced to request assistance from British troops in putting down the mutiny, and later to ask Nigeria to provide technical military assistance.

None of this was anything close to a Congo. But for any Asian, such as myself, living in Tanganyika through these troubled times, the pervasive sense of uncertainty was unsettling enough. We in the minority communities knew only too well that our continued existence in Tanganyika was almost totally dependent upon a principled approach to the issue of race on the part of the TANU leadership. Fortunately for us, on this issue (and indeed on almost all others of principle) Mwalimu

Nyerere had continued to hold firm. Shaken though he was by the events on Zanzibar and in the barracks of Dar es Salaam and Tabora, he never wavered in his belief in the rightness of an egalitarian approach. And he soon recovered from the effects of these challenges sufficiently to re-establish and reinforce his national position of pre-eminence. Working with Abeid Amani Karume, the new leader of Zanzibar, he managed to forge together the states of Tanganyika and Zanzibar into the United Republic of Tanzania, which came into being on April 24th, 1964, barely three and a half months after the uprising led by Okello. And soon after the army mutiny on the mainland, he purged the armed forces of malcontents. All this, taken together with his public declaration that Africanisation was at last dead, helped us Asian and European citizens to keep faith with the country of which we had now become citizens.

At this time my involvement in the affairs of the fledgling state was still modest, but I was doing what I could to help address some of the problems in the educational sector. In 1963, following the implementation of the government's affirmative action programme, which rightly put its emphasis upon addressing the educational needs of local people, the children of foreigners were left without a good English medium school. I discussed this matter with a few expatriate friends, and eventually twenty of us decided to establish the equivalent of an international school in Dar es Salaam. Funds were mobilised mainly through the help of a few embassies. The US Agency for International Development (USAID) was particularly helpful. Sam Butterfield, the local director of USAID, and Ambassador E.M. Elamin of the Sudan became the subscribers of the Company. Foreign companies operating in Tanzania such as Caltex and Shell also helped with fundraising. The government supported the project, but said that its facilities should be restricted to the children of foreigners.

A suitable piece of land was found, and the school was constructed. I was appointed the school's first treasurer, and George Panayotopolous its first secretary. The latter was away for some time, and it fell on my shoulders to officiate concurrently as secretary and treasurer. Subsequently I was offered the chairmanship of the limited company under which the school was established, but turned the job down, my Tanzanian citizenship being, in my view, a disabling constraint. However, I remained on the Board for two decades as the only non-official Tanzanian representative, and participated in the school's successful effort to achieve its desired result on behalf of the expatriate community working and living in Tanzania.

But my active involvement in the educational sector wasn't limited to the International School. Besides having founded the Buguruni Deaf School in Dar es Salaam, which presently serves 238 students (including seventy boarders), and having been involved in the College of Business Education and its Board of Examiners as Chairman, I have been closely associated with the Dar es Salaam Secondary Education Society, which was also founded in 1963. This society owns the Shaaban Robert Secondary School in Dar es Salaam, named after the great poet whose work has touched the lives of millions of Tanzanians and many beyond our shores. From the outset the school received good support from the government and the people of Tanzania. President Benjamin Mkapa, himself a former governor of the school, once observed, 'I am quite certain that serving on the Board of Shaaban Robert School gave me a great opportunity to understand the challenge of education in our country and the substantial part that private initiative plays in answering that challenge.'

Shaaban Robert was, to my mind, a model of the kind of public/private partnership that Mkapa was alluding to my colleagues, and I put a lot of time and effort into making it succeed. We have been blessed with two excellent Head Teachers. Mrs Mary Koleth, now unfortunately no longer with us, laid the most solid of foundations in the early years with her winning combination of strict discipline and love of learning. More recently, Mr Suryakant Ramji has served the school with great distinction, first as Deputy Head for some fourteen years, and latterly as Head. It humbles me to know that my own contribution has not gone unnoticed. Ben Mkapa said at a 1988 graduation ceremony that 'Andy is a man of many parts and a variety of responsibilities. But in the midst of the demands made on his time he has always found time to work to promote many worthy causes, providing relief for the needy and reducing the pains and want and suffering in our society. I was saying to friends the other day that he must be the most versatile keeper of a diary in our country! He has found a special place in his diary for Shaaban Robert throughout these many years. Hundreds of parents and the school's many beneficiaries are deeply beholden to him.' Again in 2003, at the fortieth anniversary celebrations of Shaaban Robert Secondary School, Tanzania's Prime Minister Frederick Sumaye, paying tribute to me, said, 'While we appreciate the efforts of those who are the everyday face of the school, it is vitally important that we also recognise those who play their role behind the scenes, and one of those is Dr Chande, the Chairman of the Board of Governors of the School. I would especially like to congratulate Dr J.K. Chande not only for the milestone this school has attained, but also for his recent Knighthood. As the first Tanzanian to receive this rare honour in recent times, I am proud to say that Dr Chande cherishes his success with humility, hard work and dedication.' The school community has decided to name the multi-purpose assembly hall, which was officially inaugurated by President Mkapa in 1997, after me, and sought my permission to do so. I accepted the honour, provided it was done after my death. In a similar vein, when in the 1970s the mayor of Dar es Salaam, Mr Kitwana Kondo, approached me about allowing the Council to name a street after me, I declined, explaining that it is a family tradition not to have places named after us except posthumously.

To return to the wider changes that the country was going through, though I shared some of the anxieties of the Asian community, my own experience of President Nyerere at this time certainly made a difference to how I saw things. Despite my having declined the invitation from TANU to stand as a candidate for Tabora in 1960, any feelings of displeasure that Mwalimu might have felt about me did not carry over into government. Once established in office, President Nyerere gave me a number of official appointments of increasing importance, from the relatively minor chairmanship of the new National Museum (which had hitherto been the King George V Museum) to the post of first government board member of the newly constituted Tanzania Electric Supply Company Limited (TANESCO) when the government took over the Balfour Beatty stake in 1964.

But perhaps more important, I was able to give substance to my pre-independence assertion to Mwalimu that I would be better placed to serve the new state as a businessman than as a politician.

My post at the Museum, before and after independence, may have lacked any real significance, but it did give me the opportunity to become involved in some of the important anthropological discoveries of that time. In 1964, as Museum chairman, it fell to me to negotiate with one of the world's greatest anthropologists, Dr Louis Leakey, for the return of the *Zinjanthropus* skull, found by him and his wife Mary in the Olduvai Gorge in Northern Tanzania. Not surprisingly this was easier said than done. Despite the conditions of the excavation agreement signed by both Leakey and Oscar Kambona, the Tanzanian Minister for Education, which made it clear that Leakey could not keep significant evidence or artefacts. Leakey was, perhaps understandably, unwilling to return the skull to Tanzania. He contended that, notwithstanding his agreement with Kambona, he had an over-riding responsibility to the international scientific community to safeguard the skull for posterity. It was my job to convince him that returning the skull to Tanzania and keeping it safe for posterity were not two mutually contradictory aims.

I had a number of meetings with Dr Leakey in an attempt to assuage him, and we were eventually able to work out arrangements that satisfied his scientific concerns. These included constructing a secure air conditioned room with a safe at the Museum, and employing a qualified ethnographer to facilitate scientific access and research.

After this agreement in principle was reached with Dr Leakey, the Museum Board, under my direction, began to look for ways of funding this deal. The Museum was then a part of the Ministry for Social Welfare, Sports, and Culture, and the major budget of the Ministry went toward non-cultural activities. I called on Minister Mgonja, and he told me that the allocation from the Treasury was so small that it was simply not possible to provide further support for the Museum. My plea for ensuring that the heritage of Tanzania was safeguarded fell on deaf ears. With the Minister's knowledge I therefore went to see President Nyerere, who welcomed the agreement with Dr Leakey, but advised me to continue my efforts to mobilise funds from the business community rather than the government. Eventually these efforts were successful, with solid support from Williamson Diamonds, Gailey and Roberts (Unilever Group), and several other sources. These contributions not only fulfilled the terms of the Leakey agreement but also paid for a 'Hall of Man', which was designed at cost price by French and Hastings, a local architectural practice. At the Hall's official opening several years later, presided over by President Mwinyi, Dr Richard Leakey, Louis's son, gave an excellent keynote address in Kiswahili.

Meanwhile, the Museum Board, with the kind help of the Danish government, obtained the services of an ethnographer named Meyer Hesselberg, who had just completed an extended assignment in Ghana. In order to expedite his arrival I took a shortcut. Instead of formally requesting technical assistance from the Treasury, I asked Dr Wilbert Chagula, Principal of the Dar es Salaam University College, to make a formal request to the Danish Embassy that Hesselberg be allowed to accept the status of lecturer at the College whilst working at the Museum. Both College and Embassy complied with my suggestion. Housing was provided with the help of the Housing Committee, chaired by the Permanent Secretary David Mwakosya, with Bernard Mulokozi pushing the Museum's case. About three months after his arrival, Hesselberg approached the Treasury for permission to import a duty-free motor car. This application, unsurprisingly, at last brought Hesselberg's presence in Tanzania to the notice of the Treasury. I was summoned by Jacob Namfua, Permanent Secretary in the Treasury, and asked to explain how many governments were running the country. Eventually, by spelling out the details of what had become an almost unending saga, I was able to smooth all ruffled feathers, and Namfua gracefully accepted the fait accompli.

The skull is still in its vault in the National Museum even today, as well as an exact replica donated by the Leakeys and on permanent display in the Museum Hall. There have been other, even more momentous discoveries since, at the Gorge and elsewhere, but I will never forget my first encounter with *Zinjanthropus*, the bleached and, to my mind, reassuringly ordinary-looking skull of one of mankind's earliest known ancestors.

In 1965 I was appointed to take part in a three-man delegation to the United Arab Republic (UAR) to negotiate the first bilateral trade and cultural agreement. The Tanzanian team consisted of Jerry Kasambala, Minister for Commerce and Cooperatives, Uli Mwambungu, Permanent Secretary in the Ministry, and myself, with Nasor El-Buali supporting the delegation as secretary. We travelled to Cairo on United Arab Airlines in the company of Ahmed Shafik Mustafa, from the UAR Embassy in Dar es Salaam, a man of distinction who went on to be his country's ambassador to the UK. As we anticipated no formalities that evening, drinks flowed freely on the plane, so I must confess that we were all a bit worse for wear by the time we arrived in Cairo. There we were met by Egyptian Minister for External Trade, a Mr Shukr, but after the initial pleasantries we were left to stew in our own juices for an unconscionably long time in the VIP lounge. Eventually I asked our escort what was going on. Mr Mustafa made some enquiries and came back to say that the Tanzanian Minister did not have a valid yellow fever vaccination certificate. The local health officials were therefore creating difficulties, saying that they could only issue a waiver on instructions from the Egyptian Health Minister himself, who at the time was attending a wedding reception and therefore not contactable. Eventually a compromise was cobbled together and we were allowed to leave the airport.

At Shepherd's Hotel, I was further amazed at the stamina of the certificateless Minister. Despite the long flight, the long wait, and everything he had consumed along the way, he still readily accepted our hosts' offer to spend a few hours at the local Sahara City Night Club. We all crawled back to our rooms in the early morning and got what sleep we could. The following morning at 9:00 a.m. sharp, the Minister, replete with dark glasses, after hurriedly downing two large pitchers of milk, gave one of the most brilliant extemporaneous speeches I have ever heard, putting forward in the most cogent terms Tanzania's proposals for negotiations. Later on that day, when we were ushered into the presence of the late, great President Abdul Nasser to deliver a personal message from Mwalimu Nyerere, the Minister again conducted himself in an exemplary way. Nasser himself seemed distracted, anxious to move us on, seemingly knowing little about our part of the world. But for all that, we all knew we were in the presence of a most able statesman. Three days later we returned to Dar es Salaam, with the agreement in the Minister's pocket.

It was also in 1965, when I was visiting Port of Spain, that I was booked to fly to Caracas, Venezuela. I left the hotel in good time to get to the airport, but I was delayed by heavy traffic and was late for check-in for the Venezuelan flight. The plane was still on the ground, but the check-in clerk declined to accept me. I met the duty manager, and he, while very understanding, insisted that as the passenger manifest was closed it was now impossible to include me. He suggested that I fly KLM, which was due to leave about ninety minutes later. I told him that I had friends expecting me at the Caracas Hilton. Furthermore, I was not sure that KLM would have traffic rights to pick up passengers between Trinidad and Venezuela. The manager assured me that I needn't worry, I would definitely be on the KLM flight. He offered to let my friends know about the flight changes, so I gave him names and contact numbers. KLM arrived and soon I was on my way to Caracas. When I reached the Hilton it was clear that my friends had not been told of my flight changes. However, during the course of the evening it emerged that the missed Venezuelan flight had been hijacked to Cuba! God was certainly looking over my shoulder that day.

Another early example of my involvement in the affairs of state was the constructive role I was able to play in defusing private sector criticism of the government over the vexed issue of land ownership. In Tanganyika, unlike neighbouring Kenya in its subsequent de-colonisation, the issue of land ownership had not been resolved in the negotiations leading up to the handover of power. When Tewa Said Tewa, Minister for Lands in the Tanganyikan government, abolished the old freehold system and replaced it with long-term leaseholding from the state, the reaction from the local business community was sharply hostile. At that time, and in common with most other private sector economies, the commercial banks operating in Tanganyika had extended credit to the private sector using the ownership of land and property as collateral. The new law threatened to precipitate foreclosures on existing loans as well as close off all future lending. Therefore, in my capacity as a key member of the main chambers of commerce in Dar es Salaam, I got in touch with the two leading local lenders, Standard Bank of South Africa

Ltd. and Barclays, and asked their managers if the deeds that they were holding as collateral would be downgraded as a result of the new government's land law. When I was told categorically that they would not, I was able to report to the local chambers of commerce that there was no risk that existing loans would be called in. Consequently, much of the hostility in the local business community toward the new landholding system was dissipated.

My extensive East African business experience, and the network of business relationships that had accrued from my regional commercial operations, were also of use to the fledgling Tanganyikan — later Tanzanian — state. Following the creation of the East African Community (EAC), comprising Tanzania, Uganda, and Kenya, I was made a member of the Bureau of East African Affairs (BEAA), which convened at State House. In the aftermath of Ian Smith's Unilateral Declaration of Independence (UDI) in Rhodesia, the question of Chinese assistance for the construction of the Tanzania-Zambia railway became a significant issue. I suggested to Dickson Nkembo, the chairman of BEAA, that the practical arrangement would be for Tanzania to own the railway from Dar es Salaam to the Zambian border, and Zambia to own the extension into its territory, with each state accepting its respective share of responsibility for the repayment of a loan from China. I also suggested that President Kaunda might wish to consider seeking financing from a friendly country to construct a quay at Dar es Salaam port, to be owned by the Zambian government. However, neither suggestion was ever raised for discussion.

Later, I was nominated by the government to serve on the boards of the East African Railways Corporation (EARC), the East African Harbours Corporation (EAHC), and East African Cargo Handling Services Limited. I was particularly pleased to be nominated as a Board Director of EARC and, after the breakup of the EAC, as Chairman of Tanzania Railways Corporation, a capacity in which I am still serving, twelve years later. These appointments brought to my mind the experience I had gained as one of the six advisers to the general manager of East African Railways and Ports Services in the late 1950s. Immediately after the breakup of EAC I was appointed by President Nyerere as the first Chairman of Air Tanzania Corporation, and later as Chairman of Tanzania Harbours Authority. He had agreed to my request that I serve as non-executive chairman on both boards.

All of this activity in the service of the state was a reflection of the trend in public policy. By the mid-1960s, the high-level political confrontation over race was effectively over. So was the national debate about human capacity, the government having embarked upon an ambitious programme of job-related training alongside a long-overdue expansion of the secondary and tertiary education sectors for Africans. The last of my three pre-independence concerns, the fundamental weakness of the local economy, was now coming to the fore.

President Nyerere had been cogitating about all this for many years. His university years in Britain and the subsequent development of his close links to the Fabian wing of the British Labour Party had given him much food for thought. Soon after independence he had given voice to his still embryonic economic philosophy in an essay entitled 'African Socialism'. In this he expressed his deeply held conviction that socialism had been the natural order of the pre-colonial system in Africa. In those times, he asserted, 'everyone was a worker.... Not only was the capitalist, or the landed exploiter, unknown, but ... capitalism was impossible. In the old days the African never aspired to the possession of personal wealth for the purposes of dominating any of his fellows. He never had labourers or "factory hands" to do his work for him. But then came the foreign capitalists. They were wealthy. They were powerful. And the African naturally wanted to start being wealthy.'

This line of thinking formed the basis for his re-education of the TANU grassroots from 1962 onwards. He taught them that African Socialism was founded on principles of mutual respect, shared property, and the willingness of all members of society to work for the common good. Once adopted by Tanganyika, this brand of socialism would lead the country toward prosperity and social equality, toward a state of familyhood known as *Ujamaa*. As Mwalimu said in his pamphlet on *Ujamaa* published that same year, 'Socialism is an attitude of mind ... a belief in the oneness of man and the common historical destiny of mankind. Its basis, in other words, is human equality.'

The concept of *Ujamaa* continued to develop over the coming years, growing in Mwalimu's mind as his experience of government, and of the wider world, increased. To my mind, two unrelated events in 1965 made an important contribution to the future development of *Ujamaa*. In that year, the President paid the first of what turned out to be many visits to Chairman Mao's China. Almost at the same time, Ian Smith made his infamous Unilateral Declaration of Independence (UDI) on behalf of Rhodesia, thereby plunging the Commonwealth into crisis, and precipitating a major rift between the anglophone countries of sub-Saharan Africa and the former colonial power. Nowhere in Africa other than perhaps in Rhodesia did Harold Wilson's pusillanimous approach to UDI find favour. But the Tanzanian reaction was undoubtedly the fiercest. When it became clear that the *Tiger* talks, and indeed everything else that the Wilson government was doing short of a concerted and effective policy response, were unlikely to get anywhere at all, Mwalimu ordered an immediate break in diplomatic relations with Britain. By going this far, alone among all the anglophone African states, Mwalimu precipitated a further decline in the wind-down of British investment in, and trading with, Tanzania—which had been, admittedly, modest. For a developed economy in good shape, such action would have mattered very little, given that the British had never taken the local Tanzanian economy as seriously as that of Kenya or even Uganda. But in the parlous economic conditions of Tanzania in the mid-1960s, the gap left by the two-year break in relations with the British (and its effects, which lasted considerably longer) simply couldn't be filled quickly enough, whatever the Nordic and Chinese and Eastern Bloc countries might have offered by way of compensation. The break in relations marked a political watershed in Tanzania between the emergent state, still over-dependent on the colonial power, and the newly confident sub-regional power, soon to assert itself as the Front Line State and a champion of the New International Economic Order. But it also made a huge difference, in my view, to Mwalimu's economic philosophy. The effects of the falling-out with London made him realise that he now had little or nothing to lose from a much more radical approach to the country's woes. With Britain effectively out of the picture, Mwalimu was free at last to set out his socialist vision in its purest form without fear of political or economic reprisals by London. Difficult times demanded radical measures.

And so, to me it was no accident that the Arusha Declaration emerged during that two-year break in relations with London. On February 5th, 1967, following a four-day meeting of the TANU National Executive Committee in that beautiful northern city, the many components of Mwalimu's evolving vision of African Socialism were finally incorporated into a single policy document.

The Arusha Declaration ran to only two pages, but its impact upon the future of Tanzania was to be utterly profound. Within a few days, the consequences were already being felt across the government and the private sector. And over the next few years, the philosophy of national self-reliance enshrined in the Arusha Declaration was to be translated into a succession of laws, five-year plans, and far-reaching policy reforms that touched the lives of each and every Tanzanian.

When one re-reads the Declaration almost forty years on, the overwhelming sense of frustration at Tanzania's economic plight comes through in every line. With its lack of money, its scant industrial infrastructure, and its shortage of skilled people, the country was in a situation of virtual bankruptcy and near total dependency, and no one had yet come close to discovering the means of emerging from it. According to the Declaration, reliance on money was not the answer: 'It is obvious that in the past we have chosen the wrong weapon for our struggle, because we chose money as our weapon. We are trying to overcome our economic weakness by using the weapons of the economically strong.' Nor was recourse to foreign assistance the solution: 'We are mistaken when we imagine that we shall get money from foreign countries, firstly because, to say the truth, we cannot get enough money for our development, and secondly, because even if we could get it, such complete dependence on outside help would have endangered our independence and the other policies of our country.' Nor was industrial development the answer: 'Even if we could get the necessary assistance [with industrial development] dependence on it could interfere with our policy of socialism.' And so instead, the Declaration identified hard work, intelligence, and the land as the lynchpins of the country's future development. This was best summed up in the peroration, which ran, 'From now on we shall stand upright and walk forward on our feet rather than look at this problem upside down. Industries will come, and money will come, but the foundation is the people and their hard work, especially in agriculture. This is the meaning of self-reliance.'

The impact of the Declaration was both local and global, for quite aside from the domestic impact of the laws and edicts that would flow directly from the Arusha Declaration, the document was the first step in confirming Mwalimu's eminence, some would argue pre-eminence, in the nascent debate on the New International Economic Order. The Nordic countries, then as now world leaders in the provision of development aid, became even more enthusiastic supporters of Tanzania post-Arusha. The declaration also reinforced the growing affinity with the socialist states of Europe and Asia (plus Cuba). And Arusha itself gained a near mythical status, no longer as the setting for John Wayne B-movies, as it had been in the early 1960s, but as a watchword for global social justice, spawning thousands of academic treatises, inspiring imitation the world over, and even giving rise to the Arusha Centre for Social Justice, which exists even today in Alberta, Canada.

But I was clearly much more concerned about the effects of the Declaration closer to home. The local business community, already jittery, was now formally put on notice that a vigorous shakeup of the prevailing economic order was just around the corner. This can hardly have come as much of a surprise. For while the 1960s had been a period of expansion in the foodstuffs and construction sectors at least, including for my own Chande Industries Limited, there was no hiding the fact that the market system, even in the diluted form in which it then operated in Tanzania, was anathema to both the TANU leadership and their followers. Already in previous months I had had a number of specific reminders from government ministers about the direction I should be taking in respect of hiring, promotion, and procurement. I clearly recall the ministers for both Finance and Industries advising me in no uncertain terms to 'cast my net more widely' (i.e., don't buy British) when it came to purchasing milling equipment from abroad. Increasingly the talk in Dar es Salaam was of nationalisation of strategic sectors and industries.

The twenty-four hours following the publication of the Arusha Declaration saw rumour and counter-rumour swirling around Dar es Salaam. Jayli and I had previously booked a trip to Mauritius to celebrate her birthday, and whilst there I was scheduled to officiate at a meeting of the Association of Round Tables in Eastern Africa, but the new situation prompted me to cancel these plans. It was fortunate that I did, because in the late afternoon of the ninth of February, barely four days after the Arusha Declaration had been published, I was told to present myself at the office of the Minister for Commence at eleven o'clock sharp the following morning.

SEVEN

THE CHALLENGE OF NATIONALISATION

I didn't get much sleep during the night of the ninth of February. Despite feeling tired and over-anxious, I went in to work the next morning as usual, to my offices alongside the milling operations on the old Pugu Road. I stood on the carpet in front of my desk, looking out across the road at the site of the new Tazara Railway Station and wondering what exactly was going to happen next.

I didn't have to wait long before I found out. Just before eleven o'clock I presented myself at the front gates of the Ministry for Commerce and was ushered into an upstairs conference room. There, along one side of the table, were gathered many of my colleagues from the milling industry. Jack Jones, the CEO of the largest of the corporations (and head of the only company bigger than mine), was on hand, as were representatives of the other six milling operations. On the other side of the table were two empty seats. These were soon to be filled by Abdul Rahman Mohamed Babu, the Minister for Commerce, and by an officer from the Ministry for Home Affairs. Meanwhile, just outside the door, a man in a plain clothes could be seen loitering, a policeman by the look of him, an intelligence officer almost certainly.

As soon as he came in and sat down, Babu opened the meeting without much ado. He wished us all good morning, in English, and then picked up the paper in front of him. It was a brief prepared statement saying that all the shares in our respective milling companies would henceforth be vested in the Treasury Registrar, effective noon that day. Existing shareholders would be given 'full and fair' compensation. That was it. Babu finished as abruptly as he had started. All of our companies had been nationalised in under a minute.

On our side of the table, we all sat looking ahead in stunned silence. I stared across at Minister Babu, in his open-necked short-sleeved shirt, and saw him looking down at an unopened packet of Sportsman's cigarettes on the table in front of him. Then, to my left, Jack Jones suddenly spoke up.

'Are we allowed to ask questions?' He sounded agitated, if not aggrieved.

'No,' said Babu quietly, calmly spreading his hands out on the table.

'Could we at least have a copy of the statement?' I asked. 'I'll need it, in order to give an accurate briefing to Sir James Simpson, my company's chairman in Uganda.'

Babu looked up and across at his colleague from the Ministry for Home Affairs. They stared at each other for a moment, as if transferring their thoughts back and forth, and then Babu nodded silently at his fellow minister. He turned back to us and addressed me in person. 'Okay,' he said, and the two men on the other side of the table got up and left the room to prepare a set of copies.

This being a government office in Tanzania in 1967, it took much much longer to prepare the copies than it ever had to draft them and convey their original message. While Babu and his silent partner were out of the room, there was precious little in the way of conversation among the eight of us still sitting motionless on the other side of the table. We were all in shock, and besides, everything anyone could say had been said.

It was shortly before noon when we finally left the Ministry building, all clutching envelopes containing our respective copies of Babu's statement. We all went our separate ways, not stopping even to share commiserations, and I went back to my office, only to find armed uniformed policemen stationed around the building. They hadn't been there when I'd left at half past ten, I was sure of that. Their presence around me now, silent but menacing, was just another sign that the government would be leaving nothing about this particular nationalisation to chance.

The first thing I did when I got back to my office was to speak to my brother Chuni, telling him everything that had happened. Then I put in a telephone call to Sir James Simpson in Kampala. Sir James knew Tanzania well, having worked in the oil industry in Tanganyika prior to independence. But his response to my call that day betrayed a profound lack of understanding of the current situation. When I had recounted to him all that had happened that morning, including the fact that armed guards were around the building, his first words were, 'This is outright robbery.' He then advised me to go and see the President immediately to find out from him exactly which law gave him the right to summarily nationalise the milling industry. At that point, conscious of the painstaking preparation the government had made, which almost certainly included the tapping of my telephone line, I put the receiver down. But within a couple of minutes the indefatigable Simpson came back on the line, complaining that we had been cut off. I then explained to him that even if there wasn't a law explicitly sanctioning the nationalisation of the milling industry, it wouldn't take long to draft and pass one. I then rang off again and called Jayli's brother Jayant in Uganda.

To their enormous credit, he and his younger brother Manubhai understood the reality of the situation immediately. After all, President Milton Obote of Uganda had for some time been talking of something similar, a Common Man's Charter, which would put all of the means of production under the ownership of the state. He assured me that the Madhvani family would do whatever they could to assist me. They would send a plane from Uganda, not least to pick up the books of the other subsidiary companies in their group that had their headquarters in my building, such as Kilimanjaro Breweries. He would also talk to Edgar Wadley, a chartered accountant in the UK who had worked for him in the past. If there was anything else that needed doing on the financial side, Edgar would probably know about it.

Jayant rang off and I began to think about clearing up the papers in my office. I rang the buzzer on my desk to summon an office clerk. No one came. I rang again, and when nothing happened, the reality of what was happening to me finally hit home, triggered, as is so often the case, not by some profound event, but by the most mundane. I took a deep breath and stood up, looking out the window once more at the Tazara Station. My brothers and I were now in the same financial boat, up the same creek, if you like, and without a paddle between us, for neither of us had any financial assets other than the capital of the company that the state had just taken from us. Neither of us even had so much as a bank account, accustomed as we were to drawing money from the company accountant as and when we needed it. The company's cashier acted as our banker, receiving our monthly emoluments and making payments on our behalf.

My brother was younger, single, and perhaps more canny than I was. Unlike me, he had refused to take up the post-independence offer of Tanzanian citizenship, opting to remain a British citizen, with a British passport. Now, angered as he was by the government's decision to nationalise us, it didn't take him long to decide on his next course of action. He would leave Tanzania for good.

Having rung Jayli to put her in the picture, I stayed in my office on the old Pugu Road until around seven o'clock, separating out my personal papers from the commercial correspondence of the firms that were headquartered there. All too aware of the armed guards, who were still stationed outside the building, I made no effort to take my personal papers out of the office that evening. Instead I put them in a pile on my desk, alongside the other separated piles of business papers. As I left the building, I was acutely conscious of being watched, of having been formally put under surveillance.

By the time I arrived home that evening, I must admit that I felt close to the breaking-point. My mind was racing, and all manner of foolish speculations tumbled through my head. The one image that kept coming back to me time and again was of my father, and how everything he had achieved in Tanzania on the family's behalf had come to naught. Over forty-seven years, two generations of my family had laboured long and hard, painstakingly building up a business founded on thrift, a sense of fair play toward employees and suppliers alike, and what today would be characterised as a true sense of corporate responsibility. Like so many Indian businessmen, we had ploughed back almost every penny we had earned into the company, always prizing future growth over any thought of personal consumption. Our efforts had generated several fortunes, but all of them had gone back into the business, and now those fortunes had been plucked by the state, like so much low-hanging fruit. I found myself wondering if my belief in the willingness of the Tanzanian state to let me continue my business activities without any form of hindrance had been but a symptom of a wider *naïveté* on my part. After all, at least my brother had had the prescience to anticipate the possibility of some future disaster, and had hung onto his British passport. I, by contrast, was a fully fledged Tanzanian citizen, with no future means of support.

Such was my state of mind when I got home that evening. The world seemed to be closing in on me. I no longer knew what I was doing or thinking. But Jayli stopped me from losing my grip, from pacing the room, from pushing myself into an unreasoned frenzy. She talked to me, calmly, sensibly, articulately, and as the night wore on her wisdom and resilience and reassurance began to bring me to my senses. As she said at one point during our long conversation that night, what God has seen fit to take away, he will one day give back. I began to recall that life, after all, must have a divine purpose, that I had been through troubles before and surmounted them, and that it was paramount for me to stay calm and avoid rash decisions that I might always regret. Above all, Jayli brought home to me the fact that the education of our children, the most important thing in the world to the both of us, was already guaranteed by the trust fund my father-in-law had set up for this purpose. Everything else in our lives of a lesser priority would come back into perspective over time.

Thus steadied, I went in to work the next morning as usual, arriving at the building at around nine o'clock, again finding the building ringed by armed guards. Inside, in my office, a stranger was standing by my desk, bending over and carefully examining the contents of my waste-paper basket. As I walked in through the door, he quickly stood up straight and stepped forward to introduce himself. He said his name was Hironimus Msefya, and that he had just been appointed by the President as chairman of my company. I asked him whether he wanted to go out and about and meet the staff. 'No,' he replied. 'I wanted to meet you first.'

I spent much of the next hour talking to Msefya. It soon transpired that he was a purely political appointee, a former MP with no experience whatsoever of the milling industry. He was an amiable fellow, though, and showed no sign of any personal or, indeed, corporate malice toward me. After he left my office that morning, without ever introducing himself to the rest of the employees, I rarely saw him again around the building.

After he had gone, I continued the job of putting my papers in order. Meanwhile, in Karimjee Hall, the seat of the national parliament, my prediction to Sir James Simpson of the day before was coming to pass. In an emergency session of parliament, a new bill to nationalise the milling industry was introduced on the floor of the House by Commerce Minister Babu. The bill specified, in line with the prepared statement of the previous day, that 'full and fair' compensation would be paid to all shareholders of the milling companies. It went on to state that employee emoluments and benefits under state ownership would be 'no less favourable' than they had been previously. The bill concluded by calling on owners and management to comply with 'the national interest' to ensure a smooth transition from the old regime to the new. Debate on the bill was perfunctory and it was passed into law that day without a single dissenting vote. When I heard of this on the radio that evening, I couldn't suppress a wry smile. If I had taken up Mwalimu's earlier offer of a TANU seat in Tabora, I would have ended up being a party to my own bankruptcy.

On the following day, I was ready to get back to business. I called a meeting of staff, to talk to them about my future plans, but also to hear their concerns. I found the Asians among them still in a state of shock, worrying, as they were, about their own futures in the country. The local African staff were much more sanguine. Indeed, some of the African workers were so thrilled at the news that their government had begun to take control of the means of production that they no longer felt any need to do their daily work.

That afternoon, a Wednesday, I was summoned to State House to see the President. Unlike on previous occasions when I had called on him at home or in the office, Mwalimu was sitting at the table in the Cabinet room, and a young note-taker sat on a chair in the corner. And unusual for a Tanzanian President, Mwalimu didn't get up when I entered the room, instead motioning to me to sit down on one of the chairs near him.

He began the meeting with an apology. He told me how sorry he was that he had had to take the decision to nationalise my company. But I had to understand that the milling industry, in buying grain from the peasants for sale to consumers, played a sizeable role in the provision of the Tanzanian staple diet. Under the terms of the Arusha Declaration, this sector of the economy had to be brought under public ownership. Hence the rapid decision to nationalise.

He then went on to ask me about my future plans. Had I got any, and what were they?

I replied by telling him that in my view he had just made a great mistake. Nationalisation was not the answer to Tanzania's economic problems. History would be the judge as to which one of us was right.

Mwalimu visibly bridled at that. 'Never mind history,' he snapped. 'What do you want to do? If you'd like a post in the government, perhaps in the foreign service, I'm sure that can be quickly arranged.'

It was my turn to give a brisk answer. I had no interest in the foreign service (after all, I had recently turned down the offer of a job with UNIDO). 'I want to continue to run this company, for as long as I am allowed to.'

Mwalimu smiled at this. '*Endelea* [carry on],' he replied. He added that measures would be put in place to ensure that the family's claim for compensation would be settled fully, fairly, and expeditiously.

I went back to my office and found that the workers were still more interested in celebrating nationalisation than getting back to work. I immediately called a meeting of the shop stewards and told them, 'Yes, the company now belongs to the state, but that means it belongs to you and me. If the workers cannot work as they did previously, then my position will be made untenable, and I will have to go back and talk to the President, who presumably will bring someone else in to run the place.' I asked the shop stewards to go and talk to the workers and put all this to them. They did, and from then on the workforce knuckled down, and never needed another reminder of their duty.

When I reached the end of another day, again I felt exhausted. Yet although it didn't feel as if we had returned to business as usual, and probably never would again for a long, long time, at least the company was up and running again, the closest approximation to normality there had been all week.

Kanku Chande, J.K. Chande's mother.

Keshavji Chande, J.K. Chande's father, 1957.

The present station building has its completion report dated 1925 and was preceded by grass-thatched mud buildings. Tabora/Igusule (second station after Bukene) on the Mwanza line was constructed by the Germans between 1914 and 1916. The railway reached Tabora in 1912 and Kigoma in 1914. In 1951, the Chande Brothers applied for a siding to their godowns at Bukene.

Andy Chande's parents on the right with his grandmother and uncle on the left, along with his youngest sister and youngest brother.

Andy Chande with his youngest brother Suryakant in 1944.

Andy Chande as a schoolboy in 1944.

Andy Chande in his school days with his friends from St. Peter's Boys' School and Kimmins Girls' Schools in Panchgani, Satara District, India, 1946.

Keshavji Chande and Rumkunver Chande, the author's stepmother, in 1956.

Jayantilal (Andy) Chande and Jayalaxmi (Jayli) Madhvani marry on May 5th, 1955, Jinja, Uganda.

Mr Chande being greeted by Sir Edward Twining (later Lord Twining) Governor of Tanganyika in 1956.

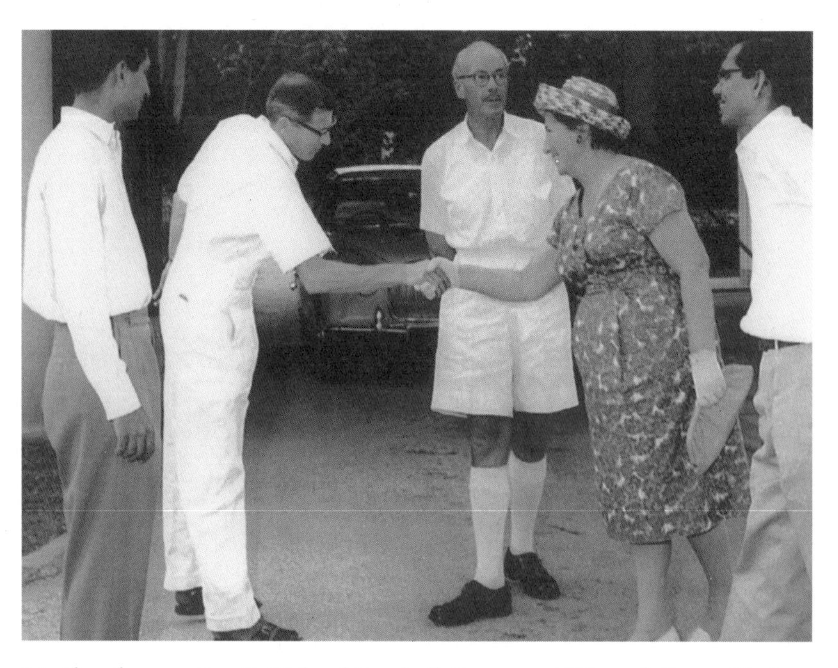

Mr Chande escorting Sir Richard Turnbull, Governor of Tanganyika and Lady Turnbull to the head office of Chande Industries Ltd. in 1959.

Clerk Mr Fenwick Klenell administers the oath to Mr Chande as a Member of Tanganyika's Legislative Council on April 28th, 1959. On his left is Chief Kidaha Makwaia; on the right are George Houry, Q.C. and Sir Charles Philips, and in the background, Amir Karimjee and Joan Davis.

His Royal Highness Prince Philip, The Duke of Edinburgh, speaking with Mr and Mrs Chande on the Independence Day of Tanzania, December 1960.

Mr and Mrs Chande being received in the State House by President Julius Nyerere, 1961.

J.K. Chande with Abdulkarim Karimjee, Speaker of Tanzania's Parliament, in 1961.

Paul Bomani, Minister for Finance and Mr William Hood, Permanent Secretary, Ministry of Commerce and Industries, with Mr Chande in 1961.

Andy Chande sits to the left of India's first Commissioner (Ambassador) accredited to Kenya, Uganda, Tanganyika, Zanzibar, Rwanda, and the Belgian Congo at a tea party in 1962.

Mr Chande as the President of Association of Chambers of Commerce and Industries of Eastern Africa receiving President Julius Nyerere at a dinner in 1964.

Andy Chande making a presentation in 1964 to Indira Gandhi, India's Minister for Information and Broadcasting (later to become Prime Minister of India).

Mr Chande with President of Tanzania, Julius Nyerere, 1964.

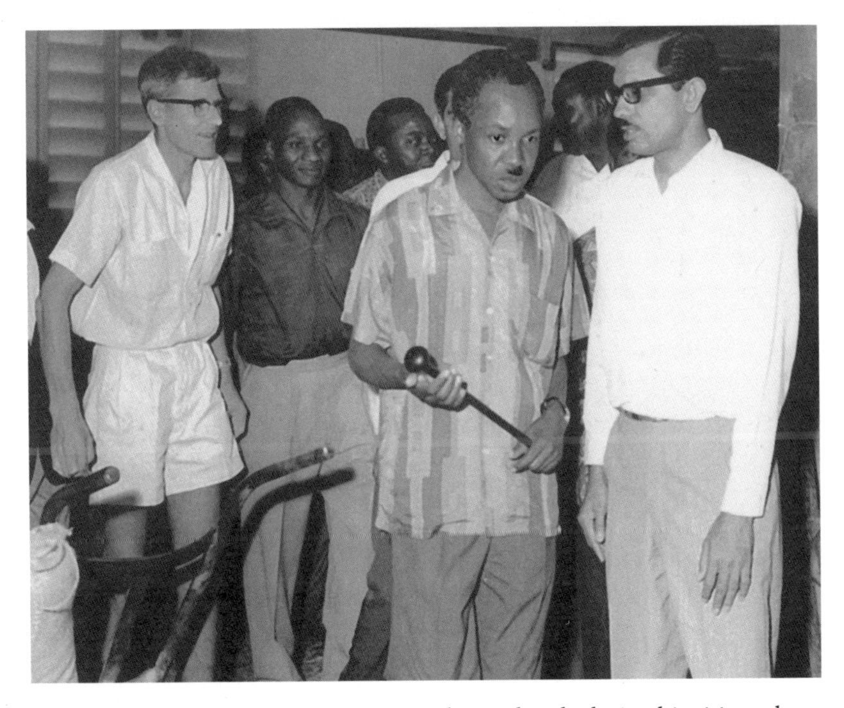

President Julius Nyerere in discussion with Mr Chande during his visit to the Chande Industries Ltd. milling company in 1964.

Andy Chande and his brother Chunilal making a presentation to Abdalla Fundikira, Minister of Justice, in 1965.

Grain milling complex of Chande Industries Ltd. in Dar es Salaam, nationalized in 1967.

Hon. Rashid Mfaume Kawawa, former Vice-President and Prime Minister of Tanzania addressing workers of the National Milling Corporation in 1968. The author is seen on his left.

Mark Newman Gilbey (of Gilbey's Gin fame), friend and business associate of Mr Chande, at his residence in 1968. Others in the photograph are the Hon. Clement George Kahama, then General Manager of National Development Corporation, Dickson Nkembo, Permanent Secretary in the office of the President, and John A, Irwin, Canadian High Commissioner.

President of Lebanon Charles Helou receiving Mr Chande when he called on him in his capacity as the World President of Round Tables and Youth Service Clubs, 1969.

In 1969, Mr Chande presents a gift to His Royal Highness Prince Albert of Belgium (now HM King of Belgium).

Derek Bryceson, Minister for Agriculture and Cooperatives, and Andy Chande in 1971.

In 1979, Mr Chande and his fellow Rotarians making a courtesy visit to the President of Kenya, Daniel Arap Moi.

Kenneth Kaunda, President of Zambia, receives the author in 1982.

President of Tanzania Ali Hassan Mwinyi recognizing the services of Mr Chande as Chairman of the National Polio Eradication Committee in 1994.

The following day my work was interrupted by yet another summons, this time from Minister for Finance Amir Jamal, a Tanzanian of Indian origin. Amir was a close confidant of the President, with a relationship that had been forged when Amir had helped in the funding of Mwalimu's successful defence team in a trial held in 1958. Amir's summons to me took the form of an invitation to take a late lunch with him at around half past three at his house in Seaview. I told him I had already eaten, but would come along all the same.

Amir's efforts to get the meeting off to a friendly and informal start didn't fare too well. When he said to me that he'd heard I'd been to see the President the previous day, I replied that I'd been summoned to State House, and had not just dropped by for a chat. Sensing my mood, Amir quickly turned to the business at hand. The President had asked him to oversee the rapid settlement of the Chande family compensation claim. A committee for this purpose was going to be appointed, and the Permanent Secretary in the Finance Ministry, Amon Nsekela, would soon be in touch with me to let me have more details of membership and remit and suchlike. I thanked Amir for this and waited for Nsekela's call. What Amir had failed to tell me, however, was that he had personally instructed the chief cashier of Chande Industries Ltd. to refuse to hand over any more money to me (or to my brother) until further notice. Similar instructions had gone out to the cashiers of all the other nationalised milling companies.

It was no surprise to me that the committee to oversee the 'rapid settlement' of my family's claims was anything but rapidly appointed. Eventually, after a delay of several weeks, the Deputy Secretary to the Treasury was appointed as chairman, with a representative each from the ministries for Industries and Finance added to the ranks. The last member to be appointed was Steen Hansen, a Danish accountant who had been seconded to the Tanzanian government by the government in Copenhagen as an adviser to the Treasury, and who later was founding CEO of the Tanzania Audit Corporation. This was hardly good news to me, given Hansen's growing reputation for his doctrinaire, almost punitive approach to the compensation issue. In the meantime, the cashier's instructions not to give me any money had been faithfully obeyed, which meant that neither my brother nor I had any money at all to pay for the daily costs of living.

Friends, especially Europeans and Africans, rallied round us. Many of my Asian friends stayed away at first, perhaps nervous of 'guilt' by association. But the efforts of friends could not keep the financial wolves from the door. Then Jayli's family came to the rescue again. Her brothers sent two cheques for twenty thousand Tanzanian shillings, one each for my brother and me, drawn on the Standard Bank of South Africa Limited in Jinja. This money, together with the continuing material assistance of many of our friends in Dar es Salaam, kept the family just above the water line until a more substantive solution to our money woes could be found.

Before long, the very process of privatisation that had ruined me became, ironically enough, a source of additional employment. The nationalisation of the banking sector followed hard on the heels of the Arusha Declaration, and for reasons best known to the Tanzanian government, perhaps because of my appointment in 1966 as Chairman-designate of the proposed East African Board of Barclays Bank DC&O, I was asked to become the CEO of the new National Bank of Commerce. I declined this offer, pointing out that until recently I had never even had a bank account. But the government persisted in wanting me to become involved, so eventually I agreed to become a member of the new board, with responsibility as vice-chairman of the Loans and Advances Committee.

The first acting general manager of the new bank, Robert Stott, was a central banker with little substantive commercial experience. It soon became clear that the combination of his obvious Englishness and his commercial inexperience was not a winning one for the Tanzanian government, and Stott was quickly shunted aside in favour of another central banker, this time a Dane named Jacobson. He did all that he possibly could under the circumstances, but found himself, like Stott before him, being constantly second-guessed in his decisions by the Board. At that time, the Board included the likes of Professor Konradsen, a Scandinavian academic whose views on the economy made Mwalimu look like a monetarist, and Professor Reginald Green, a legendary, some would say infamous, American academic who had spent several years seconded to West and East African governments thanks to the largesse of the Ford Foundation. There is a book to be written about the influence of the likes of Professor Green in Africa in the 1960s, but this is not it, and I never want to be the person to have to write it. Perhaps it is sufficient for me to point out here that, at least in the eyes of the business community in Dar es Salaam in the sixties and seventies, academically brilliant but inexperienced and sometimes perhaps misguided people such as Green gave a false veneer of credibility to some of the stranger experiments that were being conducted in the name of African Socialism.

The ongoing problems with Konradsen and the Board led Nsekela, the Chairman of the Board, to make an approach to me for help in finding an experienced new chief executive. I used my contacts in America and Europe, including David Rockefeller in New York and François Gavotty in Paris. The latter recommended one Jacques Gerbier to me. A banker with experience at the Banque Nationale de Paris who spoke fluent English, Gerbier had just finished an assignment in Madagascar, so he already had experience of working in (admittedly francophone) Africa. After Gerbier was interviewed by Ambassador Katikaza in Paris, Nsekela invited him to meet us in Dar es Salaam, and we got him to come on board. Though an odd character, strangely diffident for one so successful, he proved to be an extremely competent banker. This he needed to be, because the new National Bank of Commerce was by then the third-largest bank in the whole of Africa.

Having thus used my influence to good effect in respect of one nationalisation, you might be forgiven for thinking that the government might go easier on me back at the milling corporation. But you would be wrong. In March 1967, four weeks into the new regime, I received a message from Deputy Secretary Mayisela, from the Treasury, telling me that he wanted to see me immediately. I didn't need to be a soothsayer to know that this meeting would not be about any future plans for the milling industry, but about the Chande family's financial past.

Needless to say, I was right. When I arrived at Mayisela's office, he showed no interest at all in how the business was now running. Instead he produced company documents that he'd obtained from our accounts department showing that both my brother and I had in the distant past been granted low-interest loans from Chande Industries in order to purchase our respective homes. That sort of practice might have been okay then, Mayisela went on, but the fact was that we were all now in a different ball game. My brother and I now had to repay these loans forthwith, and I was to inform my brother accordingly.

By now I was becoming more adept at playing the new game. 'Fine,' I replied. 'I perfectly understand. You can take the repayment of my old loan out of the "full and fair" compensation you will soon be paying me for nationalising my assets.' At this Mayisela, to give him his due, smiled in acknowledgement of my gambit. He then went on to tell me, in confidence, that in calling in the loan he was only acting under instructions. To take matters forward, I should now therefore write to the Permanent Secretary, setting out my proposal for deducting the loan from the compensation payment I was soon to receive.

This I did, and was not entirely surprised to hear nothing more about the loan. The following month, however, Mayisela called me in again. This time he wanted to talk to me about my company car, an off-white Toyota Crowne de Luxe. It was hardly a luxury vehicle, even in those days, but it did have the advantage of being equipped with an air conditioner and a tiny fridge in the boot. Mayisela told me that this car rightly belonged to the state and had to be surrendered. Once I had complied with this, the new milling corporation would provide me with an alternative vehicle for official use. There was, however, one other option. If I wished I could of course buy the Toyota back from the state, at a purchase price to be set by the government.

This time I wasn't in the mood to adopt a softly-softly approach. I as good as told Mayisela where he could put his car. A few weeks later I decided to give up the Toyota and get a car that was a good deal better than might have been on offer from the government. Taking advantage of the hard times in the milling industry, I relieved my fellow victim of nationalisation, Jack Jones, of his old cream-coloured Mercedes (TDK 305) at a bargain rate, mindful of the fact that he was winding down his affairs in Tanzania.

These monthly interventions by the government did nothing for my morale. Having got their pound of flesh the first time round, they now seemed to be after the bones as well. Many of my former colleagues in the business saw in these provocations a concerted campaign to squeeze them out of the country, and most of them called it quits. Within three years of nationalisation, there was not one European left in a senior management position in the entire industry. Asians too, were thinner on the ground. But having made the momentous decision to stick it out, I personally had no problem fending off these monthly opportunistic attacks. The fact that I had been appointed as manager of my old firm on my previous salary just a week after nationalisation was, to my mind, as clear a signal as I could get that Mwalimu had been sincere in asking me to *endelea*. Moreover, the generally sympathetic approach taken by Mayisela was in keeping with a policy that was going to squeeze the fruit as dry as it could, but not bin it altogether. Besides, if they hadn't known that they needed me around to run the business at the time of nationalisation, they certainly did now. The workers wanted to work for me, whatever their rank or race. And the market had spoken for me as well, at home as well as abroad.

The first days of nationalisation had been tough for our network of international suppliers and consumers. As soon as they'd heard what had happened, they suddenly became very risk-averse. Previously I had bought almost everything I needed in the way of machinery on generous lines of credit. In February 1967, days after nationalisation, these lines of credit suddenly dried up, and the company did not have the capital reserves to make up the shortfall. My word had been my bond, but now, in the new situation, suppliers were no longer willing to accept it, arguing with some justification that as I was now a mere employee who might be around in the future when the bills came due but just as easily might not, they no longer wanted to have anything to do with credit. Indeed it was not until October 1967, when suppliers seemed finally to conclude that I was going to be around for good, that I was able to put the international side of our operations back on a sound footing. And all the time that I was trying to convince our markets of the wisdom of continuing to trade with us, the petty harassments, including phone-tapping and surveillance, didn't stop.

In October 1967, at a time when I at last felt that the crisis on the business side had passed, my wife and I were invited to take a trip to New York as a guest of Trans World Airlines, which had recently broken into the local market. I did not hesitate to accept their offer, because by that time I was really in need of a break. A number of other Tanzanians had been invited as well, including Hasnu Makame, the Minister for Tourism and Natural Resources, and we all flew off together in high spirits. On the third day of our trip, just after we had arrived in New York via Athens, I received a message from the President's secretary in Dar es Salaam. Mwalimu wanted to see me immediately. I got back to the secretary and told him to explain to the President that I was out of the country, and that I'd see him as soon as I got back. But as is so often the case in such situations, the secretary didn't want to tell his boss the bad news that I couldn't see him immediately, let alone the reason why. In desperation, I sent a message back to the Permanent Secretary in the State House, explaining that I was in New York as a guest of TWA; that I was more than prepared to leave immediately for Dar es Salaam, but that I would have to travel by another airline (the TWA flights were weekly) and would have to spend money I didn't have to travel at full fare. Eventually, after an agonising wait, a message came back telling me to stay on in New York, and come see the President on my return to Dar es Salaam.

Unsurprisingly, the rest of my stay in New York was pretty miserable. What should have been a break turned into another four days of torment. Try as I might, I couldn't work out why the President wanted to see me so urgently, and my mind filled up with all sorts of awful hypotheses. When the week was finally up, I travelled back to Dar es Salaam in a state of high anxiety, and on landing I immediately phoned State House. It turned out that the President wasn't there, having left Tanzania for a summit of the Non-Aligned Movement. He had, however, left instructions with his office for me to go and see Derek Bryceson, the Minister for Agriculture. When I got to Bryceson's office I found that he too was unavailable, being in a meeting with the Swedish Ambassador. But David Mawakosya, the Permanent Secretary at the Agriculture Ministry, noting my obvious agitation, not to mention my jet lag, sat me down in the outer office and told me that the President had instructed the Minister to tell me that he wanted my help in creating a homogeneous unit out of the eight nationalised milling companies, and in managing it.

After all of the agonies I had been through in New York, this news came as something of an anti-climax. After nine months in which I had been pestered and pilloried and made penniless, I was unprepared for such an eventuality. Never in my wildest imaginings in New York had I considered the possibility that the summons from the President would be for anything other than a dressing-down, or a further rebuff. Instead, I was now being asked to become CEO of a new national milling conglomerate, with the terms and conditions of the contracts to be handled directly by the President.

When I was finally ushered in to see Bryceson, I told him that I'd need time to think about the offer before getting back to him.

Bryceson looked surprised. 'Why do you need time to think it over?' he asked.

'Because I need to think through the concept of amalgamation,' I replied.

'Do you have any other reservations?' Bryceson asked, though he didn't look as if he wanted to hear any.

'Well,' I continued, 'Mine was only the second-largest of the milling companies. At the largest, there are still five people on secondment from the former parent company. The moment all of the firms are consolidated these will leave, and much know-how will be lost. For example, I know nothing of provender milling, the manufacture of foodstuffs for farm animals and domestic pets.'

'What else?' It was Bryceson's turn to grow agitated.

'Well, a circular has just been sent out by SCOPO [the Standing Committee on Parastatal Organisations]. This in effect revises downwards the salaries in the nationalised industries in line with the new national prices and incomes policy. If employers stick to the letter of this new circular, then the prospects for promotion for staff are zero.'

Bryceson fell silent. But Mawakosya, his Permanent Secretary, piped up. 'Anything else?'

'Yes.'

'What?'

'The Labour and Immigration departments are taking between four and six months to process applications for work permits. I can't recruit the staff I need that way.'

'Send the applications to me from now on. I'll see them through,' said Mawakosya. 'Anything else?'

'I still need time to think it over.'

Bryceson's face fell still further.

On returning home, I felt restless and troubled. At the end of a troublesome week, and at the end of a transatlantic journey, I was not in the best state of mind to make momentous decisions. At a time when officials in several government ministries were making it very difficult for me to run my own milling operations, I was being asked to take on the massive additional task of consolidating and rebuilding the entire industrial sector. I talked things through with Jayli, and that helped a lot, though my mind was still far from being made up. But sleep proved elusive, until finally, at two o'clock in the morning, I resorted to taking some sleeping pills.

The next day, a Saturday, I didn't wake up until around midday. I felt awful, still jet-lagged, and under the influence of sleeping pills I wasn't used to taking. But when I got up and went into the shower, I suddenly realised that I had at last made up my mind as to what to do. There is a Gujarati proverb that says that if a barber has already shaved half of your face, you should let him finish the job, irrespective of any dangers you might run. It was like Hobson's choice, really. I had no option but to do what the President was asking me to do.

The following Monday, the Permanent Secretary in the Ministry for Agriculture called me into his office. He said that he had heard of my concerns about the proposed appointment and he sympathised with them. He then went on to list a number of things that the government was prepared to do to help me out. First, they would ask me, and not some government official, to prepare the first draft of the legislation creating this new consolidated corporation. It didn't matter if I didn't use the correct legal terminology. The important thing was to get the content right, to make the draft bill my charter of operations, and to let them worry about the legalese. Secondly, the government would sit down and talk to me at length before any names were put forward for the new corporation's board of directors. Thirdly, the government would take a pro-active approach to the new SCOPO directive on wages in nationalised industries. If necessary they would hold special meetings with the workers in the milling industry to see what could be done to improve promotion incentives.

I thanked him for all this, and said that the assistance offered would almost certainly be needed. I then went on to say that I had decided to take the job.

Thus ended the most turbulent nine months of my life. In that time, I had stood powerless as everything my family had worked so hard to build up over two generations had been taken away from us at the stroke of a pen. I had seen my brother take the momentous decision to leave Tanzania for good. I had seen my family suffer the torments of not knowing how we were going to keep a roof over our heads. And having lost pretty much everything I had owned, including my own company, I now found myself agreeing to run the entire milling industry on behalf of the very government that had nationalised my assets.

They say that experience is the best teacher. Well, I learned a lot that year, about myself, about Jayli, about the young country of which I had become a citizen. In going through such torments, I came to appreciate much more keenly than ever before what was important in my life and what was not. Throughout 1967, Jayli had remained calm and focussed and strong when all around her was in chaos, and that strength of character of hers helped pull me through. I too discovered previously unfathomed depths of fortitude, an ability to weather a storm without compromising on matters of principle. Perhaps most important of all, I came to recognise that the journey that had started all those years before in Bukene could not be broken, even by a cataclysm such as this. Tanzania was my home, my country, for good and for ill, and in order to be re-baptised as a true Tanzanian, I had had to experience vicariously, if only for a few months, the life that has been the lot of so many of my fellow countrymen since the first colonial incursions into East Africa. By sharing the harsh experience of so many of my countrymen, I finally came to comprehend that their reality consisted of an uncertain present and an even more uncertain future. Like them, I learned to accept my lot, whatever it might be, with patience, with dignity, without rancour, and with hope for the future.

One last ironical postscript relating to the events of 1967 is worth recording. The only treasured possession that we had in Tanzania that we were not prepared for the government to get its hands on was Jayli's jewellery. They weren't worth that much, just a few trinkets that I had given her, or had been passed on through her family. But these few items were of priceless sentimental value, and we both wanted to keep them safe. And so we arranged for them to be sent out to Jayli's family in Uganda, to be held by them until such time as we were ready for their return. Little did we anticipate the advent of Idi Amin, who in 1971 ordered the entire Asian community out of Uganda on twenty-four hours' notice, with only one suitcase per person. Thus it was that Jayli's jewellery was finally lost, a further reminder, if ever we needed one, of the rightness of Jayli's fatalistic philosophy concerning God's granting and then taking away again.

EIGHT

... AND WINE AND BREAD AND BOXES

In the late 1960s Burt Bacharach and Hal David, the legendary American songwriting duo, came up with a beautiful and poignant love song entitled 'Trains and Boats and Planes'. For all they knew, they might have been writing that song just for me, because the title at least almost perfectly describes the events in my life as the process of nationalisation kick-started by the Arusha Declaration began to deepen. As Bacharach and David were crooning their hit across the international airwaves, I found myself being co-opted into senior positions on the boards of the East African Railways Corporation and the East African Harbours Corporation. Unfortunately, 'Trains and Boats and Provender Milling' doesn't have quite the same ring about it. Unbeknownst to Burt and Hal, at the time that I was assuming responsibility for much of Tanzania's international transportation network I was also still in charge of the National Milling Corporation of Tanzania, thanks to Parliamentary Act No. 19 of 1968, which I had helped to draft, at Mwalimu's request. My plate was full to overflowing.

And yet it could have been even fuller had I not had the foresight to incorporate into that National Milling Corporation legislation a clause specifically aimed at preventing ministerial micro-management of the day-to-day running of the business. For while I might have been a fairly fresh recruit to the ranks of African Socialism, my many years in the private sector, and as a member of both EXCO and LEGCO, had taught me more than a thing or two about the way government works in a country like Tanzania. The temptation for senior officials, let alone ministers, to get involved in the detailed workings of a strategic sector of the economy, especially a newly nationalised one, was going to be almost impossible to resist. Hence my drafting of a clause to close off the avenue to micro-management. I may have opened the door to the possibility that the minister responsible, in this case the minister for Agriculture, would, in certain circumstances, have an absolute right, indeed duty, to issue directives of a general nature. But the Act went on to make it clear that any ministerial directives of a more specific nature were *ultra vires*.

In drafting these clauses I did not have any particular situation or individual in mind. After all, I had known the minister responsible, Derek Bryceson, Minister for Agriculture, for many years as both friend and colleague (not least when we had served together on the restructured EXCO, which ran concurrently with the Council of Ministers in the run-up to independence). The clause was, if you like, a general safeguard against specific directives, not against those of a general nature. And yet within a year or so of assuming responsibility for the entire national milling industry I found myself glad that I had had the foresight to think of it.

As I have already made clear, I had never anticipated a fundamental difference of opinion with the Minister for Agriculture, let alone a series of them culminating in his departure from office. Derek Bryceson and his first wife Bobbi were very good friends of ours, enjoyable company yet serious people with a deep-seated commitment to the kind of nation that Mwalimu was in the process of building. Indeed Derek prided himself on being extremely close to Mwalimu, who also happened to be the Brycesons' next-door neighbour. The relationship with his neighbour and friend and long-time political ally was one that Derek guarded closely, and he gave the strong impression to me and to others around Dar es Salaam that his was the closest of relationships between the leader and a non-ethnic Tanzanian. Most days, whatever the pressures of business, Derek managed to find time to chew the fat with his illustrious neighbour. Most days Derek was able to reinforce his position of eminence as the leading non-Tanzanian in the government machine. For in that era of instant political alliances, he and Mwalimu went back a very long way, to the pre-independence days of TANU, and the closeness of that political and personal link was exemplified by the fact that Derek was the only European appointed to a senior position in the newly independent government, and had been chosen by Mwalimu to take on one of the most sensitive and important portfolios in his first cabinet. Incidentally, Derek received the largest number of votes in the 1960 election.

It was therefore extremely awkward, not to say unfortunate, that I seemed to get off on the wrong foot with Derek from the outset. My approach with him, as with others up to and including the President himself, was always founded on absolute candour, a principle that I had nurtured from my earliest days in private enterprise. From the day I took over the milling industry, I was always brutally frank with Derek in my current assessment of the situation. I would tell him what I thought was going right, but I would also ventilate my concerns as to the prospects for an early positive return from the tortuous process of integrating nine industrial concerns of varying size and efficiency and utility. Looking back, I think that my openness about the difficulties as well as the potential of the new situation I found myself in unsettled the Minister. Perhaps he had too much else on his plate to let me belabour him about my own parochial concerns. Perhaps the only news about the newly nationalised food sector he wanted to hear, and pass on, was good news. Whatever the reasons, I quickly found that a gap was opening up between us.

Even before taking charge of the national milling industry, I had told Derek that I was sceptical about the likelihood of a smooth absorption of some of the milling activities, such as the provender milling process, about which I knew next to nothing. He, in turn, confided in his Permanent Secretary that I was getting worked up about nothing; after all, he told him, 'Milling is milling.' I had learnt that earlier Derek had commissioned an American consultant to advise the government on restructuring the milling industry after the takeover by the state. The consultant had spent nearly a month in Kilimanjaro Hotel carrying out some 'studies'. Other than Derek and his Permanent Secretary, no one has seen the consultant's report, which is probably gathering dust in the archives of the Ministry. I heard rumours that the consultant had found the industry so complex and its plants so widespread that it would require the services of at least fourteen skilled expatriates. One thing is certain: the consultant improved his golf during his stay in Tanzania.

Almost my first official act on assuming my responsibilities in January 1968 was to remind the Minister of my concerns about the potentially devastating knock-on effect that the government's new Income and Wages Policy would have for promotion prospects in the newly nationalised milling industry. He in turn told his Permanent Secretary that this was an issue he should address. Thankfully the Permanent Secretary understood what I was driving at. Hence he busied himself in digging me out of that particular hole, to the point where a workable compromise was eventually hammered out. He did likewise when I went to seek his help on problems over work permits for expatriate staff. And then along came the dispute over the government-owned winery at Dodoma.

Now Tanzania has never featured on any wine buff's world map. South Africa, yes, Tanzania, well, no. And yet out in the dry arid plains of Dodoma, where the Gogo tribe once held sway, a small but symbolically significant centre of wine production had been established by Italian missionaries in the 1950s. Nothing much really flourishes around Dodoma apart from tomatoes and grapes, and I suppose that goes a long way toward explaining the Italian connection. But whatever the reasons for its foundation, the Dodoma operation seemed in many respects to be much like any other fledgling winery in the developing world. There were the jokes by the local wine buffs at the expense of the early output. There was the necessarily heavy reliance on European expertise and equipment. In one particular, however, the Dodoma vineyards were utterly and completely unique. Unlike their counterparts in, say, Chile or South Africa, or even Australia, the Dodoma grapes were grown not on the sheltered slopes of a sun-drenched hill, but in a prison, on the fenced-off farms that surrounded and formed part of Kingolwira Jail.

Now this unusual provenance of the grapes was never the main issue for me when the notion of my running the Dodoma winery was first mooted. My prime concern was the lack of congruence between the demands of running a national milling corporation and the re-establishment of a small-scale winemaking industry. I had already allowed the government to extend the definition of milling to encompass the production of fruit squashes and canned vegetables. Now I was being asked to take on, and turn around the fortunes of, an industry about which I knew absolutely nothing, and whose link back to milling was even more tenuous than that of syrup or tinned fruit. As usual, I knew nothing about the plans being hatched by the government until the twelfth hour, and even then it was only by chance. I was on a visit to London when a friend of mine told me that the Ministry for Agriculture was in the process of transferring the Dodoma vineyards into my milling empire. Being in London, at a time when communications between the UK and Tanzania were not so good, I could do nothing about the situation but worry. But as soon as I got back to Dar es Salaam, even before I had had a chance to put in for a call on the Minister, I was quickly put out of my misery. I received an immediate summons to call upon the Minister for Agriculture at my earliest convenience, to 'discuss the Dodoma winery'.

When I got to the Minister's office the following morning, the Minister, perhaps already mindful of our increasingly difficult relationship, didn't waste any time rehearsing the genesis of the proposal. Without any sort of preamble, he gave me the unwelcome news of the proposed transfer, and not only that, he handed it on not as something for discussion between us, but as a fait accompli. 'At Mwalimu's behest the cabinet has made the decision to hand the Dodoma winery over to you,' he told me. 'If you have a problem with that, then go and talk it over with him.'

For sound tactical reasons, I didn't take up the option offered to me by Minister Bryceson, preferring to keep that in reserve. Instead, my first port of call was Tanzania's Commissioner of Prisons. Unlike the Minister, Commissioner Obadia Rugimbana was more than ready to take me through the trials and tribulations of those poor incarcerated grapes. He briefed me in detail on the existing arrangements for planting, tending, and cultivation. He told me of the difficulties finding the necessary skilled staff within his current crop of prisoners, and set out the practical problems of safely transporting the harvested crop. And as he talked, it became increasingly clear to me that Rugimbana was firmly convinced that the arrangements that had been put in place at Kingolwira were unsustainable from many points of view, not least that of prison security. This brought home to me in the most graphic possible way the contingent liabilities that came from having the local commissioner of prisons run a winery. Quite aside from the risk of losing your key staff to a mass breakout, Chateau Choky was hardly the image that any self-respecting wine distributor would want to summon up in prospective buyers.

Since the decision to transfer the vineyards and the new winery had been made by the cabinet, with Mwalimu in the chair, I needed to handle the matter somewhat diplomatically. When I saw Commissioner Rugimbana again I indicated to him that his staff might face a difficult situation, given that the employees of my corporation will be managing a farm that, although not technically owned by the Prisons Department, does come under its jurisdiction. My corporation lacked expertise in vine growing and wine making. This meant that I needed to go outside Tanzania for expertise. I was also concerned as to the reaction of the consumer if he discovered that the grapes were grown by prison labour. I worked through the ruling party machinery, and eventually the decision was reviewed, and only the winery was handed over to my corporation. I promised Commissioner Rugimbana that I would assist in getting a donor agency to train a few of his staff in viticulture. I approached M. André Naudy, the French Ambassador, a man of great culture and breeding, who was taken aback to learn that Tanzanians were trying to make wine. Ensconced in his elegant sitting room in his official residence, Naudy sat listening in silence as I poured out my winemaking tale. Perhaps in stunned and stone-faced silence would be more accurate, after I had finished telling him of the ins and outs of Kingolwira — mainly ins, given the nature of the place. He was incredulous, horror-struck even, that anyone with even a modicum of business sense should be seriously contemplating commercial winemaking in a place such as

Kingolwira in a country such as Tanzania. He declined to provide any technical assistance, but agreed to have two Tanzanians trained in viticulture in France. Within minutes of my sitting down on the Ambassador's sofa, my visions of a Pinot Noir being grafted onto the existing vines in Dodoma had suddenly evaporated. I finished my tea, made my excuses, and left.

Meanwhile, Commissioner Rugimbana was excited by the prospect of developing the prison farm and enhancing its income. A few weeks later Mwalimu visited the farm and the Commissioner put in a plea for two tractors. Mwalimu said, 'If you need it you should have it.' The farm's procurement officers went ahead and purchased two units, but without following the laid-down procedure, such as asking for more than one quotation. Much later, in response to a government enquiry, the Commissioner's representative said that Mwalimu had given the go-ahead for this purchase. However, he was told that while Mwalimu may have approved the purchase, he could not have asked anyone to ignore standard procurement procedures.

My next port of call was the Italian Ambassador. He too was a sophisticated diplomat of the old school. Roman Catholic priests from Italy were already producing red wine on a small scale at Bihavana, so here, at last, although I may have laid almost undue stress on the Italian antecedents of the original winemaking operation in Dodoma, I began to make some progress. The Ambassador heard me out, and his reaction was wholly positive, enthusiastic even. He kindly agreed to find me an expert in the art of winemaking. He also agreed to fund the expert's secondment costs. And best of all, he made good on those agreements. Within a matter of weeks, a Signor Tomosili had been identified and duly appointed, and, with the good wishes of both the Italian Ambassador and myself still ringing in his ears, he went off to make wine in Dodoma. To make my happiness, and his, even more complete, he went out to the Gogo lands in the company of two young and expert horticulturalists who had been selected for training by the French government, for by then M. Naudy had recovered from the shock of my visit sufficiently to come forward with some assistance of his own, assistance that was desperately needed.

Signor Tomosili was all that one could have hoped for in an Italian winemaker. Not only did he have a deep love for his craft, expressed in the minute pains he took over each and every stage of the process, but he was also something of a prima donna, given to unTanzanian extremes of emotion that welled up from the depths of his being each time he felt that his own sense of dignity, which he tended as carefully as any grape, had somehow been impugned. I soon became aware of the volatility of the man's temperament from the reports I received from my staff in Dodoma. Perhaps I didn't take these seriously enough, because, as we neared the bottling stage in Tomosili's first season, I sent two of my accountants up to Dodoma to make a first-hand assessment of the anticipated costs of the operation. Unfortunately, in doing this I hadn't taken sufficient account of Signor Tomosili's sensitivities. Although I had no ulterior motive in dispatching the accountants (and I would have confessed immediately if I had had one), Signor Tomosili misinterpreted my action as an indication of a profound lack of confidence in his technical capabilities. Having asked in all innocence to look at the books, the accountants found themselves on the wrong end of a diatribe that carried over into Tomosili's subsequent telephone call to the Italian Ambassador back in Dar es Salaam. We were 'impugning his honour' as a winemaker. We were trying to tell him, Tomosili, how to do his job. At this, the critical moment in the birth of his first Dodoma vintage, we were interfering.

Eventually, thanks to the good offices and considerable persuasive skills of the Italian Ambassador, I was able to calm Tomosili down, reassuring him that we had no malign interest at all in the mysteries of his craft, nor did we wish to control the enterprise in any way, and that our only interest had been in obtaining something more than a rough and ready estimate of the cost of production that season. Mollified by our combined efforts, he went back to his work and turned out the first batch of a red *vin ordinaire* in time for the official launch of the new vintage at the National Development Corporation headquarters in Dar es Salaam.

I won't go into the details of that event, if only to spare my own embarrassment and that of my countrymen. Even calling it a launch was perhaps stretching the bounds of credibility. But then, in our defence, we were sensible enough to realise the limitations of what we were doing. There was never any danger at all that we were going to put a date on any of our bottles, still less declare a Tanzanian vintage; not even the proud Tomosili would argue in favour of that. No, this Dodoma wine produced by the new regime was *vin* most *ordinaire*, and it wasn't long before it was dubbed Chateau Migraine by the expatriate community in Tanzania. I doubt that very much of the first couple of years of production got past the kitchens of Oyster Bay and Msasani. But at least we had laid solid foundations for a winery that has improved much over the years, and the hard work put in by Tomosili and his successors has confounded the perpetually low expectations of so many. Eventually a passable rosé was added to the original red, and for a long time now the wine has been eminently drinkable. Not on a par with the vineyards of the Cape, perhaps, but when you consider its antecedents, behind the gates of Kingolwira Jail, an unlikely success all the same.

Winemaking may have been an unwelcome addition to my portfolio, but at least it had no adverse impact on the main day-to-day business. Then, in quick succession, two even thornier problems arose that took my already strained relationship with the Minister for Agriculture to the breaking-point.

The first concerned the seemingly innocuous issue of the transportation of paddy from Morogoro to Dar es Salaam. Unbeknownst to anyone in the Corporation, the Ministry had identified a series of problems related to transportation that were deemed to require the services of a formal Board of Enquiry. The Board had been established under the chairmanship of the Junior Minister for Agriculture, and it had begun to take evidence based on claims of misuse. But the first I came to know that problems had been reported, let alone made the subject of an official enquiry, was when the Permanent Secretary in the Ministry for Agriculture rang me out of the blue to tell me that the Board of Enquiry had presented its findings to the Minister. As a direct result, the Permanent Secretary went on, the Minister now wanted me to terminate the employment of three of my staff, effective immediately. Shocked at this, and concerned about the damage it would do to my organisation, I asked for an immediate appointment with the Permanent Secretary.

Unsurprisingly, my meeting at the Ministry was uncomfortable for all concerned. As soon as I got there, I asked for and obtained a briefing on the background to the Enquiry. I was told about the hearings that had taken place and the conclusions that the Junior Minister had drawn. Under the circumstances, the Permanent Secretary went on, I had no option but to immediately dismiss the three staff members who had been adjudged responsible for the problems. I responded that I would be doing no such thing. Instead I challenged the justification for the claims, and the way the Ministry had gone about investigating the matter. Instead of coming to me or my senior staff when the allegations had originally surfaced, the Ministry had instead seen fit to convene a Board of Enquiry. This Board had sat in session without my knowledge, and without giving me or the Corporation an opportunity to hear out the charges and to answer them. Furthermore, the summary instruction to sack three of my staff flatly contradicted the terms of the legal charter that had established the National Milling Corporation. This, I reminded the Permanent Secretary, explicitly prevented a minister or any of his staff from issuing any directive of a specific nature to the Corporation. If the Minister, his junior colleague, or any of his senior staff were in any way dissatisfied with the performance of the Corporation under my stewardship, then it was for the Minister to ask the President, who had appointed me to the position in the first place, to remove me.

Bryceson's response to all this, as was so often the case when he found himself under pressure, was to tell me to talk to the President. To his surprise, I challenged this advice as well. Derek Bryceson, not Mwalimu, was the one who had failed to consult me on potentially serious allegations about the conduct of my business. Derek Bryceson, not Mwalimu, had been the one to go against the law in calling on me to sack my staff. It was therefore his responsibility to unpick this problem, not the President's. In the meantime, and for the reasons I had just spelled out to him, there was no prospect of my complying with his directive. With that my meeting with the Permanent Secretary came to an abrupt end.

Three days later, the Permanent Secretary, Timothy Apiyo, called me again, as if expecting that in the meantime I might have softened my stance. Again he renewed the Minister's directive to sack the three staff. Again I refused, only this time I went on to ask him to put the order in writing.

I was fully aware that in asking this I was putting Bryceson firmly on the spot. There was no earthly possibility that the Ministry would issue anything to me in writing, given what we both knew about the Milling Act. As I expected, the Minister mulled over my latest gambit for a few days, and then rang Ernest Mulokozi, the Permanent Secretary in the Prime Minister's office, who happened to be the chairman of the National Milling Corporation. That call prompted the Chairman to send me a letter asking me to summon an emergency meeting of the Milling Corporation board, to which Minister Bryceson would be invited. Faced with such a request from my chairman I had no alternative but to agree, and in doing so I decided to put the best face possible on my acceptance. In my reply I went so far as to make it clear that the Chairman's special invitee would be most welcome at this extraordinary meeting of the Board. Inwardly, however, I knew that I was now in serious danger of being outflanked, if not set up.

I had, however, made preparations for such an eventuality. My caution and care in the drafting of the Milling Corporation Law had extended to the composition of my board of directors. I had had no choice as to the chairmanship of the Corporation. But I had been lucky with the appointment of the innately sympathetic Mulokozi, and I had made sure that the rest of the Board was composed of people whom I could trust, and who in turn would trust me at almost all hazards. To these people I now addressed myself, preparing the ground for the encounter with the Minister.

On the day of the meeting, Bryceson drove himself over to our offices on the Pugu Road in his own private vehicle, as he so often did. As he somehow extricated his long frame from the front seat of his Mini Minor, I was standing at the back of his car waiting to greet him in person. Irritated as I was at the way he was handling the professional side of our relationship, I still saw him as more a friend than an adversary, an essentially good and humble man who wanted above all to do right by our leader. After we exchanged pleasantries, I escorted him up to our boardroom and formally introduced him to the rest of the directors. And then we got down to business.

Forty-five minutes was all it took for Minister Bryceson to see the writing quite plainly on the wall. To my pleasant surprise Timothy Apiyo, Permanent Secretary in the Ministry, in his capacity as a Board member, fully supported me — and in so doing was of course taking a position in direct contradiction to the one he had represented when acting as the civil service head of the Ministry. For this I was grateful to him. Minister Bryceson suddenly announced, 'Okay, that's enough. I think we've all learned our lessons from this episode, including Andy. Let's close this now.' And without further ado that's what we did. And the three members of my staff who had been targeted for dismissal never once got to know that they had been lined up by the Ministry for the chop, and never once realised how much effort had been put in on their behalf to avert disaster. I should also point out that my defence of the three wasn't merely based on a technicality, or on blind loyalty to my staff. In the run-up to the Board meeting, I had instructed a couple of trusted people within the Corporation to look into the fine detail of the allegations that had been brought before the Ministry's Board of Enquiry. My own staff concluded that without a shadow of a doubt there had been no case to answer, and that the entire set of charges had been cobbled together from circumstantial evidence and hearsay. Quite what the Ministry intended to gain from this enquiry remains a mystery to me even now. It was too weak a platform from which to mount a challenge to my authority, given the way the law had been drafted. More likely, given how things worked in Tanzania in those days, a personal grudge against one or all of the three Milling Corporation staff members had somehow been manipulated into the basis for a full-blown ministerial enquiry. Whatever the reasons, another nail had been hammered into the coffin of my friendship with Derek Bryceson.

The very last nails were, unfortunately, already close at hand. The denouement, when it came, was due to a misjudgement by the Minister, a misjudgement of the limits of my tolerance and a misjudgement of the extent of his personal importance to the President.

Having been so close to Mwalimu for so long, Bryceson had always been acutely conscious of the pressure the President was under to demonstrate to himself, as much as to anyone else, that his administration was delivering on his promises to the people. After the Arusha Declaration, the spotlight, nationally as well as internationally, fell on *Ujamaa*, and the impact it might be having on the lives of ordinary Tanzanians. It was therefore understandable that with the nationalisation of the milling industry came an opportunity for the Minister to do all that he could to help Mwalimu's cause. I understood that too, which is precisely why I had taken on that national responsibility. Derek and I should therefore have been playing together on the same side. But he persisted in making decisions in regard to the milling industry, decisions that, without any reference whatsoever to me, he saw as being in the best interests of the nation.

Matters came to a head again over the issue of rice. This time the nub of the problem was not transportation but price. Derek Bryceson had never fully understood how the market for this and other primary products worked. He assumed, wrongly as it turned out, that the eight private companies in the milling business must have been making a healthy profit out of rice in the run-up to nationalisation. It followed, then, that one of the early benefits that the people should receive from *Ujamaa* was a cut in the price of rice, and he acted accordingly. He did not consult the Corporation in advance, he just went ahead and announced the change, at the same time affirming that the price to be paid to Tanzanian farmers for the raw paddy would remain as it was. The price reduction was approved by the Economic Committee of the cabinet. There were rumours that Minister Bryceson's initial thought had been to confine this reduction to Dar es Salaam, the area of the greatest volume of rice consumption — and the location of the Minister's parliamentary constituency.

The timing of this price cut was calculated to have the most positive political impact, in that it coincided with the onset of Ramadan. Derek Bryceson would have been well aware that local Muslims preferred to break their Ramadan fast each evening with a simple meal based on rice. The price cut at that time of year caused a sudden surge in demand. So I went from making only a tiny profit on each one-hundred kilogram bag of rice to losing between twelve and fourteen shillings. I also faced an upsurge in demand that I couldn't hope to meet from local production, because after the industry was nationalised I had had to rationalise production by merging several mills.

The shock of the Minister's announcement gave me some sleepless nights. I soon realised that my options were few. Not only was the Corporation going to lose money on every sack produced but, having recently closed four of the country's eight rice mills in order to break even, I would now have to go out to costly external contracts to keep up with the expected upsurge in demand, thereby increasing my losses exponentially. The national milling industry had only just weathered the storm of enforced merger. A decision like this, if maintained, threatened to bring down the entire enterprise around my ears. Because the Corporation had borrowed funds to purchase equipment from Germany and had arranged another credit term purchase of machinery from England, its cash flow was under substantial threat. This meant renegotiation of repayment terms, possible loss of confidence in my leadership, and an impact on the overall business climate in Tanzania.

I soon realised that in order to survive I had to call on the Minister and explain my predicament. Unsurprisingly, once I made clear to him the unintended consequences of his actions, I found him defensive. He explained that technical advisers in the Ministry, after a comprehensive analysis of the rice industry, had recommended a cut in the price of rice, and a proposal based on this recommendation had been submitted to the Economic Committee of the cabinet. With no other argument to call on, the Minister made clear to me his own strongly held view that the cabinet decision was final.

I went away from that meeting in a state of some anxiety. It had taken me many months to convince my supply chain from the days of Chande Industries to agree to economically sensible deals with me in my latest incarnation. I had had to go out to the marketplace in order to replace antiquated machinery in some of the other milling businesses I had taken on. The key to financing those purchases, which in the old days of Chande Industries would have been supplied on credit, no questions asked, had been the borrowing of money against the National Milling Corporation's projected balance sheet for the next five years. The sudden swing in the rice operation of the business from a small profit to the probability of a massive deficit was putting all of my wider plans in jeopardy. Even if the expected sudden upsurge in demand did not materialize (and all of the indications coming in were to the contrary), the situation for the Corporation as a whole was unsustainable. If Bryceson wouldn't listen to my concerns — and his Permanent

Secretary came back to me the day after our meeting to tell me again that he wouldn't — then I had to take the issue up with the President.

And now, for the first time since the days of our falling out over the offer made to me to stand for TANU, I found the President unwilling to see me. I went to see Dickson Nkembo, his Permanent Secretary, to explain in some detail the background to my request for a call. When nothing came of my original request, I sent three further reminders. After a month of waiting with no word, and with money now haemorrhaging out of the Corporation's accounts, I went to see Nkembo again to tell him of my frustrations and fears, and how I was at my wits' end as to which course of action to take next. Nkembo listened carefully and took notes but made no commitments of his own.

That evening, with still no word from State House, I allowed myself to be persuaded by my friends to go out to the Simba Nightclub at the Kilimanjaro Hotel. My wife as well as my friends were becoming increasingly concerned at the visible strain I was under, and the trip to the Simba was designed to take my mind off the rice-pricing situation for a few hours at least. The Kilimanjaro was at that time the flagship hotel in Dar es Salaam, and I knew it well, as I had been chairman of the Tanzania Tourist Corporation, which owned it (it was managed by Mlonot Ltd., an Israeli company). But somehow the delights of the Simba failed to do anything that night to lift my dark mood. Despite the frivolity all around me and the best efforts of my friends, I was too wrapped up in the cares of the business to enjoy myself, or even relax. At about one o'clock in the morning, several hours ahead of my friends' intended departure time, I stepped out of the club, my party all reluctantly in tow, and moved down to the lobby of the hotel toward the news vendors, gathered in a group on the pavement. There in front of them was the latest edition of the *Sunday News*, still warm off the presses, and it was carrying a front-page exclusive about a government reshuffle. Buying a copy, I read that Mwalimu had decided to transfer the Minister for Agriculture out of the cabinet and make him the new head of the National Parks. He would be replaced by one Joseph Mungai, an MP from Mufindi, who at the time was on a course in Canada.

My first reaction on reading this news was only sadness. Whatever else others might think, Derek Bryceson had been a true friend for many years, and the move to the National Parks was an obvious demotion. True, we had not seen eye to eye since my assumption of a national role in the milling industry, but our differences were founded on a lack of transparent communication, and of basic understanding of how an industry, even a nationalised one, must be made to work, and not on the absence of a shared commitment to doing what was best for Tanzania. Even if one is a state socialist, protecting and managing a command economy, state-owned corporations still have to be run on capitalist lines.

But the differences that had grown up were clearly making either my position or his untenable. I therefore suspected that my approach to the President had been the catalyst for the sudden reshuffle. There was no guarantee that with the departure of Derek my problems were at an end, but I must confess that the news of the reshuffle, once the implications of it had finally sunk in, enabled me to relax a little at last, while I waited for the newly arrived Minister Mungai to get his feet under the cabinet table.

This I did for a fortnight, even though the debts being incurred by the rice milling operation continued to mount. At the end of the month, by which time Minister Mungai had been in his post for nearly three weeks, still nothing had been heard from him either publicly or privately about the price of rice to the consumer. I could feel another rise in my blood pressure of a sort that a trip to the Simba Night Club was never going to sort out. I therefore sought an appointment with the new minister.

His initial response, once he had heard me out, was very cautious. As he took the trouble to explain to me at great length, he was new to the job, and it represented his first cabinet position; he was still learning the details of the agricultural situation in Tanzania; he was still building his national reputation politically. Under the circumstances I could hardly expect him to turn the previous cabinet studies on their head and announce an immediate reversal of a decision by the previous incumbent, particularly as it had gone down so well in the country. I told him that I understood his predicament, but my own situation in the milling industry was becoming desperate. There was no need for any further studies; his staff were fully briefed on the situation. I also told him that I had been trying to get to see the President for well over a month, but without success. Given what the Minister had just told me, I could see no alternative but to renew my request to see Mwalimu.

Mungai was clearly uncomfortable at hearing all this. But to his credit he made no opposition to my fresh efforts to see the President. Indeed, thanks to help from him and from State House staff, I was at long last given an appointment to see the President at two o'clock one afternoon the following week. It was now fully three months since I had first raised the issue with Derek Bryceson.

I went along to the appointment at State House with a strong team from the National Milling Corporation. In addition to my deputy, there was the head of Finance and the Production Manager. When we were ushered into the Cabinet room, I found Minister Mungai on the other side of the table together with his Permanent Secretary, the Permanent Secretary to the President, and two young clerks from State House. We all sat down and awaited Mwalimu's arrival.

When Mwalimu came into the room, he sat down and asked who was going to begin. I volunteered. But before getting into the meat of my presentation I sought Mwalimu's permission to talk in English. He assented.

I began by setting out the circumstances under which I had agreed to take on the role of general manager of the National Milling Corporation. I had accepted a five-year contract to run the company under Parliamentary Act No. 19 of 1968, which clearly stated that I was to manage the company in the best mercantile traditions. Now it seemed I was being asked to run it like a Red Cross Society enterprise. I was losing money fast, and the long-term impact of the losses would be profound. I therefore had to stop now, take stock, and decide whether I, and indeed the Corporation at large, had the capacity to continue running things in the way they had been set up.

At that point, I suddenly became aware that Mwalimu wanted me to stop talking. He lowered his spectacles and looked across at me. He turned slowly to the left and then to the right, staring down the table at his colleagues. They shifted uneasily in their chairs. He turned back to me again.

'Who is asking you to change the way you manage?'

'Ministers,' I replied, thinking of Bryceson.

'Then they don't know what they are talking about,' said Mwalimu. 'I want you to generate surplus, taking into account further investment in the next .'

I smiled inwardly. Mwalimu often used 'surplus' as a euphemism for 'profit'.

'Moreover,' Mwalimu went on, 'I want you to look at the possibility of new maize mills in Dodoma and Mtwara.' At this stage Mwalimu asked Minister Mungai to review the matter and bring it back to the cabinet.

With this, Mwalimu stood up and left the room. The meeting was over. I collected my things and went downstairs to find Awinia Mushi, the Permanent Secretary at the Ministry for Agriculture, waiting for me near my car. Addressing me in Swahili, he launched an attack on the way I had spoken in the meeting.

'What kind of language was that to use in front of your Head of State?' he asked.

I looked at him impassively and replied, much more quietly, 'Mr Mushi, I can't sleep at night any more. I have here in my pocket the master key of the head office of the National Milling Corporation. If you want, I'll give it to you now, because the business is losing so much money.'

'It's not your money,' he snapped back.

'I know, I know,' I replied. 'It is the public purse. And I feel responsible for it.' And with that I walked away.

Two days later I went back to the Ministry for Agriculture to see Minister Mungai and his Permanent Secretary. Both had calmed down considerably, and Mungai opened our meeting in the constructive vein that he clearly wanted to sustain. 'OK,' he said, 'let's start again.' And over the next couple of hours we hammered out a formula between us that we all believed to be sustainable both politically and financially. No one in the meeting was in any way keen to reduce the price paid to the farmer for paddy, given what we all knew about the parlous state of Tanzanian agriculture. We all therefore agreed that a series of gradual consumer price rises was needed to put the National Milling Corporation back in 'surplus'. And Mungai proved as good as his word. While it was many months before things were back on an even keel, I was able to use my new-found understanding with the Minister to reassure all of our creditors and suppliers that there were no grounds for concern as to our five-year planning projections.

The paddy crisis was now effectively over. However, the bakery crisis was about to begin. It had always been a mystery to me why bakeries had never merited a mention in the long list of strategic industries to be nationalised that was produced in the days after the Arusha Declaration. To this day, I don't know why that was. But whatever the reasons for its original omission, that lacuna in government policy was about to be filled.

The first I knew of this was when I received a telephone call from Amir Jamal, the Tanzanian Minister for Finance. That was always his style, to go to a person directly, without getting bogged down in the bureaucracy. His reasons for calling me were soon made clear (another Jamal characteristic). 'Our' people (i.e., Indians), he told me, were cheating in their bakery businesses (the local market was then carved up between the Greek and Indian communities). While bakeries were not mentioned in my original contract, Jamal went on, they were what he called 'an ancillary business' to milling. Would I therefore take on the problems of poor quality and short measures that were endemic to bakeries across Tanzania?

I could hardly refuse. I had always seen the need for good practice in the milling industry to migrate over to bakeries. I knew from my own experience how bad the local bakeries were. I was soon to learn that the ongoing efforts to remedy the situation weren't much better.

Again the local donor community had been identified by the Tanzanian government as the key to success. A few months prior to Jamal's telephone call to me, an approach had been made to the Dutch Ambassador, who at the time was in charge of one of the larger programmes of development assistance to Tanzania. Once he had been briefed on the iniquities of the local bakery operations, he had agreed to fund the installation of a state-of-the-art Baker Perkins breadmaking production plant, together with help in training the staff to run it. But in the weeks before Jamal's phone call, those Dutch plans had begun to fall apart, as a consequence of a change in German spending priorities. The Germans had previously promised to fund the construction of a multi-purpose jetty in Tanga for the offloading, in the first instance at least, of fertiliser. But then, for reasons not known, that offer had been withdrawn at the last minute and, thankfully, the Dutch had stepped into the breach. But the consequence of their doing so was that they gave up the option of supplying the new bakery, not having the resources to do that as well as the jetty. This process of robbing Peter to pay Paul, which has bedeviled donor assistance programmes from the early days of independence right down to the present day, left the government in the lurch. Casting around to find another friendly donor to help them out, they alighted on the Canadians. At that time, under Prime Minister Pierre Trudeau, the Canadians were providing to Tanzania the highest per capita aid programme on the entire African continent. It didn't take long for the High Commissioner in Dar es Salaam to say yes, and the Canadians came on board.

The Baker Perkins plant that was to have come from the Netherlands would have been being supplied on a fifty-year credit at a low service fee. This loan in turn would have been passed to the Corporation, but the credit period would have been reduced to between seven and ten years, with interest charged by the treasury at the commercial rate applying to medium-term borrowing. The Canadian plant, which I believe was also to be produced by Baker Perkins, would cost two to three times more than the Dutch plant. The government executed the necessary agreement with the Canadian International Development Agency and a side agreement with the National Milling Corporation. There was some discontent among academics, possibly inspired by some Canadians who were concerned that Ottawa's assistance to Tanzania in the growing of wheat and its help with the baking facility would adversely affect Canadian farmers.

Before the plant was installed, the Canadians agreed to provide gratis the services of a consultant, and agreed to train two employees of the Corporation as master bakers. Without consulting the Tanzanian government or the Corporation, the Canadians sent a profile of one Mr Thoroughgood to the Corporation. When I requested that we be provided with details of at least one other candidate, I was told that Mr Thoroughgood, who had provided similar services in India, but for small-scale bakeries, was the ideal person. At the time of this discussion I happened to meet Amir Jamal, the Minister for Finance, who chastised me for unnecessarily delaying the appointment of the Canadian consultant, reminding me that Canada provided the largest per capita aid to Tanzania and that prime ministers Lester Pearson and Pierre Trudeau were good friends of Mwalimu. By the time I said yes to Jamal, the Canadians were well down the road toward approval of the project. Luckily for me, Mr Thoroughgood turned out to be both Thorough and Good. And over time, we were able to clean up the operations of the local bakery industry to the satisfaction of both the general public and the government.

The rest of my five-year tenure as general manager of the National Milling Corporation was relatively straightforward. That is not to say that I led a problem-free existence. I most assuredly did not. The old and pervasive habits of *Kinyezi* (to be roughly translated as something between '*laissez-faire*' and 'lackadaisical'), which had been characteristic of many of the smaller private milling operations, took time to wear down. But eventually I found myself able to devote an increasing amount of time to the other posts to which the government had appointed me.

The Metal Box experience emerged around this time as well. Before it too was nationalised, Metal Box Tanzania Limited had been a wholly owned subsidiary of Metal Box PLC in the UK. Following nationalisation the Tanzanian government acquired fifty percent of the shares in the local subsidiary and allowed the UK company to have a majority of one on the board of directors, with the chairman of the company to be nominated by the government. The first chairman of the company was Clement George Kahama, but he resigned when he relinquished the position of general manager of the National Development Corporation. His successor did not opt to be the chairman of Metal Box, but instead appointed one of the employees in the Corporation, a Ms Rukia Hamisi. The company continued to be managed by the UK parent company under a management and technical consultancy agreement. But the relationship between the British and Tanzanian directors was not cordial, to put it mildly, and at one meeting the British directors got up and left in high dudgeon before it was formally closed. After that the local board did not meet for over a year, even though the company continued to be run by its British manager. This situation was clearly unsatisfactory, not least for the Tanzanian government.

Eventually Ernest Mulokozi, general manager of the National Development Corporation and chairman of my own National Milling Corporation, asked me if I would be willing to take over as chairman of Metal Box Tanzania, so as to help restore the working relationship with the British parent company and local directors. At that time I was already having some difficulties with Canadian shareholders in the Bata Shoe Company, with whom I was informally negotiating so that they could remain as fifty-percent shareholders in the Tanzanian company. Because of this, and my heavy workload at the National Milling Corporation, I declined Mulokozi's offer. In doing so I was also conscious that the Tanzanian government had put my name forward as a director of the company back in 1967, only for the parent company to say that they saw a potential conflict of interest, the National Milling Corporation then being a customer of Metal Box Tanzania. But the parent company was also aware that following a disagreement between my in-laws — the Madhvanis in Uganda — and Metal Box in Kenya, the former had set up a can-making plant of their own in Uganda, mainly to serve the needs of their own companies.

In the event, neither of these reasons was sufficient to put off the government. After much toing and froing, I was eventually persuaded by the Minister for Industries to take up the chairmanship of Metal Box Tanzania for 'a couple of years'.

My first task as chairman was to meet the UK directors. Accordingly, I flew to London, and on arrival briefed our High Commissioner about my mission. The Metal Box head office was located in Reading, and it was arranged that I would be chauffeured down there by one of the company's drivers, a lady by the name of Pat Brown. I spent the entire journey trying subtly, and then not so subtly, to get a bit of inside information about the personalities at the top of the company. But Pat was a dog breeder, a fanatical one it seemed to me, because whether by accident or design she answered every one of my questions with an anecdote about one of her dogs!

Before deciding to go to Reading to meet the UK directors, I had sought technical assistance from contacts in Asia and Europe, only to find that the UK parent company was a major operator in these countries and wielded considerable influence — thereby closing the mouths of my sources. I did, however, arrange for a company in Finland to provide technical help in the unlikely event that a settlement proved elusive. This was important, since one of the major customers, Tanzania Packers Limited, a company owned by Libiegs, was buying cans from Metal Box in which to pack their meat for export to Europe, and we had to ensure that any alternative supplier was of international repute.

On my arrival in Reading I saw Tanzania's flag in the head office, which was located in Queen's House. Also, I was met by two senior employees who had served on the board of the Tanzanian subsidiary. At around ten o'clock, after coffee and pleasantries, we began our discussion. The British team was led by a Mr Willis, who, it transpired, had served with distinction in the British Army in the Far East. His approach was duly military, if not confrontational. According to the parent company, the Tanzanian attitude to the company was unbusinesslike. That was why they continued to need a majority on the local board of directors. They were not amused when I interjected to say that in my own experience, a majority was only of cosmetic advantage in this kind of situation, and that it was in the interest of both parties to work together. I went on to say that in our opinion there was a great deal of scope for development and diversification in a growing local and regional market. I then hinted that even the majority arrangement could yet be revisited by the Tanzanian government.

At that point Mr Willis broke in. 'We do not like that kind of language here,' he said, 'and we don't like to be threatened.' I smiled and attempted to get the discussion back on track. But just then, their finance director suggested that we should break for lunch.

The lunch was hosted by Sir Alex Page, the chairman of the company. We wined and dined in a pleasant atmosphere and after coffee we resumed discussion. With tempers having cooled, and each side having recognised the innate strength of the other's position, it did not take long for a mutual understanding to emerge. We broke up in handshakes and smiles. And as if to underline the importance of what we had just agreed to, I was driven back to London by one of Mr Willis's colleagues instead of the dog-loving Pat.

About a year later, when the company was considering diversification, the General Manager of the National Development Corporation Arnold Kilewo and I went back to Reading as a team. We also saw some of the Metal Box factories in the UK. We were hosted in a nice hotel in Marlow, and in the evening were entertained at a fine restaurant called the French Horn. I was asked by the host if I would select the wine. I am not much of a wine drinker and know practically nothing about wine, even though the National Milling Corporation was then producing the near-legendary Chateau Migraine. I went through the wine list until I found a bottle priced at £650 and, interested to see how the host would react, I selected it. At once it seemed that the man from Metal Box was about to have a heart attack. Within seconds I called the wine captain back and asked for a bottle of house red instead. The disappointment on the waiter's face was like nothing I have ever seen. The same could be said of the look of relief on the face of the man from Metal Box.

The disputes with Metal Box, not least their fears about an unbusinesslike approach from Tanzanians, gave me a further insight into the problems that the government was facing in trying to make a success of *Ujamaa*. Another single example is worth quoting.

The Tanzanian Harbours Authority (THA) was short of facilities for cargo handling. It therefore invited tenders, to be quoted in US dollars, for the supply of equipment and for construction to enhance existing facilities, with funding to be provided in large part by the World Bank. A European company emerged as the preferred bidder, and I was passed their tender documents for review. As I was going through them, my attention was caught by the line stating that although the cost was expressed in US dollars, it would be based on the prevailing rate of exchange. In other words, the THA was being asked to carry the exchange risk. Worried by this, I mentioned to my colleagues on the Board that we should keep a second option open against the possibility that negotiations with the European should break down over the small print in the tender.

Within two hours of my mentioning this, the European were already complaining to their contacts in the Tanzanian government that I was 'causing problems'. They tried to call on me to discuss the issue, but I felt that the Board's decision could only be reviewed by it alone, and therefore no useful purpose would have been served in meeting them. They then began to exert their influence within the World Bank. Pressure on the Tanzanian Foreign Ministry caused Cleopa Msuya, the Finance Minister, to ring Paul Mkanga, the Permanent Secretary at the Ministry for Transport, to try to find out why his officials in the Harbours Authority were 'cheeseparing' over the deal. My response, when it was asked for, was that the Board had a responsibility to operate in a fair and open manner, and that at all times it takes into account the interest of the Corporation and its stakeholders.

In the middle of this dispute over the contract with a European company, I was suddenly whisked off to New York. I had been appointed

Deputy Leader to the Preparatory Committee for the Rio Summit, and had to attend a meeting of the committee in New York. I was also elected by the G77 and China to serve as a coordinator with the G8 on the Fiscal Environmental Facility. When in New York I was asked by the Ministry for Communications and Transport to go to Washington to meet with World Bank officials, with strong advice from the Minister ringing in my ears to the effect that I should at all costs avoid a spat with the Bank. With the Egyptian Ambassador covering for me in New York during the G77-G8 negotiations, the director-general of the Tanzania Harbours Authority and I sat down in my hotel in Washington with Charles Nyirabu, the Tanzanian Ambassador to the US, and talked through the line to take with the World Bank. Nyirabu was a man of distinction, well versed in the intricacies and protocols of international finance, having served three terms as the governor of the Central Bank of Tanzania. Following our discussion, during which we found ourselves in broad agreement, he asked me whether I wanted him to accompany me on my calls the following day. Anticipating the need for a further round, I asked him to hold himself in reserve.

My concerns about the potential for a row proved to be well founded. Early into the initial session, the World Bank's representatives asserted that the tender from the European company was 'substantially responsive' to the requirements. At that point I decided to see the Executive Director of the Bank for our region, who was from Malawi. The Bank officials accused me of politicising the issue, and I contended that I had every right to, given the attitudes being struck. The meeting broke up without further ado.

That evening Nyirabu gave a dinner for my delegation, to which a number of World Bank officials were invited. Immediately prior to the dinner Nyirabu had counselled conciliation: 'Why don't you accept what the Bank has to offer?' And that evening over dinner I finally did, on the understanding that acceptance would be sweetened by an extra facility for Tanzania, together with other associated and unspecified benefits.

Once again I had demonstrated what I had always said to Mwalimu: that I wasn't cut out to be a diplomat. But more important lessons came home to me, and from what I have learnt of diplomatic practice since, they remain as relevant now as they seemed to be then. And they can all be reduced to a single and unedifying principle, namely that beggars can never be choosers, even when the shift in the climate of international opinion toward unconditional commitment for self-help might fool you into thinking otherwise. I was reminded of what Mwalimu once said: 'It is expensive to be poor.'

This dictum was never clearer than at the time of the oil shocks of the early 1970s. After the Six Days War of 1967, and especially after the Yom Kippur War of 1973, some of the socialist African nations broke relations with Israel. In recognition of this, the Arab oil-producing states decided to offer help to the African states that were going through difficult times as a result of the hike in the price of oil. Working with the Arab League, these Arab oil ministers decided to negotiate, through the Organisation of African Unity (OAU), arrangements that offered financial support to affected countries. The OAU in turn delegated the responsibility for drawing up these arrangements to a committee of five foreign ministers, chaired by Foreign Minister Mansour Khalid of the Sudan. Tanzania, a member of that committee, was represented by John Malecela, Minister of State for Foreign Affairs.

Prior to the break in diplomatic relations, Israel had been quite active in Tanzania. They were involved in the consumer cooperative movement (COSATA), and a Tel Aviv company, Mlonot Ltd, was managing the Kilimanjaro, the flagship hotel in Tanzania, as well as a Beach Hotel in Dar es Salaam. They had come into Tanzania, indeed into Africa, on a wave of post-Holocaust sympathy, as a fellow underdog, a fellow victim of the machinations of the great powers of Europe. Theodore Herzl, one of the founders of Zionism, famously said in his novel *Altneuland*, 'Once I have witnessed the redemption of the Jews, my people, I will also assist in the redemption of the Africans.'

For these reasons, many Africans had traditionally viewed the state of Israel as a country heroically surviving whilst surrounded by hostile neighbours. The Six Day War in 1967 began to change that perception. The Yom Kippur War completed the process. The perception of Israel as a socialist society with a desire to be non-aligned and accepted as an integral part of the Third World had evaporated, to be replaced by that of a state whose interests were inextricably bound up with those of the US and Britain and France and Salazar's Portugal and apartheid-dominated South Africa.

This disenchantment with Israel, indeed with the Western world more generally, was a by-product of the domestic radicalisation of many African leaders and the societies they ruled. All of this combined to make Israel's position on the continent increasingly precarious. The breaking of relations with Israel was therefore an easy way for African states to express their disillusionment with the West without suffering any serious consequences.

Following the establishment of the OAU Oil Committee, Ambassador Weidi Mwasakafyuka from the Tanzanian Ministry for Foreign

Affairs phoned me to say that the Ministry had received a communication from the Secretary-General of the OAU inviting me to serve as an adviser to Mansour Khalid's committee. My initial response was to say no; I knew nothing whatsoever about oil. The Ambassador accepted my explanation and went away, but later returned to say that the government wanted me to take up this assignment anyway, given that that it was more about the financing of oil purchases than about the oil itself. I said yes, of course, and later that afternoon he brought round to my home airline tickets to Addis Ababa, a travel allowance, and briefing papers. Two days later I flew to Addis Ababa with Minister Malecela and his team from the Ministry.

When we arrived at the hotel I received a telephone call from the office of Mr Ekangaki, the OAU Secretary-General, saying that he wanted to see me. A car was on its way to pick me up and I would accompany him to the airport to receive the Chairman of the Committee. On the way there, the Secretary-General spoke to me about his ideas for the establishment of a special bank, through which the financial support, medium- and long-term loans at zero interest and a small service fee, would be made available for oil purchases by African countries. I asked him why he wasn't thinking of using the African Development Bank as the conduit. To my mind, it was well run, and for a small fee they could do the same job, earning revenue for Africans whilst saving the costs of establishing an entirely new institution.

For whatever reason, my proposal was not received with favour. I later heard that there was a move afoot to get British firm Lornho involved in the purchase of oil and the arranging of loans with the proposed bank. But this came to nothing.

After the meeting in Addis Ababa we all went to Cairo, where, under the auspices of the Arab League, the ministers from both sides met. On the first day the minister from Ghana took the argument to the Arab ministers from the outset, bristling at what he saw as their condescension to African ministers. He raised the question of concessionary oil prices for the African states, but this fell foul of several oil ministers and the suggestion was ruled out. Though I supported his forceful approach, I took the opportunity to remind the Ghanaian minister in the subtlest way possible that the decision to break diplomatic ties with Israel had been on moral, not economic grounds. But I have to say that most of the African countries did not want to present things in that way. Feeling the pinch of the oil shock, they, perhaps understandably, wanted to be rewarded with cheap oil at a time when the rest of the world was paying through the nose for this essential commodity. The end result of this meeting was that a substantial sum of money was placed at the disposal of African countries, which would be channelled through the soon-to-be-established Arab Bank of Business Development in Africa (BADEA). This decision was then formalised at the Sixth Arab Summit Conference in Algiers in November 1973 (and the bank started operating in Khartoum, Sudan, in March 1975).

By the summer of 1972, my two younger sons had followed Manish to England to be educated. At least Anuj and Rupen left when they were nine, not seven, but their departure from the family home was no less sorrowful for all that. They first went to Stoke House Brunswick, a newly merged preparatory school near Ashhurst Wood. Eventually they followed Manish (and their cousins) to Charterhouse, where all were to find a second home in 'Lockites' House, under the benign care of the housemaster Norman Evans. Evans was a kindly chap with large ears, which earned him the predictable nickname of Dumbo, and he and his wife Margaret did everything they could to make all of our boys feel settled. This was important, because money had been tight since nationalisation. Not being able to afford regular airfares between London and Dar es Salaam in those days of high-cost travel, the boys spent most of their school holidays either with my sister in Wembley or with a Mrs Edna Gundle in Chigwell, Essex. Edna was a real find, and a one-off too, and she gave all of our boys a genuine home from home. Warm and sympathetic, but also a stickler for order (before she would agree to act on our behalf she made me sign a formal guardianship agreement, a copy of which I still have), she reinforced good habits of self-discipline in boys who had become used to the spoiling habits of their doting grandparents, aunts, and uncles. To give but one example, if they told her they wanted new shoes, they had to bring the old ones along to her for inspection. By these and other means, she helped strengthen the value systems that they hold even to this day.

My five-year term as General Manager of the National Milling Corporation was drawing to a close, as my contract stipulated that I would stand down on December 31st, 1972, and I had no intention of overstaying my welcome, whatever else anyone might say or do to make me think otherwise. There were some in the government who believed that the success of the Corporation was dependent on my presence there. The Permanent Secretary in the Office of the President and the Permanent Secretary at the Ministry for Finance were particularly apprehensive about the possible consequences of my departure, and were doing all they could to persuade the President not to release me. This caused a delay in identifying a successor and recommending him to the President, which I would have liked to have finalised by mid-1972 so as to enable him to learn the ropes. But I have to say I didn't share such views about my indispensability. By 1972, the business was well established and on a sound footing. I had a good team in place, and an obviously capable successor designate, Werner Kapinga, also a member of the Board, whom the President had appointed to the post.

I moved out of my office and invited Werner to move in. This he was reluctant to do, suggesting that I remain in the same room whilst he occupied the office across the corridor. The staff kept coming to me to solve problems, kept sending files to me for review and decision. I knew I had to make a clean break. I therefore waited until Kapinga went on a short holiday and then moved all of my effects out of the building, leaving telephone numbers where I might be contacted in the future. On his return Kapinga found himself fully in charge, and rose to the occasion. We still had lunch together every now and then (Werner, like no one else I ever knew, really loved his food). And I was appointed a member of and honorary consultant to the Board. But to all intents and purposes, my intensive, day-to-day involvement in the milling industry was, after some twenty-two years, finally and irrevocably over.

I must, however, find room for one final vignette from my days at the National Milling Corporation. Tanzanians have an irreverent sense of humour that is often lost on expatriates who come to live and work in Tanzania. George Anderson, a Briton who was working for the NMC up in Arusha, was having difficulties with two Tanzanian employees over the deductions of their loan and provident fund. The main problem was the interchangeability of their names, which caused periodic mix-ups for the payroll clerk. Eventually George became so fed up with the confusion that he told them in a moment of utter frustration that the only solution he could think of was for one of them to change his name. He forgot all about his conversation with the men until the next payroll was processed, when he suddenly ran into difficulties with his own loan deductions. He then discovered that one of the two Tanzanian employees he had spoken to had indeed taken up his advice to change his name. The man's new name? Why, George Anderson, of course.

NINE

... AND NEWSPAPERS

The company name 'Lonrho' has always had a particular significance across sub-Saharan Africa. Long before Ted Heath had characterised the activities of the UK-based mining conglomerate and its many subsidiaries as the 'unacceptable face of capitalism', and even longer before the bitter personal feud between Tiny Rowlands, Lonrho's chairman, and Mohamed Al Fayed saw a stuffed shark by the name of 'Tiny' strung up above the food hall in Harrods, the name 'Lonrho' was viewed with suspicion, if not hatred, not only by the majority of black Africans, but also by a good proportion of white settlers (who thought that Tiny was definitely 'not one of us'). The Tanzanians were no exception to these rules. Even though Lonrho was a major player in a region crying out for foreign capital investment, the Lonrho chairman was effectively *persona non grata* to everyone in the ruling Tanzanian Party from the President down to the grassroots.

And yet for all that, the early 1970s saw Lonrho gaining a strong foothold in the Tanzanian newspaper industry, and by this means inheriting me as Chairman. My involvement in the industry began in 1959, when I was invited to join the board of the Tanganyika Standard Limited. At that time, this group published two local English-language newspapers, *The Tanganyika Standard* and *The Sunday News*. The Tanganyika Standard company had been around since the early 1930s, and was part of the dominant East African Standard Group, which also included the *Uganda Argus* in Kampala and the *Mombasa Times* and *East African Standard* in Kenya. The group had been founded and was owned by Rudolf and Claude Anderson (the former was a friend, and was later involved with me in the Chamber of Commerce), Kenyan farmers with a passion for publicly expressing colonial opinion on just about everything that mattered to them dearly, from farming and tourism and industry and politics right up to the issue closest to their hearts, the future role of Europeans in Africa. Inevitably, the editorial line across the group was strongly supportive of the prevailing colonial establishment. The group's editors saw themselves and their target audience as part of a clubby elite, which indeed the editors genuinely were. No one exemplified this set of attitudes better than the editor-in-chief in Nairobi, the forceful, some said dictatorial, Colonel Kenneth Bolton.

The Standard Group did not have a monopolistic place in the Tanganyikan media market, nor was I the only Asian in a prominent role. Indeed, the Asian community as a whole had been active in the local media since the 1930s, when an Indian by the name of V.R. Boal founded the bilingual (English/Gujarati) *Tanganyikan Herald* in direct competition to the *Tanganyika Opinion*, which again was bilingual and edited by a member of the then ubiquitous Patel 'clan'. During this period one Gujarati and one English weekly were published, but both later ceased publication. One Swahili weekly was brought out by the government's Information Services Department. By the 1960s, the bilingual papers had folded under the challenge of the Standard Group, as well as that of more recent arrivals on the local scene. These latter comprised the newspapers that offered their support to the African nationalist movement: *Uhuru*, the official TANU paper, *Ngurumo*, owned and managed by an Indian, Randhir Thakar, but strongly supportive of TANU, and *The Nationalist*, perhaps the most commercially vigorous of the Standard Group's local competitors.

In 1959, I already played a prominent role in LEGCO and EXCO, the local chambers of commerce, the Rotary Club, and the Freemasons. But none of these memberships quite prepared me for the idiosyncratic brand of colonialist culture that pervaded the East African Standard Group in those days. Up in Nairobi, the Board all belonged to the elitist Muthaiga Club, whose members' private opinions of African nationalists can be easily guessed at. But the self-image of the Standard Group's journalists, who passionately believed in their own commitment to Africa, led them to reserve most of their vitriol for their fellow whites. Most Europeans who came out to East Africa on short-term contracts and picked up little or nothing of the local culture were seen as 'upstarts' or 'visitors'. Avowed white socialists, such as President Nyerere's long-serving Fabian assistant Joan Wicken, were openly criticised, in common with the likes of Tiny Rowlands, as not being 'one of us', while European journalists working on assignment in East Africa were perhaps seen as the most despicable of the lot, jetting in as they did on the BOAC VC-10 flights to cover the major stories for the newspapers and electronic media and then flying out again. These 'VC Wallahs', as they were termed, were seen by the local 'club' as neither knowing anything about Africa nor, worse still, caring.

None of that tiffin and sundowners grumbling at the Muthaiga Club ever got in the way of the business at hand, however. The board members of the *East African Standard* were much too canny to fall into the trap of producing a newspaper that would allow their many competitors or detractors to cry foul. When I joined the board of the *Standard* in 1959, it was already clear to those in charge of the Tanganyikan arm of the operation that the local political wind was beginning to blow hard in the direction of independence. Whether they privately welcomed this or not, and most didn't, they immediately recognised that their continued operation would depend on their not making enemies in the upper reaches of TANU. It was one thing for the *Tanganyika Standard* to be identified as the mouthpiece of European business interests in the country, as it certainly was, post-independence. It was quite another for the paper to be perceived as antagonistic in any way to the new African nationalist leadership. Thus it was that the pre-independence editorial line of pro-establishment, pro-market development carried over almost seamlessly to the new independent state of Tanganyika. This encouraged the new government, with its hands full elsewhere, to take a *laissez-faire* attitude to the established press. It also gave the European staff of the paper free rein to pursue their efforts to preserve a British way of life in Africa, while simultaneously encouraging as many educated Africans and Asians actively to absorb themselves into that lifestyle as wished to do so.

In the early fifties I had met A.J. Nevill, the first editor I knew. He was followed by Bill Ottowill, Ken Ridley, and finally my good friend Brendon Grimshaw, who owns Mayonne Island, off Mahe in the Seychelles, and with whom I am in regular contact. Nevill, always immaculately dressed in a white suit, once at my invitation addressed the Dar es Salaam Cultural Society, of which I was at the time the Acting Secretary. The commercial side of the newspaper company was handled by Charles Thetford, and after his departure Alan Nihill, son of Sir Barclay Nihill, Speaker of the East African Legislative Assembly, took over.

The Gymkhana Club in Dar es Salaam, neither as elitist nor as stiflingly traditional as the Muthaiga Club to the north, was the main venue for pursuing those twin aims. Invitations to visit and join it, with its golf, its cricketing, and, above all, its networking opportunities were the incentives dangled in front of potentially like-minded Africans and Asians. Once I was installed as a board member, it wasn't long before I too was invited to join. Since the constitution of the Club restricted membership to persons of pure European descent, they had created a category of 'extraordinary members' outside the constitution, and in 1961 I was the first non-white person to be made such a member. Unusually for someone who prides himself on being adept at coping with all manner of social situations, I never felt entirely comfortable at the Club, and rarely if ever went there. In fact I went there only on occasions when I was to present sports trophies, in my capacity as chairman of the board of such companies as International Computers Limited (ICL), then a gilt-edged British-owned IT company. Following the decision of Dar es Salaam's city council not to grant licences to clubs where discrimination is practised, the membership (which then included me), under David Newton, the Club's president, decided, at their annual general meeting on February 28th, 1962 (which I attended), to change the constitution and make the club facilities available to all races.

My reason for wanting to join the Gymkhana Club was to learn to play golf. When I made enquiries, David Newton told me that one Mr K.C. Fane would be able to help, but he was away on leave in the UK and was expected back in a couple of months. When Mr Fane returned he telephoned me, and the conversation went as follows: 'I understand you wish to learn how to play golf. Would you meet me at the Club for the next few weeks at 2.00 p.m. on Tuesdays and Fridays?' 'Thank you, Mr Fane, but it will be difficult for me to leave the office at that time, and in any case it will be quite hot and humid.' 'Mr Chande, forget about golf, you will never be able to learn the game.'

I was of much more use to the group in a business context. At the time of my joining the Board, the *Tanganyika Standard* was a single integrated business unit, comprising newspapers, offices, print works, and stationery manufacturers. This situation had grown up over time, and no one had seen fit to question the wisdom of such an agglomeration. As I pointed out to the directors shortly after I joined the Board, the situation was fraught with contingent liabilities, with the entire whole thus made liable to the weaknesses of any of its component parts. I therefore proposed the establishment of four stand-alone entities: Tanganyika Standard Newspapers Limited (the publisher); Printpak Tanzania Limited (the printing works); Standard Properties Limited (the estate owners); and Office and Stationery Supplies Limited (newspaper distribution and office stationery sales).

My proposal was accepted and acted upon. And the wisdom of this sub-division became more apparent as the years wore on. From 1962, the year of the legislation authorising preventive detentions, right through to February 1967, the prevailing view among the Europeans on the Board was that despite the situation, nationalisation was not yet in the cards. In the days after the Arusha Declaration, however, when my own personal sensitivity about government takeovers was at its height, Mwalimu made a public speech about *Ujamaa* to a packed crowd in Dar es Salaam that raised anxiety levels at the paper by several notches. He was in the midst of a complex disquisition about the need to bring public opinion round to the potential benefits of African Socialism when a voice in the crowd suddenly cried out, '*The Standard*! *The Standard*!' This wasn't one of our more zealous salesmen touting his wares, but a grassroots TANU activist picking up on the concerns that were rising in the party. Mwalimu immediately understood the implications of what the man had called out, and shouted back to the heckler above the rising hubbub, 'Can you edit it?' The man's answer was lost in the laughter that followed. But it wasn't lost on the Board members that the question had now been publicly asked by the President, in the sort of forum that would encourage further, potentially damaging speculation.

But in the sixties nationalisation was only a gleam in the eye. A more pressing concern for me was the balance of power within the group. In 1959, when I first joined the Board, the Kenyan part of the operation was undoubtedly the hub. In fact it went so far as to have pretensions to be the entire wheel. While Colonel Kenneth Bolton sat in Nairobi barking out the editorial line for the whole group over the telephone, an Englishman named Charles Thetford sat in a nearby office masterminding the business side of the operation. Between the two of them, they controlled everything in the group that ever moved, and expected their vassals in Dar es Salaam and Kampala to do little more than salute the company flag and obey.

True to my own nature, I bridled at this way of doing things from the outset, not least given the different needs of the different business operations for the different markets. As soon as I was appointed chairman of the Tanganyika end of the operation in 1963, I began to pick away more systematically at this Nairobi-centric view of our world, a posture that was bound to put me on a collision course with the forthright retired colonel. One classic example of the problems we ran into occurred during the absence of Brendon Grimshaw, our editor, on his annual holiday. Now Grimshaw was very able, and a difficult man to replace, even during a vacation, but I nominated his deputy, David Martin, to cover for him until his return. When Colonel Bolton was told what I had done, he reacted with characteristic fury, complaining bitterly that he should have been consulted in advance, and arguing that Martin was 'not one of us'. I ended up winning that particular round, if only because no one but Martin could get even close to filling Grimshaw's shoes. Until 1968, however, Bolton had a distinct weight advantage in most of our bouts, given that he had been an integral part of the owners' social set in Nairobi for what seemed like an eternity.

Then along came Lonrho in the person of its chairman, Tiny Rowlands, and changed the entire calculus for everyone.

Lonrho had had an interest in the media in Eastern Africa for several years. In the run-up to independence in Zambia in 1964, Tiny Rowlands had acquired *The Times of Zambia*, the *Zambia News*, and a small-circulation newspaper called the *Livingstone Mail*. He appointed a talented English newspaperman named Richard Hall as editor-in-chief of this group, and Hall set to work establishing his bona fides in the newly independent state. He gave up his British passport to become a Zambian citizen, and by dint of his sympathy toward the new Zambian administration soon managed to alienate a good deal of the local white population. Yet by the end of 1967, the ruling Zambian Party, UNIP, had turned against him, denouncing him as a stooge of British imperialism. Hall flew back to Britain and went on to write a book about his experiences, *The High Price of Principles*, which further alienated his former friends in government. Rowlands, meanwhile, having burned his fingers in Zambia, started to cast around for somewhere in Africa more stable in which to anchor a media empire.

His eyes came to rest on the Standard Group of companies. These were attractive to Rowlands for a number of reasons. Each newspaper was in a country with no recent record of poor relations between media and government. Each was the market leader in its respective country. Perhaps most important of all, each was in a country where Lonrho was looking to exploit any opportunity to widen the base of its commercial operations. Rowlands therefore promptly bought three titles from the Andersons — the *East African Standard*, the *Tanganyika Standard*, and the soon-to-fold *Uganda Argus* — and at a stroke became the most powerful newspaper proprietor in the whole of East Africa. He later also acquired a chain of hotels and lodges in Kenya, including the best-known hotel in Mombasa, Nyali Beach Hotel.

This more visible intrusion of media baron Tiny Rowlands was unwelcome to many in East Africa. Given his antecedents, Rowlands gave the colonial whites an excuse to resurrect many of their old prejudices about the Germans. He upset the business community, who felt he played the game by his own rules, not theirs. And he was viewed with suspicion by African nationalists, fearful of the potentially destabilising effects of having one so rich and so powerful operating freely in their poverty-stricken countries.

About a fortnight after the acquisition, Tiny Rowlands sent a man named the Honourable Gerald Percy to see me. The object of the mission was to see if I'd be willing to carry on as chairman of the *Tanganyika*

Standard. Conscious of Mwalimu's distrust, if not dislike, of Rowlands, and of the fact that Joan Wicken, the President's personal assistant, Amir Jamal, and Roland Brown, Tanzania's Attorney-General, shared the President's views in at least as strong a measure, I immediately realised that I had to play for time. I told Percy that I needed to think his proposition over before making a decision, and that in any case, given that I had been acting as chairman for over four years now, it might be a good time for the likes of Lonrho to find some new blood.

Not long after that meeting I went for a drink with Dickson Nkembo, the President's Permanent Secretary, and told him about Lonrho's offer. I said that I'd as good as refused, that I didn't want to stay in the job, because 'Let's face it, Tiny Rowlands is *persona non grata* in Tanzania.' A couple of days later Nkembo called me, saying that the President wanted me to call on him at State House the following day. Later that day, Nkembo rang to say that the meeting had to be called off, but that Mwalimu had left a message for me instead. The gist of it was that the Tanzanian government was keen for me to accept the Lonrho offer and to stay on as chairman of the Board. The inference was clear: if a future relationship between the government of Tanzania and Lonrho was now unavoidable, then Mwalimu wanted a known quantity, i.e., me, right at the heart of it.

I then went back to Gerald Percy and told him I was willing to carry on, subject to two conditions. First, the board of directors should have commercial freedom, and second, Colonel Bolton was to become less involved in the journalistic or staffing side of the paper. Percy was content to agree to both. The only other change envisaged from the Lonrho side was the appointment of two additional directors of their own to the Board. As far as I can recall, neither of them ever turned up for a meeting, and we continued to run the company as we had previously, minus the unwanted micro-management from the Nairobi end. We were happy, and so, it seemed, were Lonrho, given that our near monopolistic position in the marketplace allowed us to turn a fair profit.

Then, toward the end of 1969, I received a message from Paul Bomani, the Minister for Planning, asking me to call on him. When I arrived it was immediately clear from his demeanour that this was no ordinary meeting between old friends. He motioned to me to sit down and told me he wanted to address me in my capacity as chairman of the Standard Group of newspapers. The government had decided to take it over, and was proposing to put it under the control of the National Development Corporation for the purposes of operational control, with me remaining on the Board, though not as chairman.

I sat back and digested what he had said. It was no surprise to me, given all that had happened in the previous two years. At the same time, I thought it a mistake and told Bomani as much.

'Why does the government need to take control when the papers have always supported the party and the government?' If money was the reason, 'owning newspapers might not be the right thing to do. Just look at the performance of the party papers.'

I then made a suggestion. 'Why don't you appoint an editorial advisory board, which could work alongside the paper's editors? The government could appoint representatives from, say, the judiciary, academia, and the business sector, together with a handful of other wise persons, and these could work in tandem with the editor.'

It was Paul's turn to sit and think. Eventually he asked me, 'Do you think Tiny Rowlands would agree to your proposal?' I told him I didn't know, but Lonrho's interest was in the bottom line, so I was pretty sure that anything that didn't affect it would be agreeable to them. Paul nodded, and said he would call me back in a few days.

Three weeks later, Minister Bomani called me again. He told me that the government had given careful thought to my alternative proposal, but had decided to stick to their original plan. He was sorry, but they were taking us over.

'Well, if that's your decision,' I said. 'But let me ask you, do you know exactly what you will be taking over? If you take over the newspapers you'll get the teleprinters, some typewriters, the editorial desks and chairs, and some photographic equipment, negatives, and files. That's it. The printing plant does not belong to the company and neither does the property.'

Bomani's reaction was short and to the point. 'Oh, God,' he gasped, dialled a number, and hearing no response, rang off. He said he would contact me later.

Another six weeks passed before I heard from the Minister again. This conversation was even shorter than the last had been. He informed me that the government would take over all four companies and that I would stay on as a Board member, as previously proposed. Tiny Rowlands was never to know that I had found it necessary to explain the group corporate structure to the Tanzanian government, something they could have established for themselves from the Registrar of Companies anyway. Perhaps it was less cumbersome that the government chose to take over all the four companies of the group rather than just the one that published newspapers. It made for a quicker and less painful process for all concerned.

The new era found me back on the Board, and the President was appointed editor-in-chief. Brendon Grimshaw, the managing editor, who had managed to survive the Lonrho era, was moved on to lead a new public relations department charged with the unenviable task of improving the image of the National Development Corporation. His departure ceremony from *The Standard* was for me in many ways a *tableau vivant* of the end of the colonial era in Tanganyika, although it took place almost ten years after independence had actually been gained. We had drinks and small bites and gathered round in small groups making polite conversation, as one would at the Gymkhana Club at around sundown. And then, when the formalities were over and the final speeches had been made, Brendon Grimshaw, ever the gentleman, and still a close friend of mine, went round the room to say goodbye to each and every member of the staff, shaking hands with the reporters, the stenographers, the photographer, and the sub-editors, telling them all that it was their duty to stay loyal to the new management, and stiffening their sinews by telling them to look on themselves as the same winning cricketing team, albeit with a new captain. The evening was beginning to draw in. The torch was finally passing.

To whom it was passing was a question that none of us at the paper had an answer for. But we didn't have to wait long to find out. On the morning of her appointment, I was told that the government had chosen journalist and barrister Frene Ginwala, a South African of Indian extraction, to be the first editor of the new nationalised *Standard*, which was renamed the *Daily News*. And as soon as she started work, she began radicalising the politics of the paper.

One of her first acts was to fly to London, where I was staying on business, to talk through her future plans. While in London, she made the first of a number of ambitious appointments. Richard Gott was a well-known journalist and author who had made his reputation championing the cause of socialism in Latin America during the political upheavals of the 1960s. He had recently published *Guerrilla Warfare in Latin America*, and he was a man with a first-class mind and a sense of political purpose that far outstripped that of most of his left-leaning colleagues in the British press, even in those revolutionary sixties. Appointed as Foreign Editor, he was Frene Ginwala's first appointment, and in my view by far the best. But for all his gifts, he possessed neither African nor Commonwealth experience.

The changes set in train didn't stop with Richard Gott. Within months he had been joined by a friend of his, Rod Prince, a former editor of *Peace News* and a sub-editor trained by the Agence France Presse in

Paris. Another British recruit was Iain Christie, the son of an Edinburgh hotelier, who went on to broadcast for Frelimo out of Mozambique, and who later earned the distinction of being nicknamed 'Lord McHaw-Haw' by the beleaguered white community in pre-independence Rhodesia. Then Tony Hall, like Frene Ginwala an ANC supporter, came on board, together with Phillip Ocheng, a talented Kenyan writer who wrote a weekly column that targeted the wrongdoings of pretty much every politician in East Africa.

By any standards, and particularly by the *Standard*'s standards, this was a strong team. It was also packed with ideological and egocentric nitroglycerine, and it wasn't too long before the first explosion was touched off. Ironically enough, or perhaps predictably, it involved the two most talented members of the new team. At the time it was billed as an ideological clash between Ginwala and Gott, with the former objecting to the latter's editorial line, which tended to praise the achievements of Chairman Mao at the expense of Russian leaders past and present. This was always going to inflame Ms Ginwala, given the Soviet Union's solid and sustained support of the ANC. But the issue was only superficially one of politics. The egos had collided, and the town wasn't big enough for both of them. So Gott made an appointment to see the President, and began the process of talking himself out of a job.

The two men met at Mwalimu's beachside cottage just to the north of Dar es Salaam. Gott spoke at great length, in conditions of the utmost informality, about the difficulties he faced in carrying out his duties in the presence of his intellectually demanding and commanding managing editor. Surely the time had come, he went on, for the Editor-in-Chief to appoint a locally-born Tanzanian to edit the paper.

Gott must have made quite an impression on the President that weekend, for within weeks of that meeting the contracts of Ginwala, Gott, Prince, and Hall had all been re-arranged, and they left the country forthwith. Sammy Mdee, a young Tanzanian reporter with a good command of both language and newspaper practice, was appointed managing editor.

It was a curious end to what had been a most promising opening chapter in the history of the *Standard* in the new post-Arusha era. It brought the curtain down on one of the most promising editorial partnerships I ever saw in my years at the *Tanganyika Standard*. It also, thankfully, brought an end to the production of the bulky political supplements that were a feature of the Ginwala/Gott era, supplements that by now have passed into popular legend, thanks to one, a hundred-pager commemorating the anniversary of Lenin's birth, which was jettisoned into the gutters of the city in such numbers by so many of our overloaded delivery boys that it caused a temporary blockage in Dar es Salaam's drainage system.

Clearly Gott remembered his days in Dar es Salaam with fondness. Writing about them in the London *Guardian* almost thirty years later, on the occasion of the death of Mwalimu, he recalled the circumstances of his appointment, and his departure. 'Invited to Dar es Salaam, I found myself foreign editor of a state newspaper in a one-party state and was soon in trouble with the British High Commission and the American Embassy for rewriting Reuters news stories. In reports from Vietnam, we used to delete the words "Viet Cong" and replace them with "the South Vietnamese Liberation Front".'

'Nyerere,' Gott continued, 'took a relaxed attitude towards his duties (as Editor-in-Chief) but urged us not to refrain from publishing stories of Ministerial wrongdoing. And only once did he dramatically intervene. Frene (Ginwala) asked me to write an editorial condemning the action of President Numeiri of Sudan, who had just executed several members of the Sudanese Communist Party. Numeiri was one of Nyerere's few supporters in his campaign against Idi Amin in Uganda, and my outspoken editorial against Tanzania's current ally proved highly embarrassing. Frene was out of the country on the very first plane, and I left soon after.'

The departures of Gott and Ginwala, the latter moving onward and upward toward the Speaker's chair in post-apartheid South Africa, opened the door to Tanzanian journalists. The most impressive of these was to be Ben Mkapa, who had been trained on the London *Daily Mirror* with the assistance of the late Barbara Castle and her husband Ted. Ben, gifted in all things, not least in his spare and eloquent use of language, stood out from the very beginning, and it was no surprise to me, or to anyone else who saw him in operation at the *Daily News* (formerly the *Standard*), that his future trajectory would outsoar even that of Frene Ginwala, until he moved on to the foreign service, eventually becoming Foreign Minister, and deservedly attained the Presidency of Tanzania itself. We often met socially, and prior to his posting as Tanzania's High Commissioner to Nigeria, he and I served together on the board of governors of Shaaban Robert Secondary School. During the time he was Foreign Minister my old friend Malcolm McDonald, president of the Royal Commonwealth Society, who then lived in Seven Oaks, West Kent, came to stay with us on rather short notice. I invited Ben at similarly short notice to join us for dinner. It was a Sunday and his official chauffeur was not on duty, but he drove himself to our home to meet Malcolm. Malcolm (son of Ramsay McDonald) was, I believe, the youngest Secretary of State when he joined the British government.

In my latter days as chairman of the Standard Group, an issue of particular political delicacy arose. For several years, Mwalimu had been making efforts to end the Dar es Salaam-centric nature of Tanzanian life. In 1973 he made his boldest bid to date, moving the administrative capital hundreds of miles inland to Dodoma. With a new Parliament and new party headquarters under construction there, he ordered Prime Minister Salim Ahmed Salim to explore with me the possibility of moving the newspaper to Dodoma as well. Knowing that I had to choose my words carefully, given the head of political steam that was building behind the Dodoma project, I said that a move of this sort could be effected, but to make it work would be costly. A new printing press would have to be acquired and installed. New premises would have to be rented, bought, or built. Suitable accommodation would have to be provided for the staff and their families. And the existing telecommunications systems would have to be upgraded and modernised.

Perhaps unsurprisingly, the move was never made. But my own departure was imminent. Reginald Mengi, an astute and able businessman from the Kilimanjaro Region, who was to become a rising star in the local media market, was appointed to replace me as chairman. I left with good memories, and no regrets. The days of the 'cricketing' editorial staff, and of Tiny Rowlands, were now thankfully behind us. With people like Mkapa at the helm, and with Mengi coming forward, I was no longer needed as I once had been. The fortunes of the Standard Group were no longer dependent upon events in Nairobi or London. Tanzanians were now at last rightly carrying all the load. A few months later I read a short news item reporting that Mengi had resigned as chairman to pursue the setting up of his own media company.

TEN

FREEMASONRY

While the late 1960s were a time of anxiety for many in the Asian community in Tanzania, the early 1970s brought a new source of concern, this time over the border in Uganda. The coming to power of General Idi Amin ushered in a new and violent era in that country's history. And it wasn't long before he took his own virulent brand of Africanisation to a devastating conclusion. New, draconian citizenship laws forced a mass exodus of foreigners, mostly British citizens of Indian origin, from the country, bringing considerable hardship to most of those affected. Among those who were asked to leave at very short notice and with only a suitcase full of possessions were members of Jayli's family, even though some of them had been Ugandan citizens — their status as citizens having been summarily revoked by Idi Amin by means of a televised announcement.

Jayli's brother Manubhai was one of those whose citizenship was revoked, and the next day he was summoned by the Minister for Home Affairs, who advised him that he was being placed under detention. Manubhai's chauffeur was instructed to drive, under escort, from the Minister's office to the notorious Makindye prison. Both spent the night in jail. Manubhai's family was advised late in the evening about his being jailed. The chauffeur was released after two days, but Manubhai and his Mercedes 500 continued to be detained. The warders cleaned the car every day, and Manubhai was treated with extraordinary respect. Vegetarian food was brought from home, as well as a copy of the Bhagvad Gita, the Hindu scripture. The presence of the British journalist Sandy Gall and a few others in the neighbouring cells and the resulting constant media focus in the UK ensured that all of them survived the terrifying ordeal. Manubhai himself, a man of belief and of a gentle and kind disposition, managed to keep his spirits up. But prison left its mark. Some of his family members left the country, and after three weeks in detention he was released and asked to leave the country as well. Both the British High Commissioner and the US Ambassador offered assistance.

The impact on the families was, as I have said, often devastating, but the wider effects for the Ugandan economy were also considerable. Jayli's

Andy Chande in the regalia of the Head of Freemasonry in East Africa (comprising Tanzania, Kenya, Uganda, and the Seychelles) in 1986.

Manish, Anuj, and Rupen, the three sons of Mr and Mrs Chande, in 1978.

Mr Gerald Nevill, former District Grand Master of East Africa, United Grand Lodge of England, with Mr Chande in 1987.

J.K. Chande addressing a meeting of Freemasons in Nairobi, Kenya, in 1989.

Shri Pramukh Swami Maharaj, the Head of the Swaminarayan sect, bestows blessings on the author when His Holiness visited Dar es Salaam in 1995.

The author with Ambassador Salim Ahmed Salim, Prime Minister of Tanganyika and Secretary General of the Organization of African Unity, in 1997.

Dr Chande receiving an Honorary Doctorate in Business Administration from the International Management Centres, Buckingham, England in 1995 from the Chancellor of International Academy of Management Mr Ivor Kenny of Ireland. Mr Chande's second son, Anuj, is on the left.

President Benjamin William Mkapa of Tanzania and Andy Chande engrossed in discussion, 1997.

Mr Chande with President Mkapa at the opening of the Multi-purpose Assembly Hall of Shaaban Robert Secondary School in Dar es Salaam in 1997. President Mkapa is seen shaking hands with Victor Kamesera, a Governor of the School and also the Secretary-General of one of the opposition parties.

The author addressing a gathering of Rotarians in Trivandrum, Kerala State, India, in 1997.

Andy Chande with President Nyerere (right) and President Mkapa (left) at the reopening of Singida Railway Line on July 19th, 1997.

Andy Chande with President Mkapa at the inauguration of Barclays Bank Tanzania Limited on February 27th, 2001.

The author with Zanzibar President Amani Abeid Karume and former US Ambassador Robert Royall in 2002.

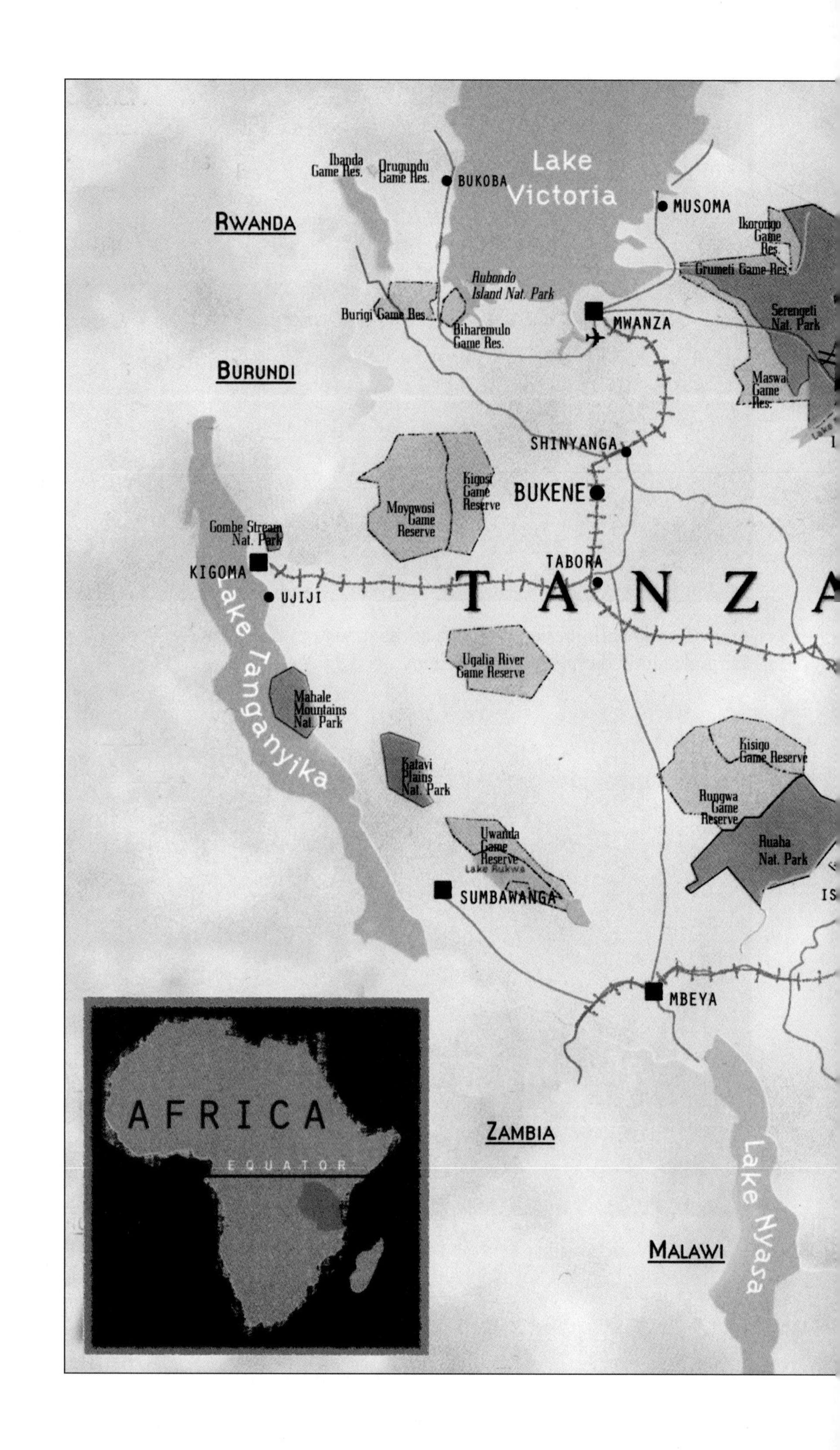

Lake Victoria
Ibanda Game Res.
Orugundu Game Res.
BUKOBA
MUSOMA
RWANDA
Ikorongo Game Res.
Grumeti Game Res.
Rubondo Island Nat. Park
Burigi Game Res.
Biharemulo Game Res.
MWANZA
Serengeti Nat. Park
BURUNDI
Maswa Game Res.
SHINYANGA
Kigosi Game Reserve
Moyowosi Game Reserve
BUKENE
Gombe Stream Nat. Park
KIGOMA
TABORA
UJIJI
T A N Z A
Lake Tanganyika
Ugalia River Game Reserve
Mahale Mountains Nat. Park
Katavi Plains Nat. Park
Kisigo Game Reserve
Rungwa Game Reserve
Ruaha Nat. Park
Uwanda Game Reserve
Lake Rukwa
SUMBAWANGA
MBEYA
AFRICA
EQUATOR
ZAMBIA
Lake Nyasa
MALAWI

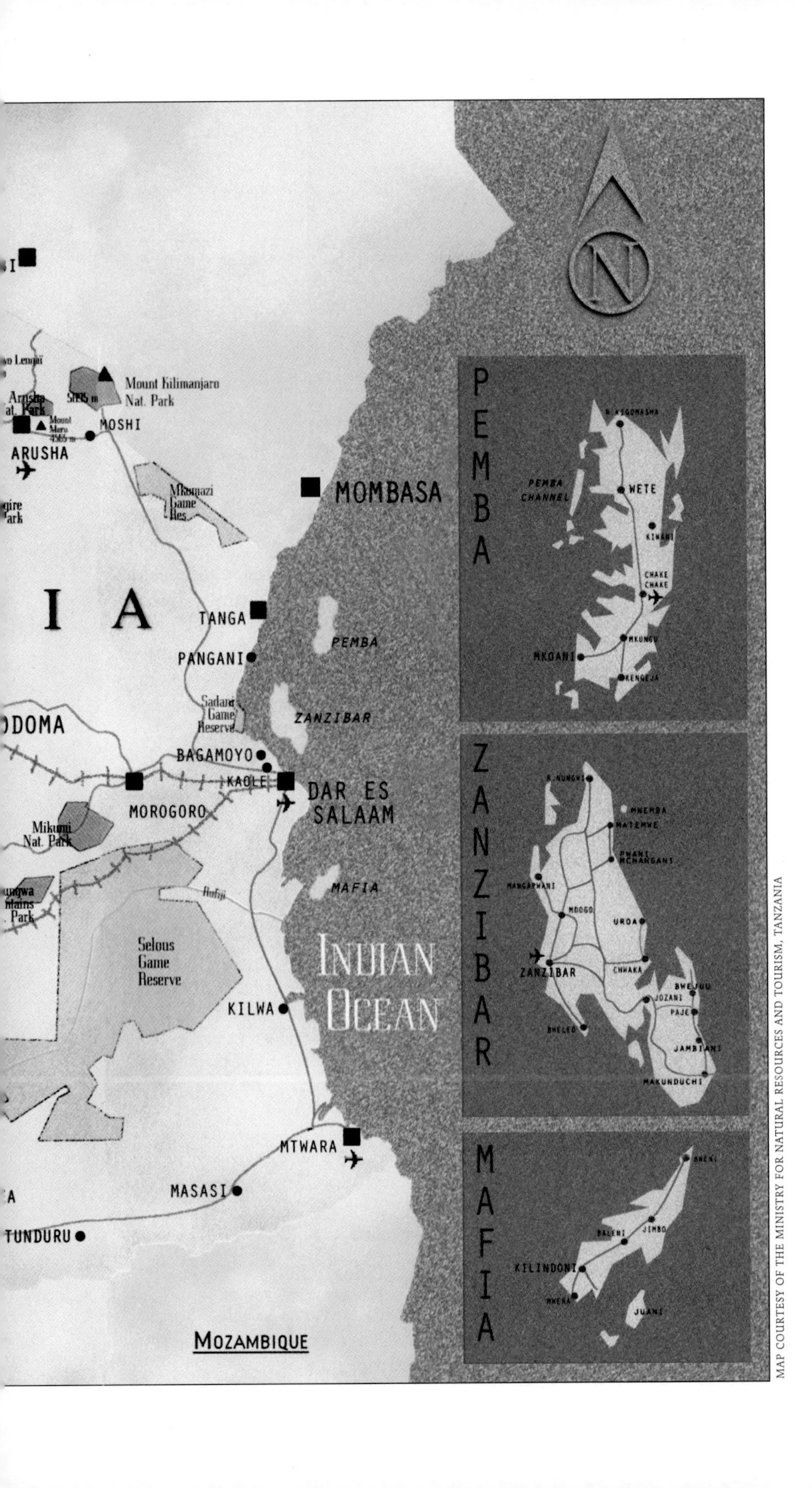

MAP COURTESY OF THE MINISTRY FOR NATURAL RESOURCES AND TOURISM, TANZANIA

President Benjamin William Mkapa is presented with crystal gifts by the author from World Rotary International, on June 12th, 2002.

This patrol boat, commissioned in January 2002, was named after Jayli in appreciation of Andy's fifteen years of service as Chairman of Tanzania Harbours Authority (now Tanzania Ports Authority).

Sir Andy Chande with Mr Richard Clarke, British High Commissioner, and President Mkapa immediately after receiving the Knighthood on August 29th, 2003.

The author with Kenya's Vice-President Hon. Moody Awori, MP in Nairobi, in 2004.

The author with participants of the International Investors' Forum in Dar es Salaam on July 17th, 2002. In the front row from left to right are: President of Zanzibar Amani Abeid Karume, President of World Bank James Wolfensohn, President of Tanzania Benjamin William Mkapa, and His Highness The Aga Khan.

On January 9th, 2005, President of India Dr Abdul Kalam presents Sir Chande with the the coveted Pravasi Bharatiya Samman Award.

The author and his wife Jayli visit the bridge on River Kwai, Kanchanaburi, Thailand, while attending the International Rotary Convention in 2005. In the background, a train moves along the Death Railway.

August 2005, J.K. Chande chatting with with Tanzania's Foreign Minister, the Hon. Jakaya Kikwete MP, the CCM's candidate in Tanzania's 2005 presidential elections.

President Mkapa of Tanzania toasting the author and his wife Jayli at the banquet to celebrate their 50th wedding anniversary on May 6th, 2005.

Sir Andy Chande, Chancellor of the International Medical and Technological University, Dar es Salaam, Tanzania, 2005.

family, for instance, was involved through its business conglomerate in the manufacturing of sugar, the brewing of beer, and the production of such goods as container glassware, matches, corrugated boxes, steel for the construction industry, tea, and textiles. At the time of the expulsions these were generating around ten percent of the GDP of Uganda.

Amin's expulsions were therefore not only racist and repugnant, but against the long-term interests of the country he now ruled. My own view is that he came to realise this before the order was implemented, but his desire to thumb his nose at the British government — part of a deeper love-hate relationship with the mother country that had taught him his military skills — kicked in at that point. For this reason, I strongly believe that, had the British government made a welcoming gesture to the departing Asians, Amin would have relented at the twelfth hour and either rescinded his order or softened it in some way. Instead, the British government, in the person of Jim Callaghan, pleaded to Amin to review his decision. In the circumstances, not least in Amin's head, that was reason enough to confirm the expulsion order.

Despite the lack of an early welcome, most of the expelled Ugandan Asians went to the UK, though a proportion went to Canada and a few to mainland Europe. The expelled Asians' settlement in the UK was facilitated by a committee under the chairmanship of the former governor of Tanganyika (and an old friend of mine) Sir Richard Turnbull. History shows how successful that forced migration was for most of those who had been expelled (as well as for their respective host nations). History also shows that Amin's despotic rule was doomed to failure, as is the case with all who prefer might to right, with Mwalimu Nyerere the eventual agent of change. In 1979, following the takeover of a part of Kagera region of Tanzania by Idi Amin's forces, the under-equipped Tanzanian army fought back like lions and pushed the Ugandans out of Tanzania. But Mwalimu did not stop there. Persuaded of the need for regime change in Uganda, he ordered his forces to press on all the way into Kampala, and they toppled Amin.

There was great relief and joy when the news came of the overthrow of Amin. A small number of those Asians who had been expelled returned to repossess the properties that had been confiscated. Families from the larger industrial groups like the Madhvanis and the Mehtas took back their assets and made substantial financial investments to rehabilitate and further develop their industries, a trend that intensified when, after Lule, Binaisa, and Obote, President Museveni came to power. I happened to be at a meeting in Neasden, England, in the 1980s, when President Museveni addressed about 2,000 ex-Uganda Asians, calling upon them to return to the old country and contribute to the economic reconstruction of Uganda. Looking back to the Amin era, the irrepressible President told his former countrymen, 'All this time we were fighting in a bush, whilst you were all happily settled in Shepherd's Bush.' The Madhvanis went back, and eventually a member of the dynasty, Nimisha Madhvani-Chandaria, was appointed by Museveni as First Secretary in the Uganda Embassy in Washington DC, with a mission to attract new investment — and is still there, with the rank of Counsellor.

When the furore of Amin's expulsions had died down, my thoughts quickly returned to my own future career.

Once I stepped down from running the National Milling Corporation, at the end of December 1972, I never again had a full-time job. That is not to say, however, that I ever lacked employment. That has never been the case, and I guess it never will be. But having invested so much of my effort and energy into the family business only to see it swallowed up in one bite by the state, I decided that my future working life would be run in a manner of my own choosing, on my terms, and at a pace to suit myself. Above all, I wanted the freedom of choice that would only come from involvement in what rapidly became a bewildering array of diverse projects. From the beginning of 1973, I set out to prove to myself and to others that the skills I had acquired in the family business were readily transferable elsewhere. And in doing so I wanted to continue to make good on the promise I had made to Mwalimu all those years ago, to put my talents and experience, such as they were, at the service of our fledgling state.

Now at last a free agent, I continued to deepen my involvement in the work of the many state and parastatal organisations that had emerged in the wake of the Arusha Declaration. From trains and boats and planes and mills, and then banks and newspapers, my responsibilities broadened to encompass lotteries, tourism, roads, construction, hospitals, water, and environmental protection, to name but a few. There are stories to tell about each of them, but those concerning environmental protection are perhaps dearest to my heart. However, before I move on to that ever-more-complex relationship between man and nature, which has increasingly occupied my attention since my teenage years in Bukene, I want to turn back to my involvement in what I have often described as 'non-gainful' activities. 'Non-gainful' is perhaps an inaccurate description, for while it is true in the narrowest sense that those activities did not generate income, the rewards that have accrued from them over the past fifty or so years have been without compare, and beyond price.

I have already written at length about the way my father, Keshavji, imbued me with a rigorous work ethic. His efforts were so successful that I have never been able to offer up half measures in any job I have taken on, or indeed accept them from other people. But my father gave me a far greater gift, one born of his intense spirituality. From childhood, he made me keenly aware that all human beings have higher responsibilities, first and foremost to God, but then also to people less fortunate than oneself. Sad to relate, I have never found it in me to take religion as seriously as my father did, though I do continue to believe in God. But throughout my working life I have stayed true to his humanistic principles, and have applied them whenever I could, and to the best of my ability.

My early days as a Rotarian have already been recounted. But before I joined the Rotary movement, I had begun to develop an interest in Freemasonry. This was largely thanks to the irreproachable conduct and humble demeanour of two of my closest friends at that time, Bob Campbell Ritchie, an Englishman, and John MacLean, a Scotsman. At first I knew nothing of their involvement in Masonic activity. To me they were friends who happened to be in government service, one of them in the colonial civil service, the other working for the railways. But as I got to know them more closely, I came to realise that each Monday evening after work Bob and John would go off together to mysterious meetings at a building close to the seafront in Dar es Salaam. Gradually, as my own curiosity deepened, they began to tell me something of what was going on. They were Freemasons, and pretty soon I wanted to be one too.

Unfortunately, we were all living in colonial Tanganyika in the early 1950s, and there was no chance at all that either Bob or John would be able to help me enter their seafront lodge as an initiate. It was whites only, you see, and then only whites of a certain type. But being my friends, they still wanted to help, so they put me in touch with Sheikh Mustafa and Jivraj Patel, fellow Masons who in time were to become my brethren. It was Mustafa and Patel who told me that a total of four tiers of Masonic lodges were operating in Tanganyika at that time, and that these closely mirrored both the class system that existed within the expatriate European society and, below that, the colonial segregationist pattern, indeed policy, of 'separate development'.

This meant that the first and foremost lodge in Dar es Salaam was reserved for the top echelon of Tanganyikan society, the white English elite. A second lodge was set aside for the European business community. A third was composed mostly of Scotsmen, though for what reasons

I never quite found out. Finally there was the fourth, the Guiding Star Lodge, which was reserved for Indians like Mustafa and Patel and myself. No fifth lodge existed then, which meant that black Africans had no chance at all of joining in.

This form of apartheid was no surprise to me. What did come as a shock, though, was the difficulty I had in gaining entry to the Guiding Star. No one had forewarned me about the pains that were taken in assessing the suitability of all would-be initiates, irrespective of their financial circumstances or standing in society. Instead of receiving an early invitation to join them, as I had clearly expected, I was made to wait for almost two years while my suitability as a Mason was assessed. During that time my daily activities, inside and outside of work, were carefully scrutinised. So too were the activities and opinions of my immediate family and close friends. Though I was the scion of one of the foremost Indian business families in East Africa, there were no short cuts for me, there was no easy access. It was only on October 25th, 1954, that I was at last initiated into the Guiding Star Lodge No. 5299. Just over fifty years later, the self-same lodge was to organise a gala banquet to mark the occasion of my fifty years of membership. On that occasion, the lodge gave a number of small gifts, which I will always cherish, and the night was marked with an excellent programme, which included fireworks and a well-produced souvenir of the occasion containing information about my Masonic career.

This lodge remained Indian-only for another ten years, until the Masonic Order in Tanzania at last woke up to the fact that independence had been granted two years previously. Indeed, it took longer than that for the colonial-era four-tiered arrangement of Masonic lodges across the capital to dissolve into something more representative of modern, multi-ethnic Tanzania — a change that had occurred some years earlier in the local Rotarian movement and other such voluntary bodies. A few members of Dar es Salaam lodge — all of them European businessmen — who wished to move the home of the lodge to London requested that the United Grand Lodge of England amend the warrant that authorized the members to meet in Dar es Salaam, but the effort proved futile. On the other hand, the Masons were still in advance of much of the rest of Tanganyikan elite society, as my experiences at the *Tanganyika Standard* were in due course to bring home to me.

When I took my first steps to becoming a Freemason, I could not help being conscious that I was being initiated into a strange and exclusive private world. For while Freemasonry has been in existence in its current form for almost three hundred years now (the two main lodge movements were unified in England in 1715), the air of mystery that hangs round it has if anything intensified in recent years. Freemasonry had existed in my part of the world for fifty years, the first 'Lodge East Africa' having been established in Zanzibar in 1904, but it had taken a further twenty-one years for the first lodge — for which, amid much pomp and circumstance, the governor had laid the foundation stone — to be built on the mainland on what was then the capital's Main Avenue (now known as Sokoine Drive).

Since the 1920s, the number of Masons in Tanzania, and in East Africa generally, has continued to rise. The same upward trend is evident in Asia, South America, and latterly in post-Communist Eastern Europe. But elsewhere, especially in Western Europe, North America, and Australia, membership has been steadily falling, producing a drop from a post-First World War peak of seven million globally to around five million. Even so, the contribution that those five million brethren make to the Order and to society more generally is huge. Annually they contribute to charity, through the work organised by their lodges, around US$400 million. In Tanganyika, and latterly in Tanzania, the Kindwitiwi Leprosy Centre in Utete, the Mother Theresa Home for Children, the Pongwe School for the Blind in Tanga Region, the Arusha Orphanage, the Mnazi Mmoja Hospital in Zanzibar, and the Buguruni School for the Deaf have been but a few of the many recent recipients of generous and sustained Masonic support. Of these, the Buguruni School is undoubtedly closest to my heart, I having been the founder and then chief fundraiser, tub-thumper, and friend in high places for the school for the past thirty years.

And yet, in spite of all that worthy activity, for all the time that I have been a Freemason the 'Antient Order' has often suffered grievously at the hands of the Western media. From being a society whose philanthropic and uplifting purpose was widely appreciated, as it was for much of the eighteenth, nineteenth, and early twentieth centuries, it has been reduced by unrelenting press criticism of a most unhelpful and unfair kind to a shadowy, conspiratorial body shrouded in mystery and intrigue.

Freemasonry itself contributed to the post-war collapse of its public image. The systematic wartime persecution of Freemasons across mainland Europe, from Vichy France, through Nazi Germany and Fascist Italy, right across to the communist Soviet Union and its satellites-to-be, led the then Grand Master of the Order to decide that Freemasonry should retreat from the public gaze. This difficult decision to make the Order more 'private', as the only means of protecting the lives and livelihoods of its most vulnerable brothers, left Freemasonry more generally wide open to the attacks of those wishing to libel it, and worse. A profusion of damaging myths, many of them the work of our wartime enemies, took root in the Western popular consciousness, partly because of the Order's refusal of all invitations to issue corrective public statements. The claims, many of which were Nazi-inspired, ranged from the frankly preposterous (that Freemasonry was in some way part of a Zionist conspiracy to take over the planet) to the much more mundane, and thus probably more pernicious (that Freemasonry was the primary means of manipulating the workplace to the exclusive benefit of the Masonic brethren). Neither of these allegations, nor many of those that fell in between, are anywhere close to the truth, yet in spite of their gross inaccuracy, the Order, by its public silence throughout the late 1940s and the 1950s, allowed these most damaging allegations to establish themselves almost as fact.

The adverse effects of this distorted picture were most keenly felt in Europe and North America. Here in Africa, and in Asia and Latin America as well, Freemasonry never suffered from the same degree of misrepresentation as it did elsewhere in the developed world, in spite of the efforts of individual Catholic priests to discourage attendance by Catholics at lodge meetings. Indeed, it was only as I began to take on wider responsibilities within the Order, first at District level and later internationally, that I became fully apprised of the extent of this gap between what Freemasons actually believe and do, and how their actions and intentions are perceived by many Western outsiders.

To begin to understand the Order more clearly, and thus perhaps to start to close that gap between perception and reality, one must return to the guiding principles of the Freemasonry, the very tenets of morality and virtue that drew me into my first discussions of organised philanthropy with Messrs Campbell Ritchie and MacLean back in the early 1950s. At that time, I began to realise that Freemasonry is, at its heart, a science of life, whose purpose is to spiritualise man and make him what he must become, an integrated individual. Much of this underlying purpose of integration is veiled in allegory, which perhaps goes some way to explaining the mythology that has attached to the Order's workings. But those rituals have been developed with the express and, to my mind, noble intention of cultivating and improving the human mind, spirit, and personality. Thus, in the first degree toward initiation, the guiding principles of moral truth and virtue upon which Freemasonry is based are suitably impressed on the mind of the aspirant member, or candidate. The second degree of the Order stresses the development of talents and skills in the arts and sciences in order to play as useful a role in life as possible. The third degree provides for an opportunity to contemplate the last few hours of one's existence, however fanciful or far off this might actually seem. By these means, the initiate is taught how to live life to its fullest potential, in a manner consistent with the Order's three guiding principles, 'Brotherly Love, Relief, and Truth', while at the same time recognising, and thereby beginning to come to terms with, the inevitability of death.

These three principles, once unwrapped from the symbolism of the builder's art that enshrouds so much of Masonic ritual, were what intrigued me most when I first got to know some of the finer details about the 'Antient Order'. In the Masonic scheme of things, the principle of 'Brotherly Love' teaches all of our brethren to regard the entire human species as a single family created by an Almighty Being. 'Relief', meanwhile, brings home a message that mirrors the creed passed down to me by my father, namely that the relief of the distressed, whether it be the relief of material poverty or the soothing of troubled and unhappy minds, is a duty incumbent upon us all. 'Truth', the third and perhaps the most important principle, is a divine attribute and, to a Mason, the foundation of every human virtue. 'To be a good man and true' is the lesson that is taught to each and every initiate at an early stage, a time-honoured saying of the broadest applicability, which is put forward as a means of regulating and if necessary reordering the course of one's life and actions on the basis of the Order's four cardinal virtues: temperance, fortitude, prudence, and justice. And all of these principles and virtues have an applicability that encompasses not only the philosophical teachings of the ancients, from the Greeks to Buddha to Zoroaster, but also all of the established religions. Contrary to the propaganda of the Italian Fascists, and indeed countless others since, Freemasonry is not a tool of religion; but neither, in contrast, is it anti-religious. Indeed, Masonry explicitly welcomes all men irrespective of their religious creeds, and makes no subsequent effort to change their faith or influence their worship. It simply tries to make them better men.

This then was the world that I was initiated into in 1954, and it has been a significant part of my life ever since. During this time, it has been my privilege to witness the selflessness of the Order in providing succour to the needy across East Africa and beyond. During this time, I have come to recognise the importance of the Order's teachings in developing a sense of virtue and truth in oneself and in one's fellow man. My spirit, my mind, and my soul have been enriched by my involvement in Freemasonry, and this enrichment stands in stark contradiction to the assumptions one finds in the Western popular press. Helping our fellows to help others, not helping ourselves, has been my experience throughout my many years as a Mason.

Having held positions of increased seniority within the Guiding Star Lodge in the late 1950s and early 1960s, I was appointed its Worshipful Master in 1967, at a time when I had also recently been made President of the Association of Round Tables of East Africa. The following year, having earlier been made the first non-white member of the Round Table, I became the first World President of the Round Table movement and affiliated organisations to come from a non-white background, a fact that gave this prestigious role an even greater profile than is customary. This in turn led to extensive travelling, media exposure, and representational commitments. In 1970 I completed my year of service as International President of the World Council of Young Men's Service Clubs, and the following year, on my enforced retirement from that movement on the grounds of age, I became an Honorary Life Vice Chairman of the Association of Round Tables of East Africa. In 1970 I joined the Rotary Club of Dar es Salaam, a first step toward becoming Governor, responsible for seventy-eight clubs across large parts of Africa. In 1972, I made my first step toward a wider Masonic role with my appointment as a District Officer, working with the regional Masonic headquarters in Nairobi, which then oversaw the twenty-eight or so lodges across East Africa.

As I was given greater responsibility, I made sure that I did what I could to demystify the Order in the eyes of the general public. In my experience, people are inclined to be suspicious or fearful of those things of which they are ignorant. Thus, when asked about Freemasonry, I have always made a point of telling the questioner about the principles of the institution, emphasising that ours is not a secret society, that its membership is widely known, and that the Order does not meet in secret places, but in meeting halls, registered by the government, that are clearly identified. As I said earlier, the association with mystery came during the Second World War, when we tried to protect our members in France, Italy, and Germany against action by the Axis powers. Since then we have gone totally public and have always endeavoured to dispel suspicion, and to show that ours is an institution that takes a good man and seeks to makes him better.

Unfortunately, not everyone has been convinced by this line of argument. In 1994, for example, eight years after I was appointed District Grand Master for the whole of East Africa, President Moi of Kenya established an official commission to look into allegations of the use of witchcraft as a means of influencing decision-making in Kenyan public life. To my concern, but perhaps not to my surprise, I was called to appear before the commission in my capacity as District Grand Master, to testify as a material witness.

This was not the first time in recent memory that allegations of Masonic conspiracies in politics have arisen. Few can ever forget the P2 scandal in Italy, when the unsanctioned activities of a misguided few brought shame on the hitherto apolitical image of Masonic lodges worldwide. In Kenya, however, the allegations of Masonic support for members of one tribe who were in opposition to the government were quickly proved to be groundless. Although I did not receive a final copy of the Commission's report, and none was made public, the fact of our exoneration can be deduced from the positive anecdotal feedback we got from the government, the absence of any public criticism arising from the report, and the continued non-interference in the activities of the Kenyan lodges on the part of the Kenyan government. And in a perverse way, the fact that allegations were made against the Masonic Order in Kenya were a blessing in disguise, providing, as they did, an opportunity to restate in public and in private the fact that in Freemasonry, your politics are your private business, as is your religion, and they are not matters for discussion, still less action, within your lodge.

I never ran into any similar political problem with the governments in Uganda or the Seychelles, nor in Tanzania, even at the height of African Socialist fervour in the heady days after the Arusha Declaration. This was because Mwalimu had looked quite closely into the background of the voluntary organisations operating in Tanzania at the time of independence, and had reached the conclusion that all of them, to a greater or lesser degree, were operating in a philanthropic manner. Only twice did I find our lodges coming under any form of governmental scrutiny, and on both occasions the attempts at interference were of the most prosaic kind and quickly came to naught.

The first time round, an officer from the Department of Antiquities, fresh from a recent fraternal visit to the Soviet Union, asked to pay a call on me at Masonic headquarters in Dar es Salaam in order to be briefed on our organisation and its activities. While inside the building, that Tanzanian government official couldn't help noticing the comfy armchairs, with their pristine white cushions, that sat at the back of the Masonic Hall. Soon his questions drifted away from the finer detail of our charitable donations and toward these chairs and cushions. He began asking me about them. I explained to him that these chairs had been around for many years, that they were not exclusively for the use of our brethren, and that they were often used at LEGCO when they were loaned out. Undeterred, this official went back to his office and started a lengthy correspondence about the future destiny of the building and of some of the items he saw, a correspondence that eventually came to nothing, but copies of which I kept hold of in my own files to keep me amused in times of boredom.

The second brush with Tanzanian officialdom came about when the state electricity company, TANESCO, became interested in establishing a training school. While sitting on the board of TANESCO, I had been perhaps the most vocal advocate of such a facility, not knowing at the time that others in the upper echelons of TANESCO were by then looking covetously at the plot of land that we owned and that housed our national headquarters in Dar es Salaam. Suddenly and without warning, during the course of one of my frequent overseas visits, TANESCO obtained an order for the compulsory acquisition for public purpose of our headquarters and land, and that order subsequently appeared in the local official gazette. This compulsory acquisition order came with a twist, in that the victims of this manoeuvre were given a ninety-day grace period in which to lodge an appeal. On my return to Tanzania I was briefed about this unwelcome turn of events, and although we were time-barred I immediately prepared the necessary paperwork for our appeal, for good measure adding voluminous chapter and verse on the history of Freemasonry in East Africa.

Not long after I had submitted the necessary (and unnecessary) documents to the President, the Permanent Secretary at State House rang me to say that the compulsory acquisition in favour of TANESCO had been summarily overturned by Mwalimu himself. TANESCO had been told to look elsewhere for a site for the training school that I had been pressing for, and we could return to our normal routine. And that was that.

To be a Mason is to submit oneself to a lengthy, indeed never-ending process of learning and scrutiny. Over the past fifty years, my extended apprenticeship within the Masonic Order has seen me attain numerous degrees, of increasing rank and importance, besides serving as the District Grand Master of East Africa (Tanzania, Kenya, Uganda, and the Seychelles) for nineteen years. To name but a few, I have served as Junior and then Senior Grand Warden in the Grand Lodge of Mark Master Masons of England and Wales — the first time the position has ever been offered to a non-UK resident. I have been installed as Worshipful Commander in the Donyo Sabuk Lodge of Royal Ark Mariner, and have held Royal Ark Mariner Grand Rank since 1990. I am the Grand Superintendent in and over East Africa in the Supreme Grand Chapter of Royal Arch Masons of England, having held a Grand Office since 1980 and District Office since 1972. In 2000, I was the Deputy Grand Sword Bearer in the Supreme Grand Chapter, and I am still the Honorary Grand Chancellor in the Supreme Grand Chapter of Scotland. In 1987 I was admitted to the degree of St Lawrence the Martyr, the degree of the Knight of Constantinople, the Holy Order of Grand High Priest, the Grand Tilers of Solomon, and created a Knight of Illustrious Order of the Red Cross of Babylon. In 1988, I joined the Grand Masters Council No. 1 of Royal, Select and Super Excellent Masters of England and Wales, and was admitted to the degree of Most Excellent Master. The following year I was admitted as indentured apprentice in the Worshipful Society of Freemasons, Channel Row Assemblage.

To an outsider, a lay reader of these recollections, little if any of that will mean anything at all. To a brother Mason, however, the significance of those arcane titles will be immediately apparent. But to both lay and Masonic reader, the fact of the long process of Masonic apprenticeship raises a number of fundamental questions, of which the first and most obvious is why someone like myself, who has attained positions of seniority in business, in society, and in institutions, would submit himself so readily and with such diligence to a fifty-year apprenticeship of such a demanding kind.

It is a fair question, and one that many an aspirant Mason must have posed to himself. The answer lies in the nature of the Order, and in the nature of the individual initiated into it.

Apprenticeship, from its earliest beginnings in the European Middle Ages, has always involved ritual learning, self-discipline, and humility. That of the Freemasons, derived as it is from the apprenticeship models of the early master builders, is in essence no different. I have always believed that, irrespective of one's previous accomplishments in life, be they in the arts, the sciences, politics, the military, or commerce, a commitment to life-long learning, kinship, self-disciplined behaviour, and proper humility can only be conducive to further success. To work for the benefit of the community, and especially the less advantaged members of it, as Freemasons, and indeed Rotarians, are committed to do, is well and good. But to do such voluntary work on the basis of a firm foundation of morality and truth is something else altogether. It offers much to the recipient, but it requires much more of the giver. Contrary to popular myth, Freemasonry is not a vehicle for self-aggrandisement. It never has been and it never will be, and that is why the process of vetting for any prospective initiate is so lengthy and searching. Whenever I speak or write about Freemasonry, I stress this point most firmly. Freemasonry is also about service to the community, and to mankind as a whole, through the established disciplines of the Order.

The debate about Freemasonry's contribution to society is at last taking on a more constructive tone. One obvious example from my own recent experience is the speech given by His Excellency the President of the United Republic of Tanzania on the occasion of a dinner at a hotel in Dar es Salaam on October 9th, 2004, to celebrate the one-hundredth anniversary of the founding of the first Masonic lodge in East Africa. President Mkapa quoted the words of the American writer and editor, George Horace Lorimer: 'It's good to have money and the things that money can buy, but it's good, too, to check up once in a while and make sure you haven't lost things that money can't buy.' After noting that by Tanzanian standards the assembled Masons had money, the President commended the Order for aspiring to the high ideals of a charitable and virtuous spirit, temperance, fortitude, prudence, and justice, and for setting an example to others. But then he challenged the Masonic Order to interpret its creed of temperance, fortitude, prudence, and justice in terms of the challenges facing the world today — in other words, to address what the President saw as among today's greatest problems: the glorification of the self; the pursuit of instant gratification; spiritual implosion; and political, economic, and religious bigotry.

As always, the questions President Mkapa posed were well thought out and well put. In a similar vein, President Mwai Kibaki of Kenya complimented Freemasons in a speech read on his behalf on September 25th, 2004: 'Your members have substantially contributed to a large number of charitable and welfare organisations and on behalf of the government I thank you for your continued support to supplement the government's efforts in improving the quality of life of the people.' And at a tea party in the Freemasons Hall, Nairobi, on November 8th, 2004, Vice-President Moody Awori of Kenya said, 'The devotion to help our people, particularly those members of our society who are considered less fortunate, is a demonstration of your creed of temperance, fortitude, and sacrifice to uplift their lives.' We Masons exhort ourselves to fulfil our duties to God, to the authorities of the countries in which we reside, and to family. The world would indeed be a better place if all of us could honestly say that we do that.

Much has changed since I joined the Masons back in 1954. Stepping down now as District Grand Master of East Africa after nineteen years of continuous service in that position, I look back with satisfaction on the contributions our members have made to the development of the Order, but above all I take pride in the commitment they have demonstrated to the well-being of their communities. The Masonic Order is always responsive to the needs of people in difficulty. In Tanzania the tragic loss of the MV *Bukoba* on Lake Victoria in 1996 brought forth a rapid and generous response from Masons in East Africa and the UK. But it also brought home to me the costs, and risks, of endemic poverty. The MV *Bukoba* was owned by Tanzania Railways Corporation, of which I was Chairman. I learnt of the sinking of this vessel through CNN as my Rotary friends and I were chatting after dinner in the guest house of the Union Bank of Nigeria in Kano, where we were staying. I immediately returned to Tanzania via London in order to be with my colleagues, so that arrangements could be made to assist the families of those who died or had been injured. As the death toll mounted into the hundreds I was infuriated, and horrified, to learn that none of the vessels owned by the Corporation were covered by any form of insurance. As the *Bukoba* tragedy unfolded, I was told by the management of the TRC that the previous board had decided that none of their vessels should be insured — not even against third-party risk — because of a chronic lack of funds (an appalling oversight I subsequently verified by examining the minutes of the meeting of the Board of Directors). Poverty thereby begat tragedy, and yet more poverty.

The same ready response as was made to the *Bukoba* tragedy was given to the bombings of the US Embassies in Dar es Salaam and Nairobi in 1998. On both occasions, the relief given by the Order took the form of sustained support for the families most affected, and the schooling of children who lost parents in the 1998 bombings is still being funded by local Masons. The same picture can be drawn on a global scale. The recent Tsunami Appeal saw Freemasonry formally inject over half a million pounds into the global appeals for relief, on top of the many millions raised by Masons individually all over the world. The duty that lodges take on to care for their districts, large or small, continues to be discharged with vigour and compassion. All such outward signs are encouraging, and to be applauded.

And yet, as President Mkapa warned us as East African Masons at our centenary dinner in Dar es Salaam in 2004, there is no room for complacency when faced with the challenges of self-absorption and self-delusion that abound in the twenty-first century. As he rightly said, 'We need not just charity, but caring.' This is at the heart of why I joined Freemasonry and, indeed, the Rotary, and it should remain as an example to all who join the Order, or yet aspire to. As I said in a recent article on Freemasonry,

> Freemasonry is a life to be lived and not a formality to be observed; it is a life grounded in religion, organised in morality, mellowed by good fellowship, humanised in charity and dedicated to serve. The teachings of Freemasonry are not for today but are forever. It is a force for good and stability and it teaches its members tolerance, dignity and respect for the individual.

Because I have lived all my working life in East Africa, where the Hobbesian notion that life is 'nasty, brutish and short' has been confounded by the great and abiding humanity of the Tanzanian people and their leaders, the continuing need for compassionate self-discipline is all too readily apparent to me. I can only ask that my brother Freemasons continue to bear that in mind when going about their apprenticeships, and their daily lives. And, more generally, none of us can elude the challenge to make ourselves better people, by whatever means is at our disposal. To paraphrase the President, and George Lorimer, check up, once in a while, to make sure that you have not lost those things and those human values that money cannot buy!

ELEVEN

"MISTER CORPORATION"

Corporations, corporations, corporations. Any state based on the proposition that the means of production must be controlled by the state, be it Marxist, Maoist, or just plain socialist, quickly turns into a land full of 'corporations'. Tanzania in the 1970s and 1980s was no exception to this rule.

In the heyday of his Tanganyikan business career, my father Keshavji was known affectionately across Tanganyika as 'Mister Milling'. Given my wholehearted commitment to service of the new African Socialist state being erected by Mwalimu Nyerere, my nickname in independent Tanzania should have been 'Mister Corporation'. In the space of a few short years I found myself appointed by the President as chairman of the following major corporations: Air Tanzania Corporation; the Tanzania Tourist Corporation (TTC); the Tanzania Harbours Authority; the Tanzania Railways Corporation; Tanzania Standard Newspapers Limited; State Travel Services Limited; Tanzania Hotels Investment Limited; Printpak Tanzania Limited; National Distributors Limited; Tanganyika Development Finance Company Limited; General Agriculture Products Exports Corporation; Tanzania Shoe Company; Tanzania Wood Industries Corporation; Tanzania Film Company; the National Urban Water Authority; Tanzania Distilleries; the National Insurance Corporation of Tanzania; and Tanzania Elimu Supplies. And that doesn't include my various board responsibilities elsewhere, or my chairmanship of non-profit foundations, such as Museum and Library services and the African Medical and Research Foundation.

There was no magic formula to running any of these corporations successfully. They were like any other business, really, requiring the fundamental skills of making the capital and the staff work as effectively as possible. Sometimes there was a need for diplomatic skills of a sort that I doubted I really possessed. The sorting out of the disputes that arose at the time of the creation of the Air Tanzania Corporation is a good example.

In the aftermath of the breakup of the East African Community, Tanzania established its own organisations to run rail, road, port, and air services. President Nyerere appointed me Chairman of Air Tanzania Corporation — an office I accepted only on the condition that it would be a non-executive post (at a time when the Minister for Transport and Communications was keen to have a full-time chairman). Of all the East African corporations relating to transport and communications, Air Tanzania inherited the most experienced staff, as a result of the collapse of East African Airways. Indeed, a few of the senior employees, such as Silva Rwebangira, were well-known personalities in the international airlines arena. But while the staff were committed to making a success of the Tanzania's own fledgling national airline, they found themselves working under the most trying circumstances. First and foremost among these was the need to resettle the families of EAA staff from Nairobi, together with such connected issues as children's education, the transport of personal belongings, and vehicles. The Tanzanian government was sympathetic to their plight, but found itself in a very difficult situation, in which it had to find extra money to cater for a whole raft of newly created organizations following the collapse of the EAC. Pending the distribution of assets of the collapsed Community, which inevitably took longer to finalise than everyone had hoped, significant additional money had somehow to be provided by the Tanzanian government (and in my view, the direct and indirect cost to Tanzania of the breakup of East African Community was around US$900 million). Understandably, there was a great deal of anxiety, and to some extent resentment, on the part of the airline employees while all this was being sorted out. I recall going to an evening meeting with the pilots, flight engineers, first officers, and other staff, held at the Africana Beach Resort outside Dar es Salaam, where many of them had been temporarily housed since their enforced return from Nairobi. I was accompanied by Michael Shirima, the Operations Director of Air Tanzania Corporation — now, incidentally, a major shareholder and chairman of the board of the successful Precision Airlines, of which Kenya Airways is a shareholder. After dinner with the senior staff (at which we wisely provided free drinks), we went to a meeting with all the rest of the employees. The meeting was conducted in a good spirit, in spite of the difficulties they were all facing. We eventually came to a close at around two in the morning, and as Michael and I left to return home we felt that we had achieved a great deal. Even then the Standing Committee on Parastatals (SCOPO) threatened to undo much of our good work when they tried to link up the salaries of cabin crew with those in other sectors in the hospitality industry. Only after we explained to them the inconvenience airline hostesses experience and the risks they take as a matter of routine, and pointed out that they need to be able to handle emergency situations and that they undergo medical check-ups every six months did SCOPO agreed to improve their salary package.

Such were some of the situations requiring diplomatic and commercial skills that I was asked to deal with on behalf of the government. But on some issues, mere business skills and a commitment to work hard for the state were simply not enough. In these, a sense of vocation was needed, and that was no more in evidence than in my work on what is now commonly termed 'sustainability'.

'Sustainability', the art of existing today in a way that safeguards tomorrow, is a concept that was in the lifeblood of everyone prior to the industrial revolution. The hunters and gatherers, the medieval farmers, the tribesmen of yore, none of these needed to be educated in the subtleties of sustainable management of their local environment. They may have lived off the land, but they did so in a way that didn't cast a shadow on succeeding generations.

The industrial revolution, and the societal changes spawned by it, changed the nature of man's relationship with his environment. No longer was it possible for man to assume that his productive activity would remain in a state of balance with nature. Resources, first mineral, then animal and vegetable, began to be consumed at a rate that brought into being the twin spectres of exhaustion and extinction. A two-tier world emerged, in which the rich got richer and the poor, if they were lucky, stayed where they were. And in this two-tier world, the rich grabbed hold of the resources of the weak and defenceless, using conquest and colonisation as the means of keeping down the immediate cost of this rapacious consumption.

Then, in time, the world changed again, politically this time, and the foundations of unchecked colonial consumption were at last swept away. But in their place came a new form of exploitation, one rooted less in might and more in hypocrisy, which manifested itself in the attitudes of industrial countries, who asserted to themselves the right to consume and pollute without care for the long-term consequences to others. The flip side of this irresponsibility came in the form of First World exhortations to Third-World countries to limit the consumption of their own natural resources, on the grounds that they had a special responsibility to keep their own rivers and forests and savannahs as nature intended. This meant that it was fine for parts of Pennsylvania, or Lancashire, or the Ruhr, to be natural wastelands, brownfield monuments to the industrial gods, just as long as the Tanzanias, the Brazils, the Madagascars of this world could be shamed and browbeaten into keeping their own territory in a pristine condition, to cleanse the air and provide playgrounds in which the rich could spot and hunt their 'charismatic' species.

All of that would sound laughable if it weren't all nearly true. As a resident of Tanganyika in the 1950s, I had grown used to hearing the colonial administrators talking of keeping Tanganyika industry-free, in the name of 'zoo-tourism'. But I never expected that this sort of double standard would live on into the twenty-first century, laying traps for the unwary proponents of 'eco-tourism', establishing unequal rights for rich and poor, and saddling the poorest of us with the ultimate responsibility of somehow saving the planet by staying poor in perpetuity.

Many years ago, I was only dimly aware of this inherent tension between the needs of peoples in developing countries and those of our fragile eco-system. As a teenager in Bukene, I watched the people working for my father's company as they gathered in the evenings to cook their meals in the open air. No stoves for them, no ovens, no electricity. Just wood, sometimes charcoal if they were lucky, heaped in age-old triangular patterns under metal and earthenware cooking pots. Then I was struck not by the effect their wood gathering was having on the local forests and woods, but by the inefficiency of their methods of cooking food. A lot of wood, a lot of charcoal, went into very few meals.

In time this quasi-industrial concern for their methods evolved into a more sustained concern for the environment. I came to see that even in Bukene the traditional harmony between man and nature could not be sustained indefinitely. Even in the absence of any sort of significant industrialisation, the very growth of population that was a relentless feature of Tanganyika in the twentieth century was putting too much pressure on the local natural resources. In a country without access to enough clean water, enough trees near to population centres, enough food to feed every mouth adequately, nature, in all its forms, was vulnerable. Even in Tanzania, one of the cradles of civilisation, where the tradition of good husbandry of the environment has been one of the defining characteristics of all tribes, where the sympathetic traditions of the Hadza people shine out across the world as a beacon even now, and where land, always plentiful, has never been at a premium — even in Tanzania, the future risks are all around us. I thought, 'Imagine, then, what is happening, what has already happened, elsewhere.' Such musings as these became a deepening preoccupation, and then, ultimately, the source of a lifelong vocation.

The first opportunity to put some of my concerns into practice came when I was appointed to chair the Tanzania Tourist Corporation.

At that time, in the late 1960s, the ethos was very much one of zoo-tourism. But thanks to undercapacity in the Tanzanian system, coupled with the fact that a preponderance of European tour companies were based in and operating out of Nairobi, the profits from the Tanzanian 'zoo' weren't ending up in Tanzanian pockets. My immediate priorities were therefore twofold: to encourage the overseas tour operators and their customers to look at Tanzania as a holiday destination in its own right, and not merely as some adjunct of Kenya; and to attempt to break the stranglehold that the beach holiday resorts of the Seychelles and Mombasa had on the British and American markets.

Neither of these was anything like straightforward. For many years now the safari packages to East Africa out of the UK and the US had followed a set pattern. The beach element of the holiday would be in Mombasa. Then the tourists would be bussed over the Kenyan border to the National Parks of Northern Tanzania — to the Serengeti, to Ngorongoro, to Lake Manyara — for a few days of wildlife watching before being bussed back to their hotels in Nairobi and Mombasa. Often they returned to Namanga unaware that they had crossed the border into Tanzania, and rarely if ever did they spend any money in our country, preferring to buy any souvenirs that they wanted in the many stalls in the streets around the New Stanley Hotel in Nairobi. Because the Tanzania Tourist Corporation had only a thousand beds at its disposal throughout the country, and had to rely upon management agreements with foreign corporations to maintain the appropriate quality at some of the prestige locations, such as the Hotels Meru (Danish), Kilimanjaro (Israeli), and New Africa (British), because there was a very limited number of beach resorts on Zanzibar and even fewer back on the mainland, and because the Kenyans were masters of an aggressive marketing campaign (which led many to believe that Mount Kilimanjaro was actually in Kenya and not Tanzania), we started at a massive disadvantage.

And yet that very weakness was a great advantage in putting together a policy that attempted to resolve the inherent tension between sustainability and the generation of much-needed revenue. By marketing Tanzania as a low-volume, high-revenue destination to an elite market in North America and Europe, the risk that tourism could in some way inflict lasting damage on the natural attractions that brought the tourists to Tanzania in the first place could be minimised. With few hotel rooms and even fewer resorts, we could aim for the top of the market, and maximise per tourist returns to Tanzania, even though the trend toward mass tourism was increasing. In this context I have had discussions with immigration authorities about the possibility of having immigration officers travelling on the flights that bring in the tourists, so that they could provide entry clearance on board the aircraft, thus minimizing the time spent in immigration by tourists upon arrival.

It took a long time for this ideal combination to deliver results. The first priority was to begin the process of diverting the return from Tanzanian wildlife tourism into Tanzanian pockets. White enterprises based in Kenya and Europe had an effective stranglehold over the National Parks, so we instituted new controls over vehicular access to the Parks while at the same time making a bulk purchase of fifty Volkswagen combis. At a stroke, we began to claw back control from a set of operators who had little sympathy with, and even less stake in, us Tanzanians.

The political impact of this was important too. Jomo Kenyatta, the founding father of modern Kenya, was being hailed as the 'architect of democracy' in Africa. In contrast, Mwalimu Nyerere, lauded by the Kenyan political establishment and media for his moderating influence before and at the time of taking power, was now being condemned as a proto-communist and the host to every African 'terrorist' movement in Southern and Western Africa. Relations began to deteriorate, and it was no surprise when, in the 1970s, the East African Community, which had been set up with such high hopes in the previous decade, eventually collapsed.

The strain on relations complicated the transit of passengers between Kenya and Tanzania. This made my life difficult at times. I once had to engineer the safe passage back to Kenya of seven hundred foreign tourists who had fallen foul of one of many temporary border closures in the 1970s, a most delicate and complicated operation involving deals struck with fifty-eight Kenyan combi drivers, Arusha-based hotel managers, lawyers, Swiss Air, and eventually Mwalimu himself, a negotiation that must have taken several years off my life expectancy, and that took on at times the characteristics of a peacekeeping operation and a hostage negotiation rolled into one. But there were benefits too. Border closures made tour operators realise the wisdom of our ongoing efforts in North America and London to sell Tanzania as a sovereign state worthy of being considered a destination in its own right. And anything I could do to demonstrate to the President and his ministers that an improvement in Tanzanian tourist revenues would be at the expense of their then difficult northern neighbours would be welcomed and further encouraged.

The practicalities of running a tourist corporation alongside a milling business and God knows what else besides never once distracted me from pursuing a deepening understanding of the contingent risks to the global environment. Back in the late 1960s I became close to Paulo de Costa, a Brazilian Rotarian who at one time was World President of the Rotary Movement. I still remember vividly a trip we both took in 1989 to a conference in Nashville, Tennessee — on which occasion, incidentally, former World President of Rotary International James L. Bomar Jr arranged for me to become a Tennessee Squire, which involved my 'buying' about ten square feet of land in Moore County. Even today I get letters from the local town clerk, giving me an update on the fate of Plot No. 655, and how often it is mown or used by animals (small animals, I guess, something well short of a herd) for grazing and pasture. One evening on the terrace of Nashville's Opryland Hotel my Brazilian friend and I talked over drinks long into the night about the need to link sustainability with poverty alleviation. His motto as World President of the Rotary Movement was to be 'Preserve Planet Earth'. And in spelling out how he intended to give this view the maximum publicity, he took me back to the argument about the use of wood as fuel by the impoverished villagers of Tanzania. I told him that it was okay to talk in inspirational terms about the environment, but if there was no alternative but to chop down trees for firewood, then environmental concerns had to fall away. Paulo disagreed with me strongly. 'You cannot separate these issues in that way,' he responded vehemently, and went on to argue, with increasing conviction, that environmental protection and poverty alleviation were two sides of the very same coin. One could not be achieved without taking measures to deal with the other.

These thoughts were uppermost in my mind during my stewardship of the TTC, deep into the 1970s. Often, however, more prosaic matters pushed their way forward. A key one, oddly enough, was the need for office space. The TTC was housed in a rented building, and a very small one at that. With inadequate space for the staff, my predecessor had been obliged to take over much of the fifth floor of the neighbouring New Africa Hotel to house our overspill. As a result, the Corporation was losing valuable foreign exchange revenue.

The Board decided to look for a suitable piece of land on which to build a new headquarters. Since we were perennially short of cash, we decided to do this as a joint enterprise with the General Agricultural Export Company and the pension fund of the Cargo Handling Company of East Africa. Although cost savings would have accrued from such an enterprise, these three corporations would have made strange bedfellows, and it was something of a relief when the search for a new site proved fruitless. It was then that the Swedish Ambassador to Tanzania, at a dinner at his home, explained to me that his embassy was continuing to look after the interests of the Israeli government following the Tanzanian government's severance of diplomatic relations with Israel in the wake of the Six Day War. With no resumption in prospect, the government in Tel Aviv had decided to sell its embassy in Dar es Salaam for US$80,000, on condition that the payment would be in the hands of its Consul-General in New York within a week. Quite why the Israelis wanted to do a deal so quickly was a mystery to me (and to the Swedish Ambassador). But the opportunity and the price were, to my mind, much too good to resist. I knew at once that I had no prospect of raising that sort of money in a week, and so I asked for, and got, a week's extension, and began work to convince the Corporation to close the deal.

I called an immediate meeting of the TTC board. I outlined the proposal and the advantages it offered to us. After only a brief discussion, the Board authorised me to go ahead, subject to the agreement of the Ministry for Tourism, our parent ministry, and provided we could finance the deal, at least in part, with money from the Tourist Development Levy. The Ministry said yes, too, in record time, and the funds were remitted in good time to New York. I sat back, congratulating myself on a good bit of business done for Tanzania.

A fortnight later the Swedish Ambassador came back to me. He wasn't pleased. He told me that he had gone out on a limb to get me an extra week to find the money for the building, but I had failed to come up with it; the Israeli Consul-General in New York had not been paid. I told him that there must have been a mistake, but my defence was not convincing.

I immediately called Dickson Nkembo, the former Permanent Secretary at State House. Dickson was by then chairman of the National Bank of Commerce, which had been responsible for transmitting the funds to New York. Dickson told me that he had personally overseen the transaction, but in the light of the Swedish Ambassador's complaint he would look into the matter again and report back.

The explanation for the problem was laughably straightforward. A clerk at the Morgan Guarantee Bank in New York had received our transfer just as he was going on leave. Instead of processing it there and then, he had put it into a safe, along with a lot of other urgent papers, until his return. The National Bank of Commerce never found out what happened to the clerk — although it is tempting to imagine, given the Morgan Bank's well-earned reputation for feistiness. The money, however, was quickly freed up, and the deal was eventually completed.

I sincerely believed I had pulled off something of a coup. The building was cheap by the market prices of the day, very cheap in fact, and we would save on the rental and gain from the freed space at the New Africa Hotel. I thought I had done well by Tanzania. Others, however, clearly thought differently.

About a month after the deal was struck, I received a phone call from the Minister for Finance, Amir Jamal. He wanted to know what I was up to. Instead of promoting tourism, as I was mandated to do, I was getting involved in the real estate business. I told the Minister that this was a one-off deal, and on very favourable terms to Tanzania. Why, I had already received an offer of US$104,000 for the building, after having paid only US$80,000 for it four weeks previously. Besides, I had gone through all the proper channels. I had consulted the Board and got their agreement, and that of the parent Ministry as well. I just couldn't see what the problem was.

Amir Jamal went quiet after that. But about six months later, just before we were due to move into our new quarters, I was approached by the US Deputy Chief of Mission in Dar es Salaam Herbert Levin. I assumed he wanted to buy the building, but State Department regulations wouldn't permit that. Instead, he asked to rent it; I quoted US$25,000 a year, payable in advance. The Americans took over the building and improved it significantly with their own money; when they eventually moved out, the building reverted to the newly created Tanzania Tourist Board. Meanwhile following the improvement the rental was increased by US$10,000.

This little episode taught me a lot about the mindset of Mwalimu's government when it came to commerce. It wasn't that they didn't want to make deals that maximised advantages for Tanzania, but their innate suspicion of the marketplace, an attitude common to socialists the world over, made it difficult for them to trust in any deal that seemed to be generating a rapid 'surplus'. I recall that in the 1970s I arranged for Mtibwa Sugar Estates Ltd (a company then owned jointly by National Agricultural Food Corporation and the Madhvani Group) a loan by Williams and Glyn's Bank of Scotland to the tune of £2 million for six years at 6 percent interest per annum payable on a reducing basis, to enable Mtibwa to buy sugar machinery from Fletcher and Stewart of Derby. Finance Minister Jamal thought that there must be some catch; otherwise the Bank wouldn't provide finance on such attractive terms. On these occasions, and on others, I was able to allay their fears, and they would join me in rejoicing in their good fortune. But alas, there simply weren't enough entrepreneurs willing to work within the new system. As a result, the cautious, doctrinaire, anti-enterprise line usually won through.

When I became chairman of TTC the general manager was Gabriel Mawala, a fine man from the old school, who continued to take an interest in Tanzania's tourism development until his recent death. I recall an amusing incident. Mawala on my suggestion had asked the Permanent Secretary in the Treasury to allow the Corporation access to the Tourism Development Fund, which was held by the Exchequer. The request was turned down. Mawala's successor was Francis Byaboto, who had just retired as Permanent Secretary in the Treasury, and I asked him to reopen the matter, as I felt that we would now have a better chance. However, about six weeks later I found that his successor in the Treasury had replied to him that he could do no better than quote the contents of his own letter, which he had written when he was occupying the Treasury chair. This did not amuse Byaboto.

Some two years later Esrome Maryogo, one of President Nyerere's personal assistants, told me that the President had decided to appoint him General Manager of the Corporation, and had said that, because he had no experience in managing business corporations, I would assist him. A year or so after Maryogo took over I decided to resign from the chairmanship, and four months later Chief Adam Saki, Speaker of the National Assembly, was appointed in my place. The board was also reconstituted.

Finding a way to balance the revenue demands of the government with the protection of the local environment was never easy. Like other African countries, we suffered from poaching and illegal logging by foreign companies. But thankfully, a combination of diligent local customs and enlightened policymaking ensured that a sustainable balance was struck. The local people had no taste for bush meat, so the depredations of local wildlife for food seen in, say, the Congo never happened in Tanzania. And the tourism policy of low volume, high value generated the necessary revenue without overloading our national parks. Vigilance is still required on all fronts. With our tourist attractions co-existing alongside expanding local communities, the threat from overdevelopment by tourist operators and local villagers, even in some of our most prestigious national parks, such as Gombe, is a continuing challenge to their survival. Illegal logging, especially of teak, remains a problem, as does overuse by local communities of scarce timber for charcoal and woodcarving. Tourism in Tanzania has shown itself to be over-sensitive to the security fears of the British and Americans. And even now, in a global market worth close to US$4 trillion a year, Africa receives only four percent of the international tourist trade, and less than two percent of that four trillion dollars. But by and large, the policies laid down in Tanzania in the late sixties and seventies, policies designed to make eco-tourism in Tanzania sustainable for generations to come, have undoubtedly worked, to the point that tourism is about to become the largest earning sector in the entire Tanzanian economy.

Stepping down from the chairmanship of the TTC did not bring an end to my interest or involvement in environmental issues. The Rotarian and Round Table movements both have long and distinguished traditions of involvement in green issues, on both the local and the international stage. With 758 Rotary Clubs across Africa alone acting as partners in environmental protection, the opportunities for close partnership with government and business and local communities is considerable. Through friendship exchanges, through the Rotary Foundation's Ambassadorial Scholarships (which have been running since 1947), through corporate programmes amounting to over US$100 million annually across every relevant discipline, from poverty alleviation to disease control, the Rotary movement undoubtedly makes a difference, and has certainly helped act as a catalyst in establishing that closer linkage between protecting the environment and eradicating poverty that is so dear to my heart.

In 1989, Dr Salim Ahmed Salim, a former Prime Minister of Tanzania, was the Secretary General of the Organization of African Unity (OAU). Rotary International applied for OAU affiliation, which Dr Salim granted and he received my credentials as Rotary's first accredited representative to the OAU. A distinguished servant of Africa, when first appointed he was Tanzania's youngest diplomat. Currently, he is chairman of the Mwalimu Nyerere Foundation.

In the late 1980s, with the government having recognised my continuing deep interest and involvement in all matters environmental, I was appointed Deputy Leader of the Tanzanian Delegation to the Preparatory Commission to the Rio Earth Summit. In that capacity, I was elected by the G77 countries (and China) to act as their negotiator with the G7 (now G8) countries on the Global Environmental Facility. This ambitious programme was designed to ensure a transfer of funds to developing countries in compensation for the continued pollution of the earth by the industrialised countries. After much tough negotiating we struck a good deal. The same can be said about the whole Rio process more generally. At a time when the US administration was coming out of an anti-environmental era (which persisted throughout the two Reagan administrations), and when they were joining the Europeans and the rest of the world in celebrating the end of the Cold War, Rio seemed to mark a new beginning in the collective struggle to save our planet.

Those of us at Rio were hoping that the US delegation would be a high-powered one, led by at least Vice-President Dan Quayle, but as it turned out, even the Director responsible for the environment was not present. At an informal gathering one evening someone lamented at the apparent lack of interest by the US government; Minister Kamal Nath of India remarked, 'We should not worry of President Bush and Vice-President Quayle. We are concerned with real bushes and quails.'

It was an event of enormous significance, and even now, after the disappointments of the conspicuous failures to honour the Kyoto Agreements, Rio still stands tall as an inspiration to all those who truly care about our environment. We in Tanzania know better than most just how fragile the balance is between the workings of nature and the workings of man. It is not just a matter of our being home to the African 'Big Five' or others of the more charismatic animal species. It is not just about our hard and often painful experience in balancing the needs of impoverished local communities with those of the animals and trees that live alongside them. It is about understanding, as Africans often do better than most other peoples, that everything ultimately connects, and that actions taken elsewhere with no knowledge or thought of our fragile great continent, be they political, economic, or environmental, often have the greatest impact upon us, in Africa, mere innocent bystanders. In a globalised world, where the few effectively make the rules for the many, there is a lesson embedded in all of that, a lesson about the urgent need for a greater sense of global responsibility, in Africa, yes, but more importantly, much more importantly, in the governments and businesses of the dominant nations of the developed world.

TWELVE

THE MWINYI YEARS

As the 1980s dawned, I was still very much Tanzania's 'Mister Corporation' — indeed, one evening at a dinner party a diplomat referred to me as 'Dean of the Corporate World'. By then, however, I had long been convinced that Tanzania's socialist experiment was failing badly. More significantly, its principal architect, Mwalimu Nyerere, was coming to the same conclusion. For in spite of the injection of more than US$2 billion of donor assistance, despite the complete reorganisation of the economy, not least in agricultural production, despite intensive efforts to educate and retrain our workforce, and despite the best efforts of no less an organisation than the World Bank to assist in redeveloping our infrastructure, Tanzania in 1980 was almost as poor as it had been in 1961. In terms of distance walked by villagers to obtain clean water, in terms of variety and nutritive value of diet, in terms of life expectancy and infant mortality, indeed in terms of most of the indices used to compare economies on a global scale, Tanzania was clearly not getting any better. In fact, in all of the UN league tables that counted, we were still at the bottom with countries like Bangladesh.

The reasons for all this are not susceptible to any simple diagnosis. After all, some of the best brains on the planet had turned their attention to our troubles. One can point to our relative lack of natural resources, such as hydrocarbons. One can point to the harshness of much of our natural environment. One can point to the breakdown of our previous trading patterns, which until now had hidden many of the flaws in our economic make-up. And one can also point to the failures of socialist systems worldwide. But the factors that eventually overwhelmed Mwalimu's concept of *Ujamaa* were much more deep seated and complex even than these. I have had twenty years to think about what went wrong. The following, in no particular order, are some of the reasons why, according to my own diagnosis, my country has failed to rise to the massive economic challenges of independence.

History undoubtedly has a lot to answer for. In the sixties and seventies many Africans, many Tanzanians, were inclined to lay most of our troubles at the door of our colonial masters — in fact some are so inclined even now. Like many polemicists, they often tended to overstate their argument, seemingly as a means of absolving themselves of all responsibility for what has happened here in the past forty years or so. By over-egging the pudding, they have risked obscuring the underlying strength of their case. No, I don't think Britain is to blame for all our ills. If colonialism is a form of despotism, and it surely is, then the British were perhaps alone among all the imperialist powers in pursuing an enlightened and sympathetic form of despotism. But when one makes a cold-eyed analysis of the reasons for the failure of *Ujamaa*, it is impossible to conclude that our colonial masters did not have an enduring responsibility for some of the underlying problems.

For in truth the British rule in Tanganyika was a very half-hearted affair when compared to the settlement of, say, Kenya or Rhodesia. Perhaps it was the manner and timing of Britain's inheritance of responsibility after the First World War. Perhaps it was the terms of the League of Nations mandate. Perhaps it was the harshness of life in the Tanzanian interior, or the constant battle with infectious diseases such as malaria and sleeping sickness, or the struggle with insufficient rainfall, or the vast distance between pockets of exploitable land: all these factors had worked against any permanent settlement by expatriates from the late nineteenth century onward. Whatever the reasons, the lack of enthusiasm and commitment in the British effort was plain to see in the state of our country in 1961, when Mwalimu came to power. At that time, thanks to under-investment in the local education system, such as it was, there was only a small number of African university graduates in a population of over twenty million. The primary school system, itself almost wholly dependent upon the work of missionaries, was probably less effective in 1961 than it had been back in 1931. Tanganyika on the point of independence had a haphazard and vulnerable pattern of agricultural production that made poor use of innovation and almost none of local knowledge (of which the legendary, nay infamous, groundnuts scheme is but one obvious example). The British bequeathed us a food supply chain that had consistently emphasised production for the benefit of local European consumers at the expense of native peasant producers. We were left a skeletal administration that was capable of doing little more than implementing policies of *laissez-faire*. We inherited a transport infrastructure that was at best rudimentary, and such limited links as we had to the outside world were costly and inadequate. Our trade had been based, indeed continued to be based for some time after independence, on an antiquated and inefficient import and export regime that had been manipulated to meet the material needs of the mother country. Our mass media were in the hands of resident Europeans and under the control of non-resident Europeans, and would stay that way for almost a decade. Our economy had not been developed by either the Germans or British, was without an industrial sector to speak of, and was constrained by a culture in which private enterprise, typified by the ubiquitous *dukawallahs* [shops owned by people of Indian origin], was barely tolerated, and often despised. And so on and so on and so on.

But the weaknesses of the system bequeathed to us by the British were, as I have intimated previously, themselves in part a function of the harshness of the local environment. Nature did not see fit to bless Tanzania with vast exploitable reserves of hydrocarbons, or rich mineral deposits that could be easily accessed. Nor did it endow the new nation with an abundance of food-producing land. Tanzania may be a vast country, but its agricultural heartlands, such as they are, are widely spread, and subject to the vagaries of erratic soil fertility, uncertain rainfall, crop pests, and persistent infestation with mosquitoes, tsetse flies, and other insects. These shortcomings explained the absence of an active and entrepreneurial expatriate community. They also set limits on what could be done by the Tanzanians themselves to exploit the country's agricultural potential. Unfortunately, perhaps, such liabilities did not manage to set an upper limit on local population expansion. From the beginning of the British mandate to the year that Mwalimu stepped down as our president, there was a fivefold increase in our population, and this despite tragically high rates of infant mortality and low life expectancy. By going against the logic of our situation, this growth in population had a further negative impact on our agricultural system. In order to feed this massive expansion in population, which also saw a persistent drift of young adults, especially males, to our expanding towns and cities, such traditional local staples as sorghums and millets, which were best suited to the Tanzanian eco-system, had to be supplanted by higher-yield but more vulnerable cereals such as maize. Little wonder, then, that the hard-pressed rural communities buckled under this strain.

Then the politics of African decolonisation must be added to the equation. Tanzania came into being at the front end of a tumultuous process that spawned tribal conflicts and warfare across great swaths of sub-Saharan Africa. None of these new countries, most of them artificial constructs of past colonial occupying forces, had developed anything like a sense of national identity, with the persistently damaging consequence that true loyalties often lay in kinship rather than state. With a huge land mass and one hundred twenty different tribes contained within it,

Tanzania had a potential problem of regionalism, if not tribalism. At the same time, with eight land borders, and a narrow channel across to a colonial Arab enclave, the newly independent Tanganyika was, and still is, more vulnerable than most to the spillover effects of wars and pestilence on its doorsteps. New countries like Tanganyika also found themselves caught up in the wider game of power politics, which saw developing countries as little more than pawns to be shuttled across a board by the big powers, and which saw the Cold War being fought out by proxy across the fledgling states of Africa. And then, to cap it all, with the twin processes of decolonisation and African nationalism grinding to a sudden halt on its southern borders, Tanzania, as it became known, was, in those early uncertain post-independence years, abruptly forced to choose between its former colonial master and the freedom movements of Zimbabwe, Mozambique, and South Africa, a deeply moral choice that came with awful unintended economic consequences.

Finally, there are the dynamics of international development. Mostly this was a well-meaning exercise in trying to help new countries like Tanzania pull themselves up by their bootstraps. But because it was a new activity, and was initiated at a time of global games-playing by the great powers, the associated risks to the recipient country were never thought through as rigorously as they might have been. The World Bank under Robert McNamara rightly recognised Tanzania as a potential test bed for new paradigms of development. But as was the case in so many of the pilot projects of that idealistic era, the outcome fell far short of what was planned. All too often we found that donor countries were far more interested in the domestic kudos that came from the act of giving than from the sustainability of what they were supposedly kick-starting. Money to countries like Tanzania came in on a leash, and often a shortish one that all too often was tugged hard. Conditions, invariably linked to spending the incoming money on goods and services from the donor, undermined the efficiency and effectiveness of the programmes. Donors also replicated the mistakes of the British, deciding what should be done where and for how long, with little reference to the Tanzanians themselves. So-called experts on open-ended contracts were often foisted on Tanzania because the donors needed to find them a job somewhere. In the circumstances it is hardly surprising that the oft-quoted headline figure of US$2 billion of international aid for Tanzania from 1961 to 1985 is misleading. The actual bottom line for Tanzania was a lot, lot less than that, except in one significant and pernicious way. The amount of psychological dependence bought locally by all that donor money far exceeded two billion dollars' worth. And, sadly, some twenty years on, those attitudes are still hanging round the necks of Tanzanians. Made mendicants by imperialism and then by donor money, we still look at life as mendicants even now, and act accordingly.

By now you should be getting the picture. I write in these terms not to exculpate Mwalimu and our people from all responsibility for the failings of *Ujamaa*, but to mitigate any blame that attaches to them. Given all we know now, it seems truly miraculous that Tanzania emerged from the early days of its foundation without having suffered from civil war, or famine, or military dictatorship, or pandemic. The odds were heavily stacked against us, as the chaos elsewhere in so much of sub-Saharan Africa has undoubtedly proved.

And yet without question some mistakes were made in our early years. The process of villagisation, by which ninety percent of Tanzanian peasants were moved, without choice, to thousands of new villages often many miles away from their places of birth, ranks as one of the least defensible economic policies of the era. True, the move contributed to a homogenisation of the peoples of this country, reinforcing a valuable sense of nationhood above any previous tribal, regional, or indeed religious affiliations. But the damaging impact on an already vulnerable agricultural sector was to be profound and long-lasting. People went to areas that they didn't know, to work among new communities of virtual strangers, and the high hopes for the co-operatives being established all around them were never backed up by enough hard cash and expertise. Then there was the failure to recognise the need for businessmen to run businesses. Mwalimu's pragmatism in respect of my own involvement, in milling and elsewhere in the economy, was sadly the exception rather than the rule. Too many good businessmen, African as well as Asian, fell victim to the practice of privileging political doctrine over sound money and economic growth. The economy, even when largely run by the state, should have been geared to providing surplus. It should also have focussed on areas of greatest need and lowest external capitalisation, both actual and potential. But it wasn't. Finally, there was the over-reliance on international socialist partners, whose political stock was still high but whose economic credentials were becoming increasingly threadbare. East Germans and Cubans and Russians may have made comfortable political bedfellows in those difficult times, given the then indefensible British policies on apartheid and UDI. But the fraternal links to the Soviet bloc were, in all honesty, never likely to help lift us up from the bottom of any global economic pile.

To his eternal credit, Mwalimu recognised his own shortcomings as well as the difficulties inherent in the situation he had either inherited or had otherwise been saddled with. Unique among the African leaders of his generation, he had no intention of being President for Life, or abusing his lofty position for his own personal gain. He was a giant among men, and all the more so for acknowledging that he too was human. And by the early 1980s, he saw that the time was fast approaching for the *Uhuru* torch to be passed.

In a new nation, the act of choosing a widely acceptable successor is never going to be easy; the problem is particularly acute in a country like Tanzania, in which a historically Christian mainland had been merged with Muslim Zanzibar. In Chama Cha Mapinduzi (CCM), the successor to TANU as the party of government, there were plenty of younger politicians all too eager to try to fill Mwalimu's shoes. But of the people who now started allowing their names to surface as potential successors, few were seen by Mwalimu as having the necessary personal qualities to be deemed potential presidential material. In his mind, the needs of nationhood, the necessity of sustaining the ongoing process of forging national unity, remained uppermost. The road was pointing toward Zanzibar, and Islam.

History books have already crawled over the ins and outs of the subsequent CCM selection process. I see no point in my attempting to rehash those accounts, or to add my own gloss on them. Not having himself groomed a successor, Mwalimu was free to exert his massive influence to make sure that the choice was taken with the future interests of Tanzania as a whole uppermost in mind. The party's (and Mwalimu's) eventual choice as successor, Ali Hassan Mwinyi, left the nominating convention enjoying all of the benefits of Mwalimu's blessing, but also facing the unenviable challenge of charting a new course for the Tanzanian ship of state, first economically, and later politically.

Doing all this in the absence of Mwalimu would itself have been a daunting task. Attempting such a significant change at a time when the founding father of the country was still very much part of the landscape and casting a long shadow, not least by remaining as chairman of the ruling party, was indeed close to Herculean. For that reason alone, any assessment of President Mwinyi's two terms of office needs to take into account the circumstances in which he operated. Some commentators have tended to dismiss the Mwinyi era as a disappointment after the high water mark of Mwalimu's presidency. But I disagree. For most of the seventies, indeed up to the changeover of power in 1985, the accomplishments of Tanzania had been largely political. Economically, the country was at best treading water, though mostly it was sinking. For all his genius, Mwalimu simply couldn't make the change from command economy to something more liberal in his time in office. Instead, that onerous responsibility was left to Mwinyi and his team. I am therefore absolutely convinced of the significance of the presidency of Ali Hassan Mwinyi. It was he who took the risks, he who laid the groundwork for the significant economic and social progress that has been made since 1995, when Benjamin Mkapa became president.

My relationship with President Mwinyi was always going to be different from the one I had with his predecessor. *Ujamaa* put Mwalimu on a collision course with the local business community, and though his policies never quite drove me off the road, I was always conscious that others were not so fortunate. Mwalimu was a man of high principle, but I always found him ready to adjust his course if sufficient new evidence was put before him. Even when his own personal affections were engaged, as with Derek Bryceson, he would never shrink from doing what he thought was right for the country.

President Mwinyi was similarly committed to doing the right thing for Tanzania. He was and is a much more courtly man than Mwalimu ever was. A natural conciliator, with an innate sense of how to secure a more productive balance in the relations between faith and ethnic groups in Tanzania, he is deeply respectful in the way he treats all those who seek his advice. I may have met less frequently with him than I did with Mwalimu, but with President Mwinyi there was less need for such meetings. President Mwinyi had committed himself to an economic programme that was much closer in conception and execution to what I would have wanted to see executed some twenty years before. Besides, I consider any comparisons with Mwalimu to be grossly unfair, in that no one in Tanzania is ever likely to match, or indeed need to match, the great man's capacity for statesmanship on the national and international stage. But if he was not an international colossus like Mwalimu, President Mwinyi also (thankfully) lacked Mwalimu's capacity for confrontation. Mwalimu's criticism of him — that he ran State House like a shop — said as much about Nyerere as it did about Mwinyi, if not more, for Mwalimu often came across to those who didn't know him as a man of principle first, and principle last, even when the local economy often called for something else from him, something more pragmatic and less unbending.

Under President Mwinyi I continued to serve the state as best I could, in corporations, as always, but also on official missions, and in quiet counsel too. By then I was serving the ruling party as well. Following years of unofficial advice to the leadership on business issues, I was appointed to the board of its enterprise wing, a business arm that had been set up with the express intention of avoiding reliance upon the use of state funds for party purposes. I still used to meet up with Mwalimu now and then, maintaining our old relationship of great frankness and, I like to think, mutual trust, and I continued to benefit from his wisdom and vision, just as his successor did. And as the Mwinyi era unfolded, the Tanzanian economy gradually began to stir from its torpor.

But it is not only as the time when a new process of far-reaching economic reform began that the Mwinyi era will be remembered. Significant political developments inside the country and beyond its borders served to test the new administration in ways that could never have been anticipated when the new president came to power in 1985. The nation owes much to President Mwinyi for the change in direction and for instituting economic reforms.

The external events at first looked more like a new opportunity than a challenge, at least for the poorer countries of the developing world. The end of the Cold War at the close of the 1980s and Operation Desert Storm in early 1991 were both characterised as portents of a radical restructuring of the international political system. All the talk that was coming out of Washington and then out of London about a New World Order seemed to suggest that the curtain was about to come down on the old Cold War habits of unconstrained meddling in the internal affairs of the developing countries. This New World Order, which was billed as something of a return to first principles for the UN, only this time a revitalised and well-financed UN at the centre stage of international affairs, was of great interest and held great potential for countries like Tanzania. With an African Secretary-General and an African in charge of peacekeeping operations, there was at last a realistic prospect that even-handedness and the rule of law, not 'might makes right', would be the principles to be applied across the globe to conflict prevention, conflict resolution, and post-conflict reconstruction.

At first these bright new beginnings gave real hope to the leaders and informed thinkers in almost all developing countries. The international response to the crises in Haiti and then Bosnia at the beginning of the 1990s seemed to demonstrate a new willingness on the part of the international community to do what was necessary, more or less, to safeguard the vulnerable and uphold the law in parts of the world that previously would have been off-limits or of no real interest to the UN. Then along came the civil war in Somalia in 1992, and with it the first signs that the big powers, especially the Americans, might yet be reverting to type. However, it was not until 1994 and the outbreak of the civil war in Rwanda that the nations of the Third World in general, and the Africans in particular, began to realise that the lofty ideals and new methods of conflict resolution of the so-called New World Order were going to be applied only selectively, and that the criteria for selection would be framed so as to specifically exclude them.

The civil wars in Rwanda and Burundi, like those before them in the former Republic of Yugoslavia, had been igniting intermittently for longer than people cared to remember. Successive Tanzanian governments from 1970 onwards had had to cope with periodic waves of refugees from that part of the world, who had wandered over the common border in their thousands, often never to return to their homelands. But the war that broke out in Rwanda in 1994 following the assassination of the presidents of Rwanda and Burundi on their way back into Kigali after yet another peace-brokering summit in Tanzania, was of a ferocity that no one had ever witnessed before. President Mwinyi described it as another Bosnia on his doorstep, and in many respects he was absolutely correct. But in the most crucial particular — the speed and extent of the response of the international community to the butchering in Rwanda of first thousands and then hundreds of thousands of defenceless civilians by their neighbours and friends — the difference between Bosnia and Rwanda was stark. Whilst I was attending a regional meeting in Kigali on the eradication of polio Rwanda's Health Minister asked me if I had visited the genocide site. When I said I hadn't he arranged for me to go there. The official car that took me passed through a village named after Mandela, and on arrival at the site I found a television crew. After about fifteen minutes, when I was ready to go back to the hotel, I was offered a visitor's book and requested to put down some remarks. What could one say? I wrote, 'I hope the present and future generations of Rwandans will learn from what is at this site.' In Bosnia in 1992, after some initial hemming and hawing, both the Europeans and the North Americans committed significant money and manpower to damp down the conflict before too many lives had been lost. In Rwanda they did nothing of the sort, nothing in fact but talk.

In consequence, the Africans in general and the Tanzanians in particular had to carry whatever part of the new Rwandan burden that they could. Powerless to stop the killings, the Mwinyi government instead held open its borders to the hundreds of thousands of refugees who came flooding across into Tanzania, while redoubling its efforts at the negotiating table in Arusha. The social and financial costs of looking after the refugees, who were staying at what at the time was the second largest town in the Republic, were immense. Eventually the international community, in the form of the UN, stepped in to support and sustain this never-ending tide of human misery that flowed into Tanzania, and went on to fund and then staff the subsequent war crimes tribunal in Arusha. But by then the local damage to the UN's credibility had already been done. If indeed there was a New World Order, and there was by then decreasing evidence to support that thesis, then it was a mere repetition of the old imperialist practice of prizing European lives way above those of Africans. This lesson would carry over into all future negotiations that the governments of Mwinyi and his successor (and Mwalimu) would conduct. Whether in the Great Lakes or Burundi, the UN offered a limited amount of help, and then only at the margins.

While that depressing realisation was still sinking in, the Mwinyi government was busy preparing for Tanzania's first post-independence multi-party elections. Back in 1992, Mwalimu Nyerere had been the principal architect of the shift away from a one-party system, but it fell to the Mwinyi government to prepare for the countrywide elections in 1995. For the first time in its history, the ruling party would have to take its case to the country, and see off its rivals in seeking a popular mandate.

Opposition parties in Tanzania still contend that the CCM decision taken back in 1992 to abandon the one-party state was little more than an exercise in cynicism. I am afraid that the logic of that argument continues to escape me. An approach based on cynicism would have been so much more straightforward than that. Just call another one-party election, as the tradition had been up till then. Yet instead of staying on that old course, CCM adopted a brave new principled position that flew in the face of political trends to the north and south, a position of principle that has since opened the door to, at the very least, a future opposition victory in the Zanzibari elections. No cynic of my experience would ever have acted in such a spirit of self-sacrifice.

Whatever the opposition parties might have contended, the decision to hold multi-party elections in Tanzania in 1995 inevitably created new political dynamics in the country. But this came on top of an increasingly unpredictable struggle for the CCM presidential nomination. Having served two full terms, President Mwinyi was barred by law from seeking another. But the absence of Mwinyi from the list hardly narrowed down the field. As had been the case in 1985, at least a dozen names began to circulate as possible contenders to this highest of offices.

In the run-up to the decision by the nominating convention of CCM, Mwalimu once more demonstrated not only his commitment to moral principle but also his capacity to surprise. Out of a packed field of seasoned politicians, he let it be known that he was throwing his weight behind one of CCM's least-fancied candidates, having previously raised serious doubts about the integrity of some of the more media-friendly front-runners. The party faithful and the local press were taken aback. But, as always, Mwalimu's surprises were founded in cold hard logic.

Mwalimu's eventual nominee, the CCM candidate and soon to be third president of the United Republic of Tanzania, was none other than my old friend and colleague Benjamin William Mkapa. To many in Tanzania he may have been an unknown quantity, but for me there was no room at all for any mystery or doubt. From the day of his nomination, just as on the day of his appointment to the *Daily News* all those years before, I instinctively knew that Ben Mkapa was the right man for the right job, and at the right time, for Tanzania.

In 2005, the CCM for the first time set out to select its candidate for the presidency without Mwalimu's presence. There were eleven contenders, among whom were two serving ambassadors. President Mkapa, as chairman of the party, steered proceedings, and the party selected 54-year-old Jakaya Kikwete, who has served continuously as foreign minister since 1995. With his ability to connect with young people, he is a candidate ideally suited for the twenty-first century.

The end of the Mwinyi era also marked a personal watershed in our own lives. During the 1980s and early 1990s our three boys had come of age in every sense. All have become successful in their own fields, in some cases spectacularly so. Having qualified as an accountant in the mid-seventies, Manish had worked his way up a blue-chip accountancy firm before being appointed Finance Director, and then Chief Executive, of Imry PLC, engineering the rapid growth (including stock market flotation) of this property investment company. He later became Chief Executive of the largest property company in Europe — Landmark Securities — and then moved back to his private property development business. He is currently Chairman of NCP, the largest car park company in Europe. A member of the Commission for English Heritage, Manish takes a keen interest in community service. He is actively involved in the National Society of the Prevention of Cruelty to Children and is a Trustee of the Windsor Leadership Trust, a body formed to develop and inspire leaders for society. Anuj, like his elder brother, also qualified as an accountant; he worked for Albright and Wilson in the UK and NCR Corporation in the US before becoming the youngest partner at Grant Thornton. He has won the Lloyds TSB Professional Excellence Award and is a Member of the SME Board of the National Employment Panel as well as a Member of the London Employers' Coalition. A mentor for the Prince's Trust charity, he is involved in many charitable causes. Rupen, our youngest son, earned a Master's degree in Business Studies at London University and an MBA from the University of San Diego, California. Unlike his brothers, however, he opted to go into the non-profit sector, working with the UNA and CARE International before he set up the Aga Khan Foundation Offices in Dar es Salaam as its first Chief Executive. He is presently Manager, Professional Development Centre, Institute for Educational Development, Eastern Africa, of The Aga Khan University. An educationist, Rupen too is community service-minded.

And with all that success came an expansion of the family. Rupen has stayed a bachelor, though he is not short of female friends. Manish, the eldest, met and fell in love with Lucy Dickens, a fellow pupil of Charterhouse and incidentally the great-great-granddaughter of the renowned Victorian writer, and together they have two children, a daughter, Lonika (herself now an eighteen-year-old student at Charterhouse), and a son Josha (now sixteen and at Highgate School). They divorced last year, but whenever we are in London we meet Lucy. A former Fashion and Beauty editor of the *Brides Magazine*, Lucy is a talented writer and a distinguished artist in the medium of oil colours. She has exhibited her work to considerable critical acclaim in London's galleries. Anuj, our middle son, married Nishma, a girl he met through his London friends. Born in Mombasa, Kenya, Nishma is an interior designer. Her work includes exquisite hand-painted silk scarves as well as hessian cloth paintings. Nishma sometimes uses Lucy's studio for her work. They have a daughter Polomi, now fourteen. All of our grandchildren are blessed in being both bright and beautiful (how it pleases a grandfather to say such things), and like their fathers they often unwittingly reveal old family traits. Without wishing to single any one of them out, for they all have their own particular talents, I quote but one example: when he was just six, I took young Josha to Hamley's Toy Department store in London. Before we went in, he stopped me on the pavement, stared up at me, and said, '*Bapuji*, before I start looking around, I need to know what my budget is.' Now there speaks a true Chande.

THIRTEEN

THE MKAPA PRESIDENCY

When President Mkapa was sworn in as the third president of the United Republic in 1995, I was sixty-seven years old (well, sixty-six according to the records office in Mombasa). I still had the zest for life of a man half my age, whichever way you computed it. My body, however, sometimes disagreed, having been pushed pretty hard for the previous forty-five years.

However old I was or felt, I still had an important role to play in the economic life of the country. But in the first instance, the problems facing the incoming president were largely political. Not only did he not enjoy the popularity or control of the ruling party's grassroots that his principal challengers for the nomination continued to enjoy. Not only did he not have the authority that came with the chairmanship of the ruling party, that office still being vested in the former president. But the advent of multi-partyism had brought with it a major problem with the opposition parties. Benjamin Mkapa had won a comfortable majority in the Union presidential elections, gaining around 61 percent of the vote to 27 percent for his main challenger, Augustine Mrema. Over on Zanzibar, though, the incumbent president, Salmin Amour, had been run very close indeed by Seif Sharif Hamad, the candidate from the Civic United Front (CUF), too close for political comfort.

The narrow margin of President Amour's victory, less than a single percentage point, signalled the onset of persistent political unrest, which was to consume so much time in the next ten years of President Mkapa's tenure. The closeness of the Zanzibari presidential result, the three-day delay in announcing the winner following early speculative reports that Hamad had won, and the split in the vote between the two main islands of Zanzibar, with CUF dominant on Pemba and CCM controlling Unguja, all of these factors brought home to the Union President the difficult political reality he now faced. I knew then, and still know now from my own personal experience, dating back to before the revolution of 1964, just how volatile the close-knit communities on Zanzibar can be if push ever comes to shove. With the islands divided politically from the day of the 1995 election, just as they had been divided ethnically in previous centuries, the need for domestic as well as international statesmanship on the part of the incoming president was almost immediately apparent.

Back in 1985, President Mwinyi had been given the onerous responsibility of beginning the process of economic reform, and to his credit he had done so. But with the international community continuing to offer development assistance in ways that did not come close to maximising its impact, and with the Tanzanian economy having to drag itself out of the vortex into which it had long since plummeted, the chances of a rapid recovery during the Mwinyi years had been slim to none. I knew from the returns from the ports and the railways that domestic production and export value throughout the late 1980s and early 1990s, particularly in agriculture, were still chronically low. During that time, neighbouring countries such as Mozambique had begun to attract significant levels of external capital investment. Others, such as Kenya, were beginning to exploit their established international transport links to tap into the growing European market for African flowers and vegetables. In Uganda, as well, it was clear from the success of my wife's family's enterprises that the growth rate of GDP there was already respectable, and rising. The Tanzanian economy, meanwhile, continued to bump along the bottom. Inflation was high, thanks to a weak currency and inelastically high import levels. Growth was low, even from such a modest starting point as ours, and certainly much too low to have any redistributive effects across Tanzanian society. Central bank reserves were uncomfortably meagre. And the positive effects of such innovation as had been introduced into agricultural production were undermined by the absence of a sophisticated road network to railheads and cities. This meant not only that the profit margins of any export goods were sharply reduced by transport costs and natural wastage, but that producers in Tanzania, unlike, say, those in Kenya, could never guarantee that their goods would be in a certain place by a certain date, given the rigours of the necessarily long journeys on unmetalled rural roads.

This latter constraint, the deficiencies of the road transport network, would clearly need early high-level attention. President Mkapa certainly knew that, and made the sector a priority in his dealings with the international donors, especially with the EU. But he also knew that the main economic focus in his first five-year term of office had to be macroeconomic stability. None of the macroeconomic indicators were moving in the right direction. They needed to do so, and soon, if he was to convince both potential investors and the donor community that a dollar spent in Tanzania would bring a certain and justifiable return. To my knowledge he is one of only two state leaders who have agreed to be chairman of the Business Council. President Mkapa took over the chairmanship of the Tanzania National Business Council, has chaired six international investors round tables, and has taken a personal and keen interest in the follow-up on the decisions. When, at one of the forums, investors were considering the investor-friendliness of the World Bank, President James Wolfensohn remarked that having someone like Mkapa as head of state was additional bonus for prospective investors.

Around this time I was in Paris in my capacity as chairman of the Tanzania Railways Corporation. On the first night of this international railway jamboree, we had a formal dinner, at which the EU Commissioner and former UK Labour Party leader Neil Kinnock was the keynote speaker. Now my son Manish, a Tory supporter, would cross the world to avoid such an encounter.

I was booked into the Hilton Hotel, not far from the office of the International Railway Union, and was having a shower when the telephone in my bedroom rang. Jayli was at that time in Hong Kong, and thinking that it might be her, I rushed into the bedroom to answer. When I got to the phone I was disappointed to hear a hotel clerk on the other end of the line, telling me that my transport for the evening's reception and dinner had arrived. As I went back into the bathroom I slipped and fell in a pool of water on the floor that had previously cascaded down from my wet body. Though hurt, I managed to crawl to the telephone and tell the hotel operator what had happened. Ten minutes later, an English-speaking doctor was in my room, telling me that I had probably fractured a rib. He asked me whether I wanted to go to the British or the American hospital. In pain, I whispered, 'To the nearest one.' I was taken to a British hospital, where a lady doctor treated me. The X-rays revealed that I had a hairline fracture of a lower rib, which caused me to miss the dinner and delayed my return to London. Later on, to the chagrin no doubt of my eldest son, I heard that Mr Kinnock had delivered himself of a brilliant speech on the future of the global transport industry.

While it is one thing to recognise the need for macroeconomic reform, it is quite another to deliver it. Even in Western countries, where the average citizen has a relatively wide margin between comfort and penury, and where the state provides a sophisticated array of services in all of the social services and transportation, any government policies that sharply reduce government spending and increase taxes are met with howls of protest. In an economy such as Tanzania's in 1995, with most people living in deepest poverty, and with civil service overstaffing one of the few obvious lifelines for extended families, the new reform policies were a huge and painful gamble. In the long run, if they paid off Tanzania would at last have an economy with a potential for effective take-off. But would most Tanzanians be willing or able to wait for the long run to come about?

This then was the dilemma facing President Mkapa. True to form, he didn't duck it. Indeed, he quickly realised that there was no dilemma at all. He had no choice but to undertake a far-reaching programme of macroeconomic reform, whatever his people might think. Without it, Tanzania was economically doomed.

Over the next five years, his economic reform programme began to bite. The civil service began to be slimmed down, radically so in some ministries. Administrative measures to make government procurement transparent (and therefore less susceptible to waste and graft) were introduced, with a legal framework to follow. Similar measures were introduced in respect of government borrowing. Sound fiscal policies were introduced and adhered to, and the tax take from business and individuals, both notoriously low in comparison with that in other countries, began to rise. Huge external investment in gold mining and energy was drawn into the economy on the back of generous concessions (the President arguing, most convincingly, that it is only in such circumstances that the country's natural deposits would be exploited). Moves were made to denationalise those sectors of the economy in which private investment should always have played the prominent role (telecommunications, for example). And an anti-corruption programme was launched, with a network of new offices and officers established throughout the country.

Sitting, as I did, in the chambers of commerce and in the corporations, I could sense that this package was getting a grudging rather than an enthusiastic welcome. Almost forty years of economic under-performance, and that on the back of another seventy years of ineffective and unenthusiastic colonial economic exploitation, made the investor community extremely cautious in its responses to the Mkapa programme. The human cost of the macroeconomic package was readily quantifiable, but as yet no one was willing to count the projected returns.

I had another vantage point at that time, an international one, which allowed me to look right across the global economy and see how others in Tanzania's position were faring. In 1995 I was invited by former President Gorbachev to sit in on the 'State of the World Forum', a US-based Gorbachev Foundation initiative to study the dynamics of the post-Cold War era. Because the Foundation was based in the US, much of the polemic was about the implications of a unipolar world for the US, the UN, and the international community more generally. But in the midst of these discussions, and, in San Francisco in 1997, in the International Industrial Conference (regularly sponsored by Stanford Research Institute of Menlo Park, California, and the Conference Board of New York, of both of which I was a member), of which I had been an International Council member for over twenty years, I was able to get a clear sense of the changing international environment for developing countries. Thanks to the growing disillusionment with the UN's efforts to police the world's hot spots, largely due to the failures of some of the leading countries, the post-Cold War debate inside and outside of government was already shifting its focus. The thinkers inside the international fora, key governments, and major transnationals were becoming increasingly convinced that economic growth was a much more reliable means of avoiding conflict than any force or sanctions that the UN might (or might not) deploy. They were also becoming convinced that a truly global market was at last being established, thanks to the unlocking of the potential of the low-cost, high-productivity, and increasingly high-quality Chinese and Indian economies.

This growing fascination with the potential of the process that soon came to be known as globalisation did not at first extend to countries such as Tanzania. Again, from my vantage points outside the country, I could see that the reforms then being implemented by President Mkapa would give Tanzania the best possible opportunity to take advantage of the globalising trends in the marketplace. Some at home, still steeped in the command philosophies of the *Ujamaa* period, remained unconvinced. Just as they had always wanted to control the economy from inside government offices, they now wanted to do the same with the forces of globalisation, and somehow keep them away from the shores of Tanzania.

Thankfully, President Mkapa was a man of vision. He saw that a global market was not something you could just opt into or opt out of. It was a phenomenon that had to be dealt with and prepared for. He was also a man of strong resolve. Never one to go courting personal popularity — throughout his political career he has never resorted to the techniques of demagoguery — he stuck fast, in the teeth of growing domestic discontent, to the processes of opening up the economy and reforming the public purse. And in time the results began to show. Inflation dropped from double-digit to single-digit, and then down to less than five percent. Growth rose to around five percent. The central bank reserves built up to a comfortable level again. Public procurement and public lending were no longer subject to the previous processes of arbitrary, often inexplicable, decision-making. And the possibilities for regional economic integration were put back onto the agenda after a hiatus of twenty years, with the long-overdue re-establishment of the East African Community (EAC).

The immediate impact of this success was more international than domestic. I knew from my contacts with foreign governments and the external investor community that the changes being made were now coming to be seen as of real significance. The new macroeconomic figures had come in at a time when the donor community was reassessing the efficiency and effectiveness of its previous means of delivering international aid, and the Mkapa macroeconomic breakthroughs gave Tanzania a head start on most other recipient countries in accessing the new donor facilities. These new ways of delivering assistance, in untied, multi-year packages paid directly into the local exchequer, were as a result now piloted in Tanzania. The importance of this shift, at a time when traditional aid packages to the likes of Kenya were on the wane, cannot be underestimated. For the first time ever, the Tanzanian government could integrate a major tranche of overseas assistance into its annual budget cycles. With that sort of predictability, and with assistance being delivered in advance in cold hard cash and not just vague promises or help in kind, the multiplier effect of such assistance was suddenly realised. Thanks to the tough macroeconomic reforms instituted by the President, the old days of personal whimsy as a key determinant in delivering external assistance to Tanzania at last seemed numbered.

There was, however, an obvious downside to all this. Belt tightening for the Tanzanian government inevitably led to more of the same for the Tanzanian people. And for them the belt already felt too tight. The Mkapa programme might have pushed the macroeconomic indicators in the right direction at long last, but all of the social indices were still stuck fast, and in some instances, such as basic health and access to primary schooling, declining still further from an already low point.

I know from my many conversations with the President that he felt this dichotomy keenly. Although it hurt him to know that the Tanzanian people were continuing to suffer, there was little or nothing he could do to address their problems until he got the government financial house in order. That didn't mean that he wasn't planning for the future. As far back as 1996, he had already laid out his blueprint for future change in social conditions, whereby he aimed to create nationwide prosperity.

I was conscious of this because of my own increased involvement in the Tanzanian health sector. I have always had a close interest in the country's social services. My role in founding the deaf school and my continuous high-level involvement in the local councils for Financial Management, Secondary Education, and Business Education, most of them from the mid-1960s onwards, reflect my deep commitment to improving the local educational system at all levels and for all Tanzanians. But as the 1990s wore on, I began to take up senior positions of responsibility in the local health sector as well. I became a trustee of the Muhimbili National Hospital, the International Medical and Technological University in Dar es Salaam, the Tanzania Heart Association, the Tanzania Registered Nurses Association, the Tanzania Society for the Deaf, and the Tanzania Society for Cerebral Palsy and Mental Retardation. Some of these bodies I had already had long associations with; quite aside from my role at Buguruni Deaf School, I had been the prime mover, as both a Mason and a Rotarian, in setting up the District Nurse scheme in Tanzania. But the sudden expansion of my other roles in the mid-1990s, which has been sustained until the present day, reflected a desire to give the overloaded and underdeveloped local public health sector whatever boost I could.

I won't deny that some of this work was as difficult as any I have ever encountered. The problems at the Muhimbili Orthopaedic Institute, of which I am the chairman, had, and sometimes still have, an intractability all of their own, and I have often despaired of getting even the simplest solution to any problem adopted. But then again, I have never been a quitter. In all my years of service, only once did I ever resign from a corporation. I certainly wasn't going to give up on the health sector when it needed all the help it could get.

By the late 1990s, the health sector began to be the focus of increased government activity. Working in partnership with the local donor community, which set up baskets of funds for specific social sectors, the President was at last able to start turning his attention to addressing the deep-seated deficiencies in social provision in Tanzania. But just as this important work was building up some useful momentum, the ongoing rumbling of political discontent in Zanzibar increased. The Union presidential elections of 2000 saw the incumbent President Mkapa returned to office with an increased majority over Professor Lipumba, his main (CUF) opposition rival. But over in Zanzibar the problems that had been revealed by the 1995 election broke surface once again. The then Commonwealth Secretary-General, Chief Anyoku, had spent much of the late 1990s trying to broker an accommodation between CCM and CUF on Zanzibar, and came very close to getting a deal. But when those negotiations eventually foundered in the run-up to the 2000 campaign, the stage had been set for another trial of strength between CCM and CUF, only this time with the opposition feeling an ingrained sense of bitterness.

In 2000, CCM won the presidential elections on Zanzibar again, and Amani Abeid Karume, the son of the first president of Zanzibar, took office amid renewed opposition claims of shenanigans. I had served together with Karume on the board of East African Harbours Corporation in the 1960s, and we had become close associates. I had always found him to be of a quiet disposition and a man of integrity. The elections to the Zanzibar House of Representatives were even more fiercely disputed. The opposition cried foul, international observers reported irregularities, elected CUF representatives refused to take their seats, and in late January 2001 the whole situation came to the boil when opposition demonstrations on the streets of Stone Town in Unguja as well as in Pemba descended into chaos, and in the ensuing crackdown over thirty people, including two policemen, were killed.

The disturbances in Zanzibar were a moment of real crisis for President Mkapa. He had spent the previous five years establishing the economic credentials of Tanzania in the eyes of governments and industries in the developed world, and the killings on the streets of Zanzibar risked unpicking much if not all of his good work. This was especially so once the main Western news agencies had made their judgements. The President's interview with Tim Sebastian of the BBC, in which the latter characterised the events on Zanzibar in terms of Pol Pot's killing fields, was the harshest of lessons in the way Western news media now functioned. The deaths on Zanzibar had been a matter of national shame, just as they would have been in any other civilised country. But to extrapolate from such an event to comparisons with the sustained genocide of the likes of Pol Pot showed how little understanding of the local situation there was even at so august an institution as the BBC. With an unjustifiable anti-Mkapa slant such as that in international media reporting, the chances of getting relations with the donors back onto an even keel, let alone the Zanzibari situation, were nowhere near good.

The next few months thus saw the President's well-laid plans for Tanzania placed in jeopardy. True, international development assistance for Tanzania did not dry up (though a ban on assistance to Zanzibar was put in place). But the hitherto constructive atmosphere in which the debate on future collaboration with the donors had been conducted had been soured. President Mkapa and his closest political advisers set to work to heal the breach between the parties on Zanzibar. But the political risks he was taking in doing so did not receive the same sort of credit as those he had previously taken with the national economy. Indeed it was not until some time after an agreement had been reached with CUF, the Muafaka Agreement of October 2001, that a measure of trust was re-established between the President and the international donor community.

I would go so far as to say that the reaction to the events on Zanzibar were something of a watershed in President Mkapa's view of the donor community. This had less to do with immediate reactions than with the longer-term messages the donors sent to the President, some subliminally. The people who had been most affected by the events of January 2001 went on to demonstrate a fundamental trust in the President's bona fides during the process of negotiating, signing, and then implementing the Muafaka Agreement. The fact that CUF took those risks speaks volumes about the character of the President (for only someone of unimpeachable integrity could have healed the breach with CUF). Meanwhile, the donors showed nothing like the same trust in the President throughout that difficult time, in spite of the earlier risks he had taken in pushing through his programme of macroeconomic reform. Though he has never said anything of this to me, even in private, I think that the events of 2001 taught him more clearly than anything else just how shallow their commitment to him, and their understanding of the challenge of ruling a country like Tanzania, really was. Little wonder therefore that Mwalimu had felt himself bound, in the early years of nationhood, to assure the international community that the newly independent Tanganyika would never be 'another Congo'. Such assertions, such need for public guarantees of future good behaviour, were the rules of the international game as played by the industrialised nations then as much as now.

Whatever the disappointments of the Muafaka year, the programme of cooperation with the donor community on social services was further strengthened. The crash programme of primary school building and teacher training produced a rapid improvement in the quantity, if not quality, of primary schooling in Tanzania. Under the stewardship of Education Minister Mungai (his days in the sugar business, like mine, now long past), the President's commitment to offer free state primary education to all children has now been delivered. Ambitious programmes to reduce infectivity to malaria and AIDS through widespread access to preventive measures such as nets and condoms are now in place alongside measures to improve the standards of hospital care for all Tanzanians. The provision of potable water within acceptable distances of people's homes has at long last been made a priority, with new drainage and waterpipe systems being introduced into the capital. The privatisation of the telecommunications sector has led to an exponential growth in mobile phone ownership. Rural electrification and the construction of a new network of both rural and trunk roads is under way, and the port system in Dar es Salaam has been completely overhauled, to the point that the turnaround time compares favourably with that in every major port up the East African coastline. Everywhere you look, there is sense of forward movement and of positive change. There may be a long distance still to travel, but my abiding impression is of a country that is transforming itself for the better after too many years of standing still.

FOURTEEN

ACCOLADES ...

The journey that began in Bukene all those years ago is coming closer to an end. I write this not because I have recently received an intimation of my own mortality, but in view of the number of awards and accolades I have started to receive in the past few years. Only sportsmen and singers and a minority of the finest actors are garlanded by society when they are at the very height of their powers. The rest of us, if we get any awards at all, only receive them when we are fast approaching that final dreadful cliff edge of decrepitude.

In 1995-96 I received the President's Golden Century Citation from Rotary International for continued dedication and commitment to Rotary's growth. In 1998 I received the prestigious 'Service Above Self' award from Rotary International in recognition of all of my years of work for the Rotary Movement, having also been awarded a citation for meritorious service in 1993. In 1998 again, I was pleasantly surprised to be nominated as the International Man of the Year by the International Biographical Centre in England. It was an honour to be so selected. In 2003 I was appointed as a trustee of the prestigious US$90 million-per-year Rotary Foundation, based in Illinois, USA. I am, at the time of writing, the only person from Africa and the Middle East serving in that capacity. In 2004 I was appointed Chairman of the Rotary Foundation of the United Kingdom.

It was in the summer of 2003 that the awards process began to gather momentum. First I received the prestigious 'Hind Ratna' award from the former Indian Prime Minister, I.K. Gujral. Then I was declared to be the 'non-Resident Indian of the year' by the International Congress of Non-Resident Indians (NRI). During the same year I was given the Pride of India Gold Award at a conference organised by the NRI Institute in London. Most significantly of all, I was informed by the British government that Her Majesty Queen Elizabeth II had decided to appoint me an Honorary Knight Commander of the Most Excellent Order of the British Empire (KBE). This order, dating back in inception to 1917 and the reign of King George V, has quickly become one of the most important in British society, and I immediately recognised the award's significance to me.

According to the citation that accompanied the badge of the Order, this honour was conferred on me in recognition of the valuable services I had rendered to UK-Tanzanian relations, and to the voluntary sector worldwide. When telling me of the honour, Buckingham Palace gave me two options as to possible investiture. I could either wait for a slot in one of the regular autumn investitures in London, or I could be invested in the Order by the resident British High Commissioner to Tanzania.

Being a loyal and proud Tanzanian, my strong preference was for the latter. But before making a final decision I talked things over with Jayli, and with my children. We all agreed that a ceremony held in Dar es Salaam would be far the most appropriate in the circumstances. Not only would it act as a symbolic reaffirmation of my deep and constant attachment to the country of my citizenship, but it would also enable many more of our Tanzanian friends to share in the joyous moment of my investiture.

The date of the investiture was quickly set for August 29th, 2003. I say quickly because it soon became apparent to me that the British High Commissioner was on the point of retiring from the diplomatic service. It was agreed that the ceremony, the last official act by the outgoing High Commissioner, would be held at his official residence on Kenyatta Drive, the mansion overlooking the Indian Ocean once owned by a Greek sisal magnate. Afterwards there would be a lunch on the lawns of the house, and in the evening, a formal reception at the Royal Palm Hotel (today renamed the Mövenpick Royal Palm Hotel).

The day of the investiture itself was inevitably one of great happiness and high emotion. The sun shone brightly, and mercifully the wind dropped to a gentle breeze. At the High Commissioner's residence, over one hundred guests, including ministers, senior officials, ambassadors, business and voluntary sector colleagues, and of course our family, over from Kenya, Uganda, and London, gathered to witness the investiture. Most significantly of all, certainly in terms of protocol but also because of our long and enduring friendship, Benjamin William Mkapa, President of the United Republic of Tanzania, and his wife Mama Mkapa, together with the First Lady of Zanzibar, Mama Karume, were on hand to witness my investiture.

In his speech prior to conferring me with the honorary knighthood, Richard Clarke, the outgoing High Commissioner, spoke of the rarity of such events. In fact no Tanzanian had ever been knighted since independence. He also talked, in simple but moving terms, about my life and my contribution to voluntary work, to Tanzania, and to bilateral relations between Tanzania and the UK. And as he spoke I couldn't help but let my mind drift off into the past, to the emotions my parents would have felt at seeing that moment, and then to the more recent debt I owed to Jayli and my family. And as I sat looking across at Jayli and my three wonderful sons, the High Commissioner's speech suddenly switched focus to my family, and he paid fulsome tribute to the many sacrifices Jayli and my sons had made over the years in having 'selflessly shared' me with the world.

With that, the time for formal speechmaking was at an end. I was asked to rise, and the High Commissioner pinned to my jacket the small but ornate and beautiful badge signifying knighthood in the Most Excellent Order. There were a few wry smiles among the Tanzanians in the audience at the words 'British Empire', but I think no one felt anything but the immense national pride I felt in being so honoured.

After photographs by press and by family and friends came lunch under marquees on the lawn of the house. Under wide fringed palm and frangipani trees, the atmosphere lapsed back into easy informality, and I spent a precious couple of hours reminiscing about old times with the President in the company of relatives. I could see that President Mkapa, like my family members, was visibly moved. As we left the British residence, High Commissioner Clarke presented me with a book, signed by all attendees, on the cover of which was the Coat of Arms of Her Majesty's Government.

The reception that evening in the Royal Palm Hotel was graced by the presence of another old friend, former President Ali Hassan Mwinyi. The atmosphere again was celebratory, and memorable for very different reasons. At lunchtime the focus, my focus, had been on the act of investiture. Now, several hours later, the reception at the Royal Palm was an occasion for contemplating the joys of my family. I have a deep love for my sons, a love that is expressed within the context of a set of relationships that is very different from the one that I had with my own father. I have never expected, and not surprisingly have never received, the same level of filial respect and obedience as was required of me by my father. Jayli and I raised our sons differently, instilling good values along the way, but with a lighter touch and less emphasis upon duty and authority. As a result, our sons are happy, relaxed, and modern people.

The way they reacted at the event at the Royal Palm therefore meant so much to me. Because they had not been raised to view me as some omnipotent being, it was all the more touching to see the genuine pleasure they got at seeing 'the old man' knighted: the way Manish's voice cracked, the tears that welled up in his eyes as he spoke on behalf of the family; the same emotional reactions on the part of Anuj and Rupen as they and our three grandchildren gathered together at the front of the stage. Of all the achievements in a man's life, to love one's children unreservedly and to be loved the same way in return is the greatest.

But my happiness at receiving such an honour didn't end that evening. The following day saw the marriage of President Mkapa's son, Nicola, and my brother-in-law Manubhai Madhvani and I were privileged to be among the many hundreds of well-wishers present at the reception afterwards. In his welcoming speech to the happy couple, the President suddenly announced that the wedding was a 'second day of rejoicing. I rejoiced yesterday because I was able to witness the conferment upon a distinguished Tanzanian of a most deserved order of Knighthood in the British Empire. It was deserved because it marked a recognition of a long life of service to the people of Tanzania by a Tanzanian patriot.' He went on to pay tribute to the influence our friendship had had on the growth of his character, 'my capacity for political analysis, my understanding of the realities of the modern economic world and the betterment of our people ... a great, loyal Tanzanian who has been so instrumental in assisting me to acquire prudence, charity, magnanimity and humility.' And finally he proposed a toast in my honour.

I cannot even begin to describe the effect these words had upon me. To receive an award from a foreign government, and such a prestigious one from so great a country as Britain, is in itself a great honour. But for a loyal Tanzanian, and one who has tried his best to serve his country through thick and quite a lot of thin, to receive such a tribute from a president of the standing of President Mkapa is quite another. In the personal assessment of the outgoing British High Commissioner, President Mkapa is a man touched with greatness. Few who have followed the fortunes of Tanzania over the past ten years would dare to quibble with that. I lay no claim to having had any influence of the sort he alluded to in the wedding speech, but if Ben Mkapa is content to see me as a loyal and trusted friend and a true patriot, then that is more than enough for me.

My roll call of official honours does not quite end there. In 2005, the Indian government saw fit to confer upon me its equivalent of a knighthood. In Mumbai on January 9th, 2005, I received from A.P.J. Abdul Kalam, the President of India, the Pravasi Bharatiya Samman Award, in acknowledgement of my 'outstanding achievement in the field of Public Affairs and valuable contribution in promoting the honour and prestige of India, and in fostering the interest of overseas Indians'. This award was established very recently, and is given every other year to ten outstanding persons of Indian origin who have made their mark in the world. As I travelled to India to receive this, I could not help but be taken back to my happy school days in Poona and Panchgani. My father, Keshavji, had had to leave India to restore the family honour, and now I was going back to complete the circle. And finally, in July 2004 Dr Andrew Pocock, High Commissioner Richard Clarke's successor, invited me to plant in the gardens of his official residence a palm commemorating the knighthood bestowed on me earlier. Among those present on this occasion was the Tanzanian First Lady, Mrs Ana Mkapa, who had returned from China just a couple of hours earlier.

Family brings with it the greatest honours. And this year I celebrated an achievement that eluded both Jayli's parents and my own. On Friday, May 6th, 2005, in Dar es Salaam, we celebrated the anniversary of our marriage, which took place on May 5th, 1955. Our children had lovingly, painstakingly, and meticulously organized a series of celebratory events lasting over four days. Our second son Anuj, his wife Nishma, and their daughter Polomi had, a month earlier, come to Dar es Salaam to plan for the dinners, lunches, outings, and the rest. All three sons took on the duty of organising the celebrations with the same sense of style and precision as had been the hallmark of the original ceremony. The highlight for both of us was the 'Photographic Perspective', as they titled it, of our lives, which they presented with great polish and panache at the gala dinner at the height of the anniversary celebrations. That dinner was graced by no less than President Mkapa, former President Mwinyi, and Zanzibar President Karume, together with their spouses, plus two former prime ministers and the speakers of the National and East African Assemblies. The photos selected and screened by our sons brought me back to the many happy times Jayli and I had spent together, not least with our beloved children and grandchildren. Rupen, in his welcoming remarks, spoke with great dignity and emotion, just as Manish had done at the time of the Knighthood reception in 2003. And I took great pleasure in the kind words of President Mkapa in proposing the toast. Because they meant so much to me, I take the liberty of quoting them:

> Sir Andy has always been an outstanding leader in the Tanzanian economy and society. Indirectly, he also worked for the government through the various positions he held in Boards of Directors of Public Enterprises, Commissions and Committees, some of which he chaired. Sir Andy is an exceptionally able and humble man, not the rooster crow that 'many men' are said to be. Sir Andy has been in the thick and thin of the political and economic transformation of our country, from the colonial times,

> the independence struggle, independence, nationalisation and ultimately privatisation. He was there, and he has seen it all. And it is not just that he saw it, but at some point he personally experienced it, as when his family business was nationalised. No one will ever know the full impact and real value of the loss one suffers in such circumstances. We can, perhaps, accurately calculate the economic and material loss; but we, certainly, cannot accurately calculate the emotional and psychological sense of loss and devastation. It speaks a lot for the strong constitution of Sir Andy that he took it all in stride so very well, at least to those like me looking at him from a distance. Sir Andy did not lose heart or courage. Neither did he run away. Instead, he internalised Mwalimu Nyerere's rationale for the nationalisation process, and even remained at the helm of the family business after it became a public enterprise. He did not sabotage it; on the contrary he played a leading role in transforming it from a private to a public enterprise. Honest married men here will tell you that the higher your responsibilities and stature in society, the more you depend on your wife to give you the support to shoulder on, and the shoulder to lean on. It is a worn-out cliché, but a correct one nevertheless, that behind his success was a woman — so I join you all in paying great tribute to Sir Andy's wife, Jayli.

President and Mrs Mkapa joined us for the dance at the conclusion of the dinner. Both Jayli and I felt elated and uniquely privileged. A successful marriage is like a successful business, needing hard work, loyalty, and a fair slice of good fortune. But unlike a business, it also needs love and tolerance, the sheer joy of having married a person who is prepared to share the lows as well as the highs, someone who will support his or her partner faithfully and in full measure yet without lapsing into subservience. In Jayli, my bride fifty years ago and my bride even today, I found all that and more. And now, having celebrated fifty happy and fruitful years together, we look forward to still more from each other, and from life. We are particularly happy that our sons are also actively pursuing community service, that they have adopted that good habit of putting things back into the society they have been blessed by, a habit that I myself inherited from my own father.

Growing old sometimes feel like being on a train that is gradually picking up speed. Childhood years pass by so slowly, each day, with its small wonders unfolding, seeming more like a year. But once one is launched into adulthood, the days, then the years begin to flash past. It seems to me like only yesterday that Rupen, the baby of our family, was indeed a baby. And now look at him, and his brothers too, all grown men, and the next generation, the grandchildren, growing up as well.

And so I go back in my mind to those long childhood days in Bukene, and the house, roofed with corrugated iron, on that narrow dirt road. I run home from school just to be at my mother's side, squatting down on the concrete floor to watch her prepare the family's evening meal, chewing on the sweetmeats that she tells me she has made just for me, listening to her talking about her day, and about mine. Now I am at the railway station in the darkness of a Wednesday evening, part of an aimless crowd of villagers awaiting the arrival of the weekly passenger train, and in the hubbub of anticipation as a far-off whistle blows, I stand watching as the station master nervously brushes down his crumpled uniform one last time. Above us the stars high up in that African sky, the night still warm, still airless. And below, the ochre dust on our feet.

My long journey from Bukene is now almost over. Yet sometimes, in my heart, I know I never left.

INDEX

The first edition of *A Knight in Africa* is limited to 1,500 copies,
of which 1,390 have been casebound for general sale.
One hundred copies have been slip-cased, signed and
numbered 1 to 100 by the author, J.K. Chande,
and President William Benjamin Mkapa.
Ten have been slip-cased, signed and numbered by the
author, J.K. Chande, and President William Benjamin Mkapa,
in a limited leather fine binding.
The author will donate proceeds from all editions
to Tanzania's fund to eradicate malaria.

A Knight in Africa is set in Cartier and printed on Rolland Opaque
Vellum, Natural. The colour photographs are printed on Hanno
Art Gloss. The dust jacket is printed on Jenson Gloss.

PENUMBRA PRESS
www.penumbrapress.ca